AF252045

KINGYO

TOY TOKYO

Manami Okazaki

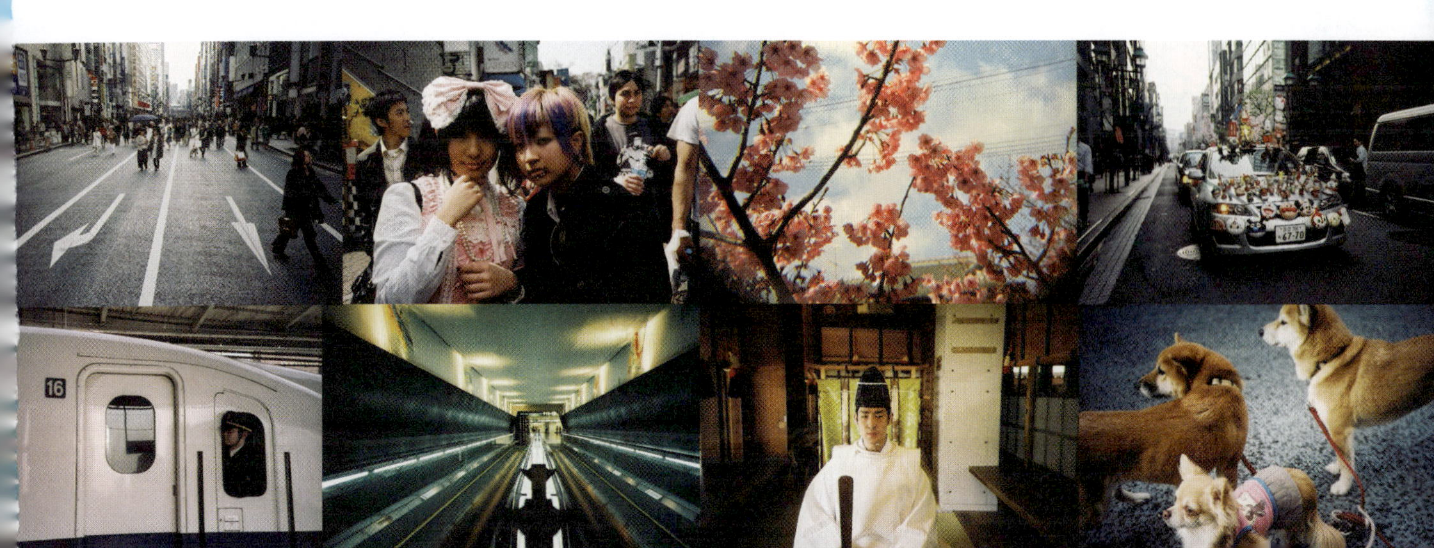

CONTENTS

Introduction

PLASTIC DREAMS

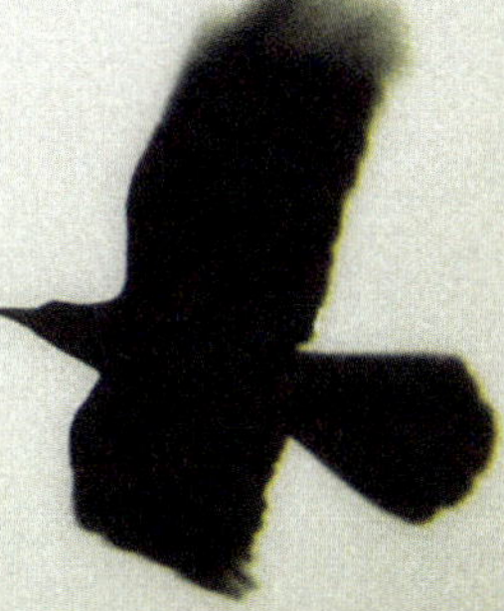

Blurry, out of focus, streaked with light and distorted. While these are adjectives you might not associate with quality photography, these are the quintessential characteristics of photography produced by toy cameras. As the technological prowess of digital SLRs and cameras intended for the prosumer advances towards image crispness, toy cameras such as the Holga, Diana, LOMO LC-A, and the range offered by Lomography offer an alternative to this never-ending quest for increased megapixels.

Typically very simply constructed, made of plastic and (as we were surprised to find out) often made by hand, these cameras have seen waves in popularity, and have now gone beyond a gimmicky novelty status to an established genre of photography - especially as renowned photographers continue to make prize-winning, iconic images with them.

As digital cameras continue to become more user-friendly, enabling the average hobbyist to take decent photos, the role of the photographer seems to be ever-questioned, and many turn to simple cameras like toys and pinholes as a means to create art when we are bombarded with digital imagery that requires no thought, nor skill. Many people liken toy photography to impressionism - the low quality of the lens, which often produces ambiguous images, has a nostalgic or dream-like atmosphere. Rather than capturing objective truth, for many photographers, they use toys to capture an image closer to perception and imagination - in fact, many photographers mentioned that they use toys to recreate an experience as they remembered it, not as it is in reality.

This book showcases the work of several photographers who have used toy cameras as a medium for self-expression. Whether toys are their main cameras, or simply a diversion from their regular work as photojournalists or commercial photographers, all their images capture something uniquely intimate, abstract or surreal.

Asides from a being toy camera book, given how suited toy cameras are to travel photography, and the conscious decision to feature a lot of photographers not native to Japan, I hope this book serves as an alternative travel photography book as well. All the photographers show ways to enjoy, experience and document travel to unfamiliar places, when one's senses are the most heightened, without having to resort to generic clichés often seen in travel photography.

Almost all the photographers I talked to appreciate the process of using a toy. Not only are they light and not intimidating (making them ideal for street photography), most of the cameras in the book use film, and cameras like the pinhole require a high degree of patience. The element of surprise and unpredictability that is inherent in toy cam photography is also something that most photographers mention - the notion of "happy accidents". An important point to add is that film is still widely available in Tokyo, and the city has a great infrastructure (shops, places to develop, camera shops, excellent toy cam and vintage cam magazines) as well as a cultish love of film, partially due to the influence of the 70s masters. Curiously, even the most jaded photographers I know well, who are utterly bored of their "professional" jobs, suddenly become enthusiastic and curious when talking about toy cameras. Lastly, while I set out to do a book on Tokyo, I started working with too many incredible photographers who were working in other cities, Kyoto, Gifu, even the countryside in Tohoku.

I hope you enjoy the book as much as I did making it!

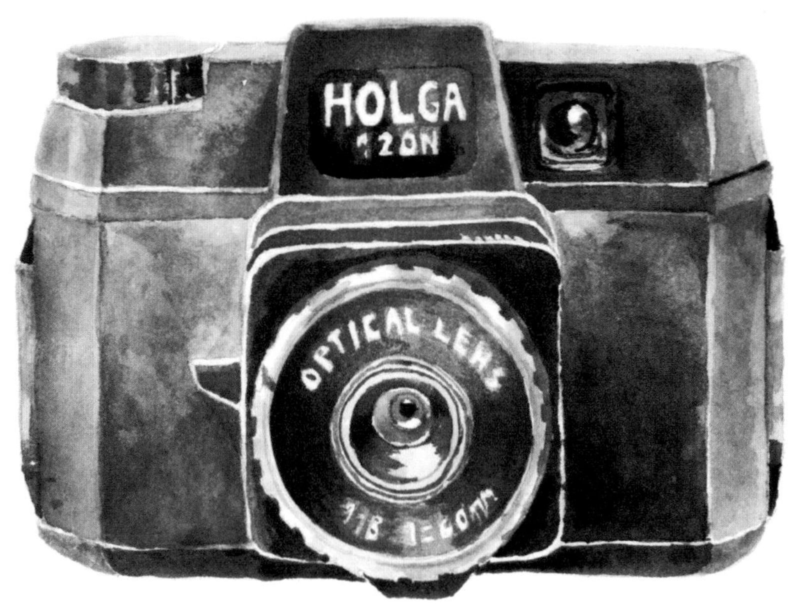
HOLGA
120N
OPTICAL LENS

HOLGA 120

The Holga is a medium format, plastic camera that uses 120 film, and shoots 12 6x6 photos, or 15 6x4.5 exposures per roll. It uses no batteries, and a simple zone focus system. The 120 is the most iconic Holga, but there are many different formats such as the 135 and the 110. Now in its 33rd year in production, Holga faces challenges in the digital age and they have a lineup of iPhone accessories and lenses for SLRs.

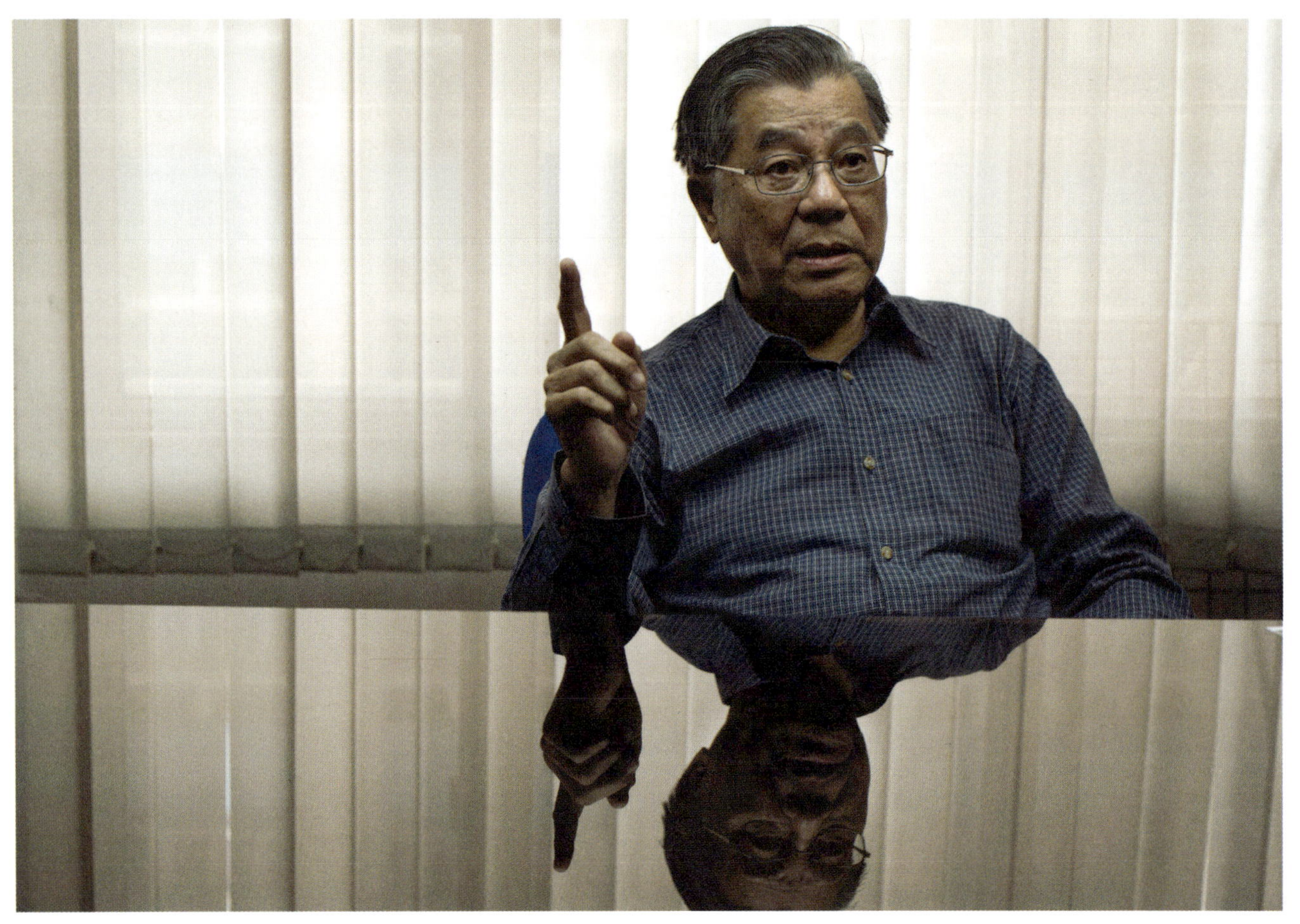

—— *interview 01* ——

T.M. LEE,

FOUNDER OF HOLGA CAMERAS

T.M. Lee, Holga founder, Christine So, Holga PR and curator.

Can you tell us how you started in the camera business?
I left China in 1964. I came back to Hong Kong, and in 1967, a Japanese camera factory called Yashica employed me as the factory manager in Hong Kong. I was not there long; I left Yashica, and we established Universal Electronics Limited by the end of 1969.

But actually, I graduated from a university in China in 1952. After that, I stayed there to teach about locomotives and cars, and cameras were not my major. Locomotives and cars are quite different to cameras, but because they are all mechanical and cameras are locomotive machines, the basics are similar!

Did Yashica have part of the production line in Hong Kong during that time?
Yashica established their first factory in Hong Kong in 1966, so they employed me. At the time, they had no production line in Hong Kong, so it was my duty to start the factory here in Kwun Tong.

Would you say most of the camera factories were based in Hong Kong at the time?
I think Yashica was the first to set up their production line in Hong Kong. I was employed as the factory manager because a company, WOC, was the sole agent for Yashica cameras at that time. It was established by my brother, so I was introduced to Yashica by him.

You started by making flash units, not cameras?
When our company started our business, we made some electronic components for receivers. First, we wanted to make electronic capacitors, but when we started production, the business was not so good, so we had to try to make other things. During that time, a Japanese technician helped us to design the flash unit. After we produced it, we found out the business was quite good and we continued. I designed the next myself, and got an award from two organizations. Because of this award, news went all over the world, and a German company, AGFA, heard about it too. They sent someone to Hong Kong and they discussed a flash unit for AGFA. After we started to make the first unit for them, they continued sending orders for us, so we enjoyed a very good period of business during the 70s. But the end of the 70s something happened: Konica built an in-built flash in their camera, and other camera companies followed the same.

When Konica built this in-built flash camera did everyone stop buying flash units straight away?
Yes, it was very fast. By the end of the 70s, in Hong Kong, there were many manufacturers making the flash unit, as I knew of about 30 manufacturers. In one or two years, there were three manufacturers left, one of them being us.

We could not depend on the flash unit to survive anymore, but we wanted to make flash units for the studio. They are more complicated and require more technique, but we made it gradually, by first making small ones, and then bigger ones.

Can you tell us about the first camera you made?
I was expecting to sell the 120 to China, because in 1980 they had already opened up their country for some time. The population is so big, so I was expecting to sell them in China. At that time, China also produced 120 film, and that is why I concentrated on making 120 cameras. I produced one with a built-in flash and one without a built-in flash.

What kind of consumer were you thinking of?
At that time, I was expecting not only one or two companies - the price is so cheap, so I was expecting that many people in China would buy it. But out of my expectations, when we introduced this camera to China, they didn't like it! They wanted only to get something from outside of China, a 135. No one ordered our camera!

Can you tell us about the camera factories in China?
The factories at that time belonged to the country, so they have a lot of capital; I think most of their equipment was imported from Russia in the 1980s. I had a chance to visit their factory - wow! Their machines at the time were very special. They could keep their workplace at a constant temperature all year long, because the dimensions of the parts change because of temperature. Their equipment was excellent.

They would also sell their cameras at a very high price, as they were not intended for common people. It was for export or for their own national companies.

So you had to change your strategy?
What could we do? We had to find another way. Later on, we introduced the camera to Europe and the States. We sent out samples all over the world; Lomography in Austria got our sample and they tried it. They found out the result was quite different and special. But we waited quite a long time - several years - and by the end of the 80s, Lomography and also the US and Japan started to order our 120. It was at the end of the 80s and early 90s that business increased. Firstly, school teachers would introduce our camera to their students, and after some time, David Burnett got a reward because he took a picture for a competition (his photo of Al Gore).

You have an in-house curator, Christine So, and you put on art shows which is really great, as not all camera companies support artists like this – why is it important to you?

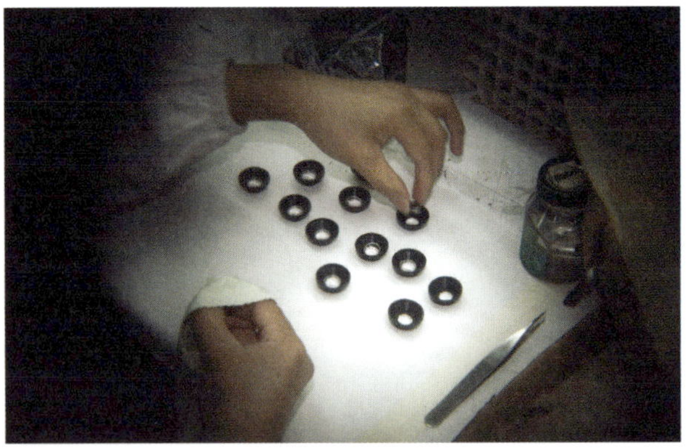

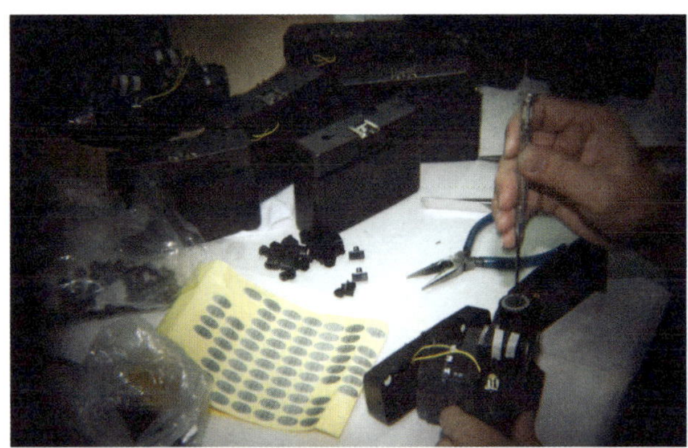

(Christine So): Lomography is valuable because they make trends but we didn't want to do the same thing. We found out that very famous photographers use Holgas, and we recognize the Holga community. So we made connections to help support the artists because we respect their work a lot; many photographers are very inspiring and use a Holga camera - such a simple camera - to produce such amazing work.

With the increase in digital technology, you had to think in new directions again.
We started to make components for digital products, for example, the iPhone. We also made a Holga lens for digital cameras, so you can change the lens.

You have had some problems with pirates and copying, is this something you can avoid?
Someone in China copied our iPhone products, and it is very difficult to stop them. It depends on how complicated your product is. If it is simple, they will copy you very fast and sell it very cheap, but if it is difficult to make, they will have problems copying it too.

Why do you think you managed to survive?
Because we want to survive! We just continue trying to develop something for the market. That is the only way to survive, it seems simple, but it is a real rule.

Can you explain the charm of a Holga?
Christine So: Holgas have special effects and photographers say each Holga is so unique, it is like a fingerprint, so you cannot make an identical photo. Each Holga has its own character. One of my friends even calls his Holga different names.

I think it is like art, some artists specialize in realism, but Holga is like abstract expressionism. It is another option for artists to express their creative expression. It doesn't have to be sharp. The beauty is that is so simple, and unpredictable. It is not perfect.

Also the Holga is so simple, and you can modify and experiment with it. There are so many possibilities to play with your Holga. A lot of artists use alternative processing as well, and spend long hours in the darkroom.

Finally, it is affordable and unbreakable. (Photographer and Lightstalkers founder) Teru Kurayama had a really bad car accident in Pakistan three years ago, and one of the drivers was killed. He said all his cameras were broken except for the Holga.

PHOTOS BY ERIC RECHSTEINER AT THE HOLGA FACTORY IN SOUTH CHINA TAKEN WITH THE HOLGA SLR LENS

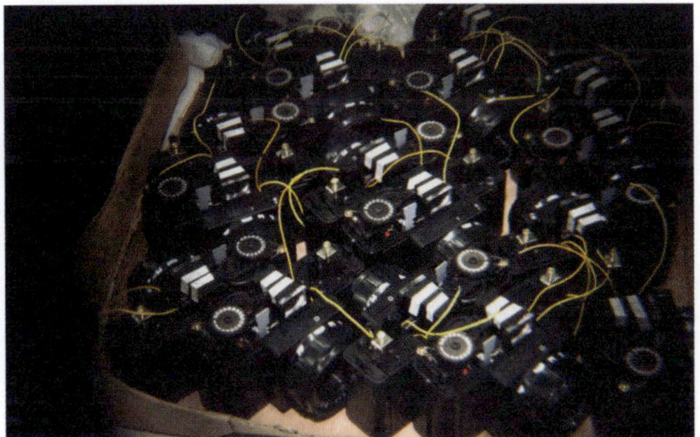

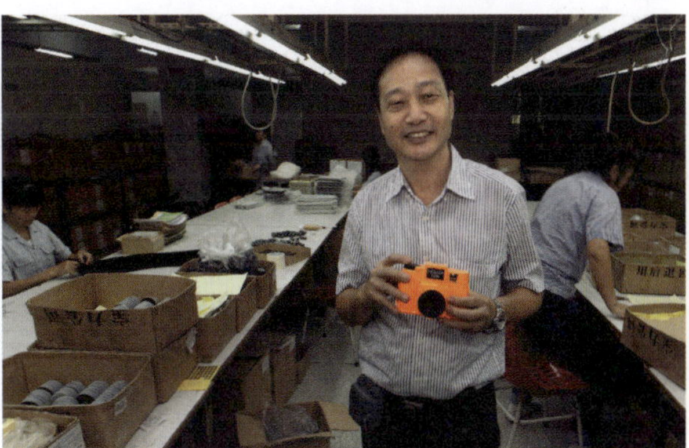

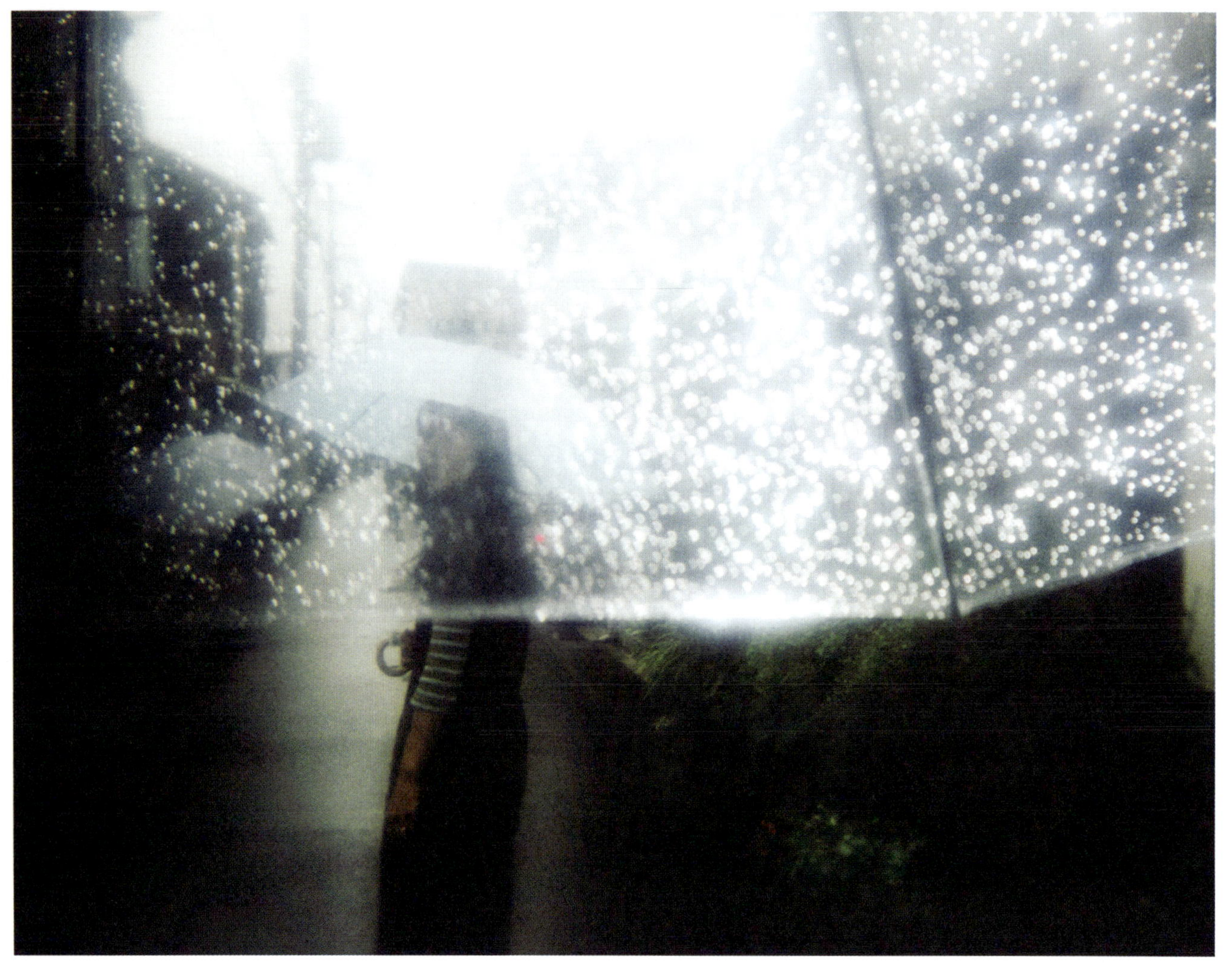

—— interview 02 ——

TAIJU FUBUKI

When did you first come across the Holga?

Originally, I was making films as a script director, and I was studying at a photography school's film division. When I graduated, I became a cameraman for TV, I wanted to do dramas, but I ended up at a sports channel, which is the complete opposite!

So it was really quite technical work.

Yes. I actually wanted to do directing and scriptwriting, and I was wondering how I ended up a cameraman, and felt quite gloomy about it. I persevered for 12 years, I was really busy, so I didn't have that much free time. I was thinking maybe I should do films as a hobby, but because you do that with a group of people, it was difficult to match up everyone's schedules. And then I discovered photography. It was something I could do on my own, and perhaps I could use photos to express myself. Up until then, I was not using (still) cameras at all; maybe I would get one or two disposable cameras a year when I was on holidays or a party.

So I went out and bought a camera, it was 1999 and I was 28 years old. The cameras I was using for work were for broadcasting, so they would take clean images. I didn't want do things that were the same as work, so I was looking for cameras that would take distorted images, so I came across Lomo and Holga cameras on the net. I was like, 'This looks great!' The images look interesting, and I was using a 8mm camera when I was in high school, like a single 8, or a super 8 and I felt that they had the atmosphere of those kinds of films.

Was there a particular director you liked?

It wasn't like I was so into a certain director. Even with photography, it isn't that I am in admiration of a particular artist. So it wasn't like I wanted to take photos like someone in particular, I just wanted to express myself.

That is really rare!

Yes for me taking photos was the means, not the goal. I think taking photos suits my personality. I like that when someone views the work, they are free to interpret the work as they like. Whereas with films, it can be problematic if you are just interpreting the story as you please! I originally wanted to make a narrative, but I came to realize that it isn't that important. I think I wanted to make things where you can get into it holistically, from the bottom of your heart.

You also run a gallery in Osaka – by having this gallery you can see the audience's reaction straight away, is that something that is appealing as well?

Yes, that is also fascinating and the amount of time the audience can look at a photo is up to them too, whereas with a film it is set, for example, you have to watch an hour-long film, in an hour. They are totally different worlds, they both use cameras and the act of shooting subjects is the same, but asides from that, I realized that they are completely different.
However, I do feel that because I came from a film background, that my logic is different to people only shooting photos. I want to take filmic photos.

So was Holga your first camera? That is amazing!

I was thinking of getting an SLR, but during that time it seemed

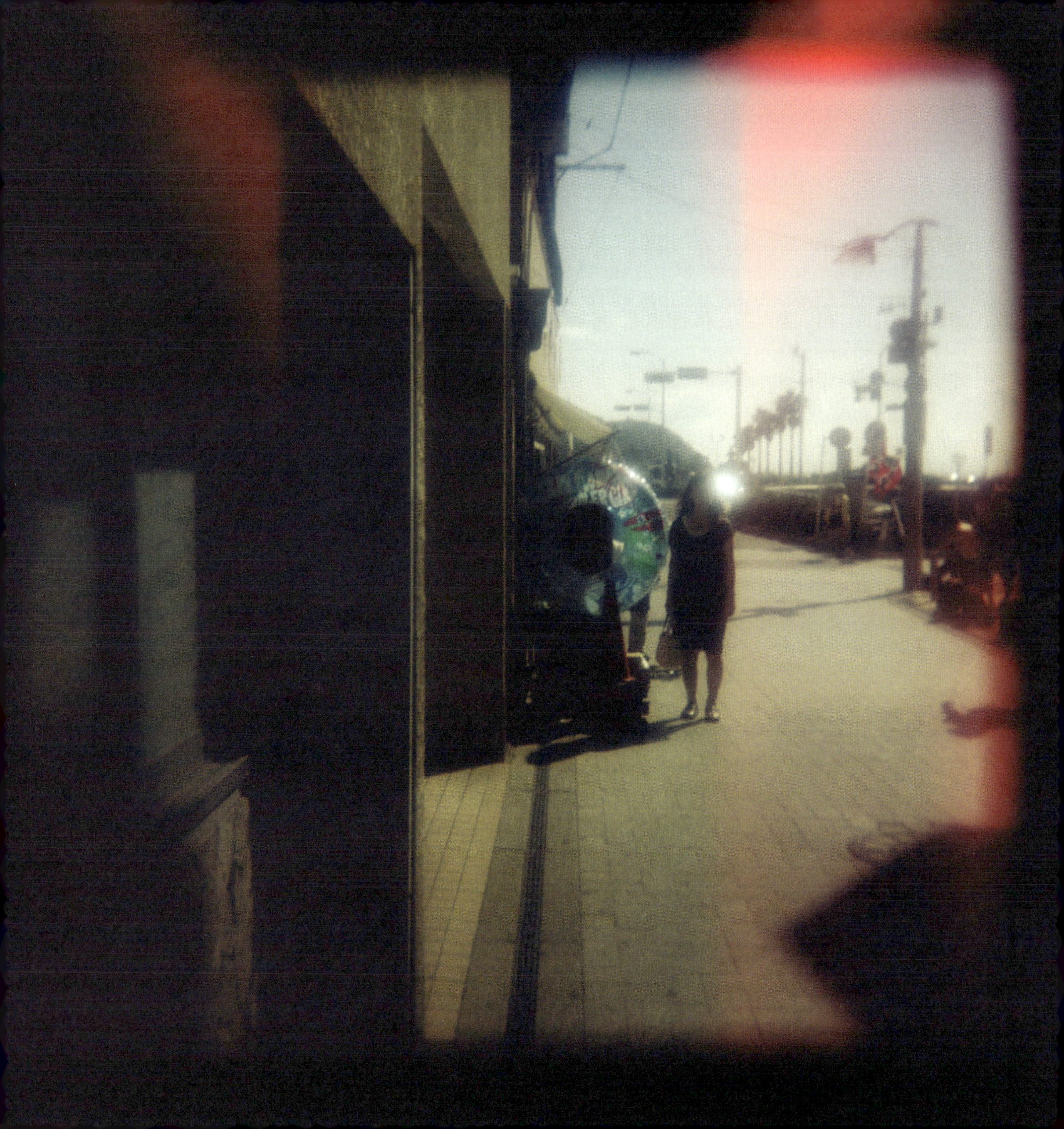

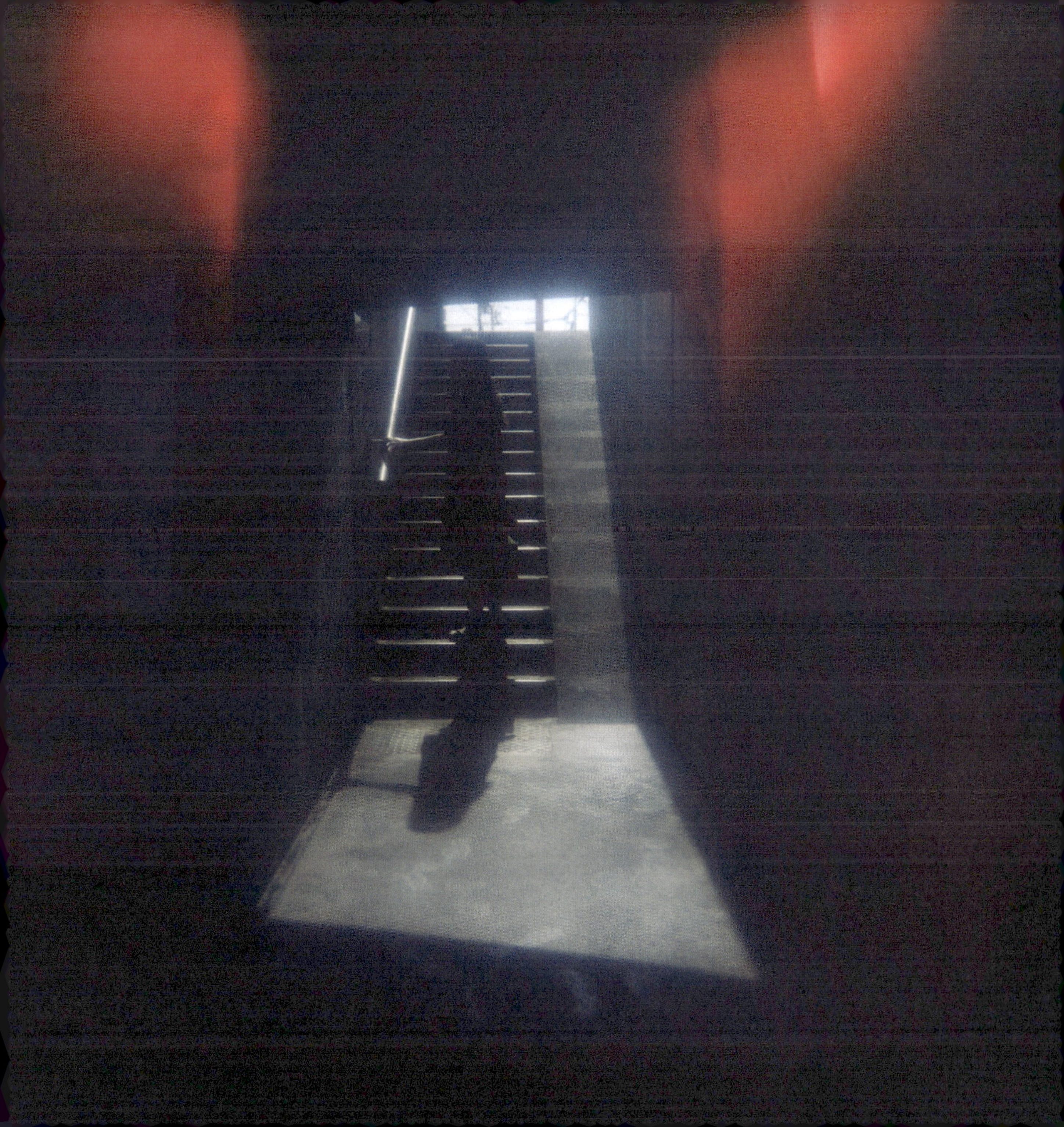

like the popular designs were made of resin and colors were in "champagne gold" and a bit rounded. There was the aesthetic lack of appeal too. I think I liked the toy cameras too, as objects.

It seems there are a lot of camera geeks within toy camera users.

Yes, in Japan, there seems to be a fashionable element and toys are cute and cheap so it is geared towards people who might not take photos normally, and they might try it out of curiosity. Then they find that taking photos is fun. I think nowadays that trend has shifted to Instagram and the iPhone though.

Could you get toy cameras easily then?

Around '99 was the first boom in Japan, it was a bit in fashion. It was a subculture, a niche product that you couldn't get in a camera shop, but you could get something over the net. And that was the start of my photography career.

There are three-year cycles in toy popularity, but nowadays, it is steady and seen as a photographic style. Instagram and toy camera modes on the phone have increased the number of people who recognize toy cameras, but when I started, there was the notion that people who are shooting with toy cameras are just fooling around. Galleries would not even look at your work, they would think it wasn't serious work. They would have not seen the work yet and they would say, "Use a real camera." But maybe because of these opinions, I wanted to use it even more.

Do you think toy cameras are strongly related to film culture?

I was using video cameras for work, so in my case I don't mind whether it is film or digital, I think you should choose freely. So even now, I shoot with film, but then I scan it, digitize it and do postproduction, and then print it, so there is definitely a computer somewhere along the line. In the past, people thought that was strange and wondered why I would use a PC halfway through, and not just do the whole lot in film. During that time PCs were pretty bad too. Holgas are not high precision so the bright spots are totally white and dark places are totally black, so I would adjust it on the computer.

Can you tell us about the Holga Association?

In 2001, I started the Holga Association and there were about 500 members around the time I wanted to do the gallery - not only Japanese people, but also overseas people like Koreans. I created it to discuss how to use a Holga, have shoots and show each other's work. We also hold exhibitions and group shows such as the Holga Expo.

With the Holga, a lot of people like to customize it to suit their own needs, what is the Holga mask that you use?

It produces this black soft atmosphere around the perimeter using paper. I am using a modified Holga. With the 120 S, the classic Holga, it is a bit different, and there was no mask, and you couldn't take the square format, and we would modify them. Back then, the way everyone was modifying them was different too, so the individual characteristics of the work were stronger, but nowadays the makers know this and put these functions onto the camera, and since then, the way people shoot has become a bit uniform.

When I first got the Holga I couldn't take the square format so I was modifying it until about 2005. From 2006 I stopped, and

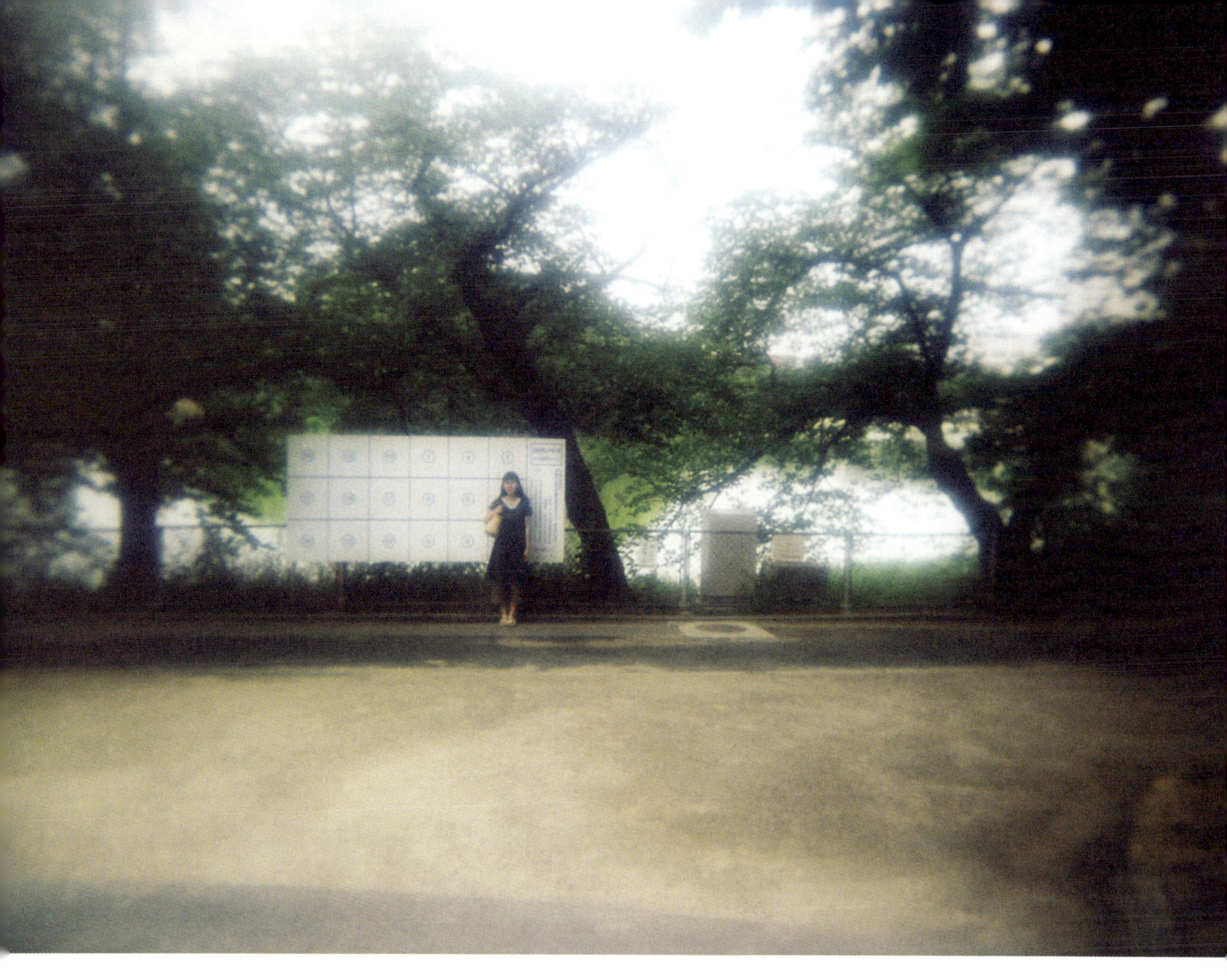

last year, I started using it again because the photos get a really nostalgic atmosphere. There was a period when I thought that photos don't need that kind of nostalgic atmosphere, but lately I have changed my perspective again and went back to how I was using the camera before, but the things I am shooting are totally different.

It is like looking into a memory box, and when the red is introduced into the photo, it can render new memories as well. With humans there are unchanging and repeating landscapes, so I wanted to explore that notion.

I am looking at the idea of "itsuka tabi" (a journey sometime), the word itsuka is both the future tense and the past tense in the Japanese language, so it could refer to a memory from my childhood, or a memory that my own child sees now, and there is this sense that there is something close by that is repeating.

Toy cameras are ambiguous, they don't take photos clearly, and therefore for someone seeing this photo, it makes it easy for the viewer to feel an affinity with it. Like the subject in the photo could be my mum, or this lake could be the one near my house. I think if the audience can feel an affinity with it, the photo goes beyond what I was simply taking.

If the outcome is so unpredictable how do you plan to take photos?

When I am shooting, I don't really have a plan, I am just walking along and shooting things I think are interesting. So my process is that I take a lot of photos, and the main thing is to select well them afterwards. So the shooting, in terms of effort is about 20% and the selection, retouching and editing is about 80%.

So the shooting is quite fast?

Well, I do take a year though. When I take it, it is a snapshot. There is no direction per se. I am looking for things that look like a stage, or a scene within a film, and then I will take a photo. Things that I am seeing for the first time, but make me feel a sense of déjà vu.

I do take things that are seemingly nothing, but things you can recognize. Things that make people think, 'I could probably have possibly taken this myself, or maybe not.' It isn't things that have a huge impact, but things that permeate under the skin. It is subtle and slowly permeates you, so it isn't a mainstream aesthetic, but I think these images remain with you.

So when I am shooting, I don't decide what kind of image the photo will be, or what meaning it is. I don't think of it like that, and don't give it a conclusion when I'm shooting.

Do you like the "accidental" aspect of shooting with a Holga?

If you use a high precision or digital camera, you can check it straight away, and once you get the shot you wanted you stop thinking. So after that, there are no surprises. There are great surprises when you develop a Holga and if you can be surprised by a photo, so will others.

Your photos have a lot of depth and detail though.

Yes, I work on them and do a lot of postproduction afterwards. But there is a misconception that Holgas take bad photos, it is just that they take ambiguous photos. So it brings out the beauty

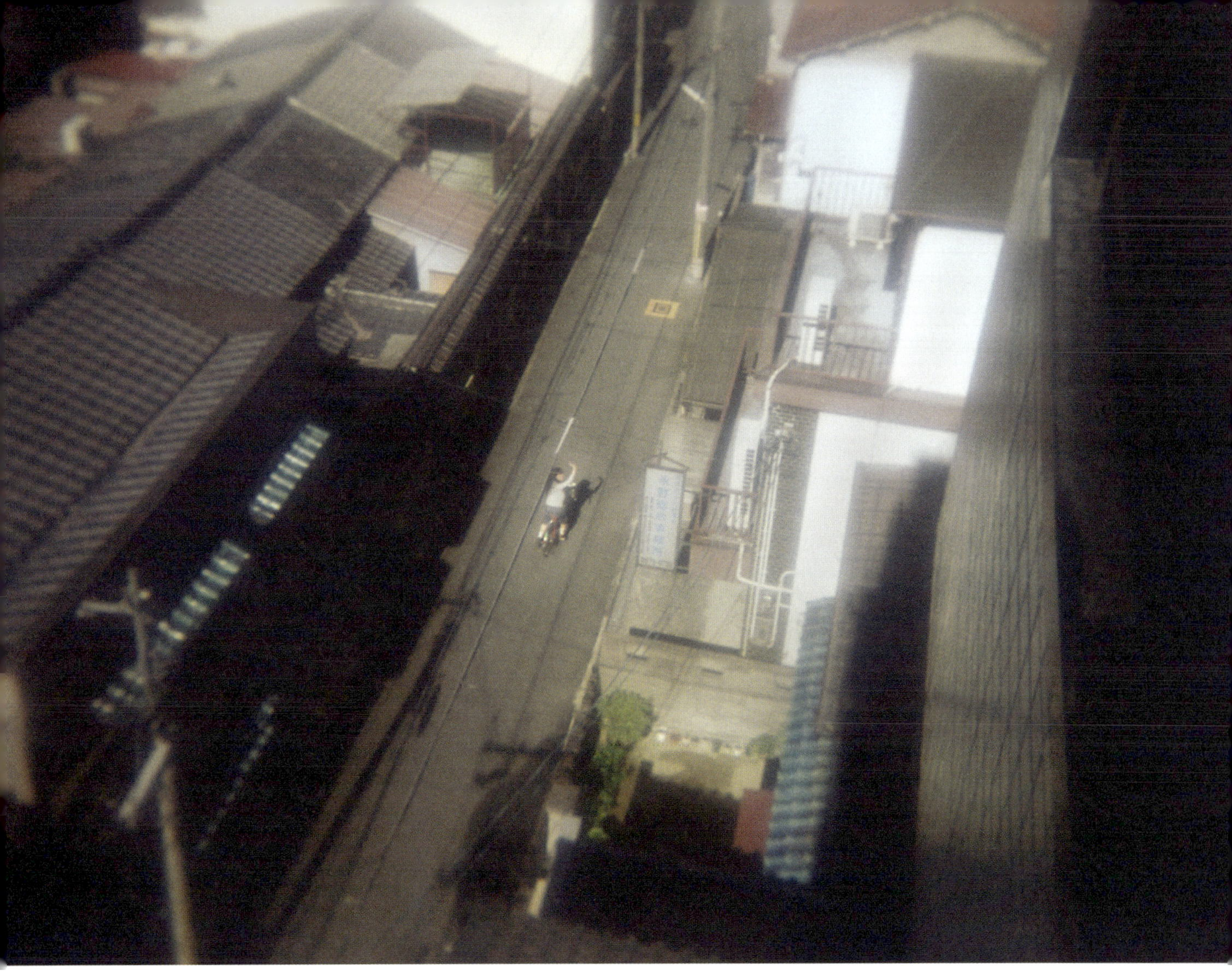

in that. But it is medium format film, so you can get detail that you can't with 35mm, that is something else I like about the Holga.

I saw on your homepage that you had a lot of retro style photos, like the downtown areas of a city.

Yes that is my old work, to take kind of old things like old streets, so I would take retro style things, and things like disappearing parts of the city. But then I progressed and decided to take aspects of my life, and my psychological state, and that had an element of nostalgia as well. So rather than the subject being old, it is the quality of light and composition that make something nostalgic. But I do admit, that you can get these kinds of things more when you go into the countryside.

Does the ambiguity add to the photo in other ways, other than nostalgia?

I was taking "happy" photos after my retro stage, so it was an expression of my everyday lifestyle, and the small moments of happiness I could find in that. I really was taking happy photos and when I did an exhibition I was wondering how I can make photos happier than these!

Then, I got sick, and in 2010 I nearly died. During this time, I wanted to do something more raw and real. On my 39th birthday, the doctor told me that I might have cancer. I recovered and I am better now, but during that time I took a lot of photos. The meaning of photos can change after we take them - if the photo is too precise, it becomes too much about my story; there is no interpretation, just like a journal of my illness! So this ambiguity is good so that people can make a connection to the work. If it is too nuanced, it is simply my story, and if it is like that, people don't empathize with the work.

I do think of how my work would be seen after I die, it is a weird feeling but I think it is amazing that what you see gets left behind. If it is too nuanced after I die, only my story remains, and I don't think that has longevity. I think it is important to think of this.

What makes you stay with a Holga after all this time?

I think the Holga is a type of product that you would never expect to be sold in Japan, it is really a camera with a lot of character! The focus is off, you can only use it when the weather is good and not dark - basically the humans should adjust to the product. It's not the product adjusting to the people, as with Japanese products! It is like a living thing, there are days the camera is in a bad mood.

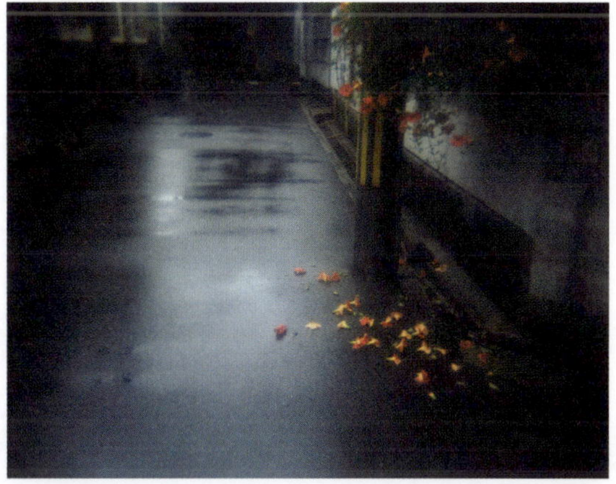

interview 03

FRED LEBAIN

Can you tell me about your background as a photographer?
I started my professional activity as a chef, before I became culinary stylist and photographer. Today, I work around still life and fashion in my studio in Paris, with digital camera, but always with an "artisan touch" – without Photoshop in most cases.

When did you first come across lo-fi photography?
By chance, while I was shopping in a flea market in NYC, and I discovered an old Holga camera, and I tried it. In a second, I decided to do a project with it; (the book) "My Travel with Holga."

I worked only with the Holga because in the 90's nobody knew this camera. It was a real challenge, and with the first click I fell in love of this camera, the crazy thing was that camera was supposed to be a professional camera, due to the size 6x6.... incredible!

What aesthetic possibilities does it open up that regular high precision cameras don't afford?
Surprises, distortions, flare, it is uncontrollable.

Is there a particular advantage in using them, in terms of the shooting process as well?
The biggest advantage of the Holga camera is that you can't be taken seriously.

Can you describe shooting in Tokyo, and what challenges it presented to you?
Tokyo was a step into my travel, I realized that it was in Tokyo that the people were the most surprised by the Holga....it was seen like a nonsense camera in the "mecca" of high tech cameras!

What can you say about the relationship between the people and the city after shooting Tokyo streets so extensively?
Tokyo is a village for me, an incredible sensation of proximity between the people and their city.

Are you able to tame the unpredictability of toy cameras to a degree?
Impossible to tame it, that is the charm of it, like a human being!

What is the relevance of cameras like Holga in the digital age?
It has a long life! Cohabitation is always possible – and one day digital cameras will be low tech, no ?

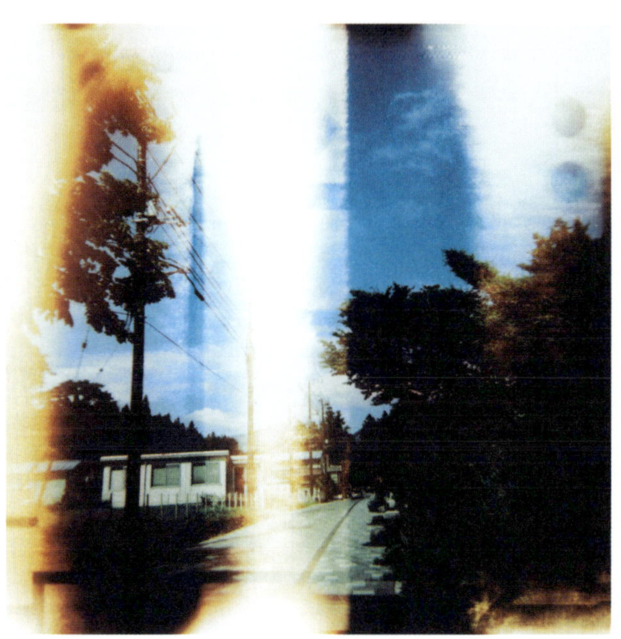

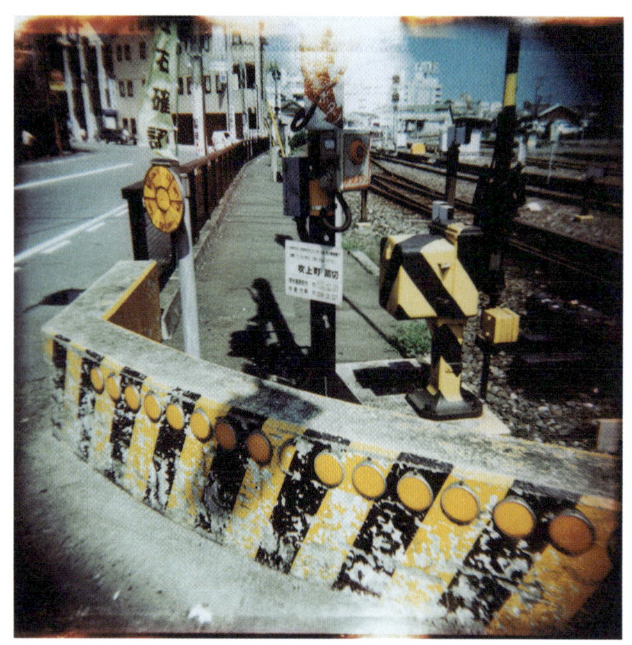
吹上町 踏切

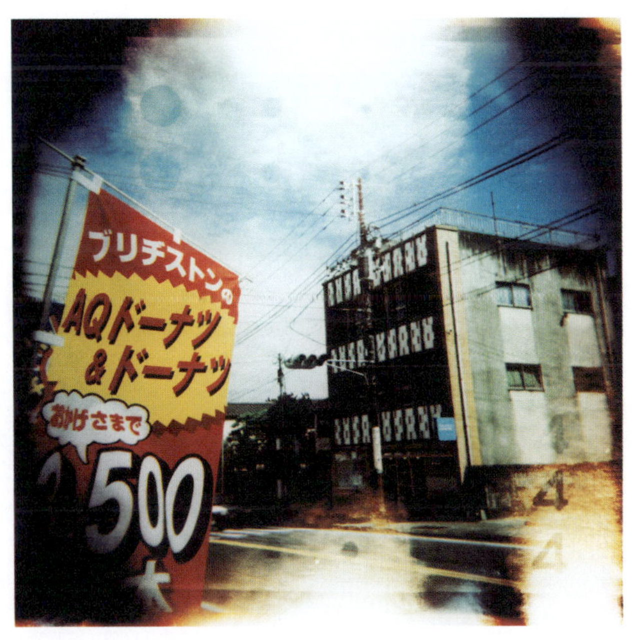
ブリヂストンの
AQドーナッツ
&ドーナッツ
おかげさまで
500

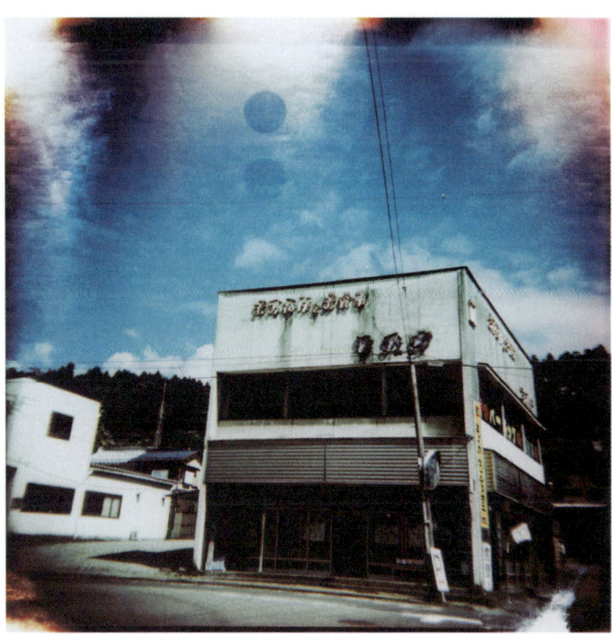

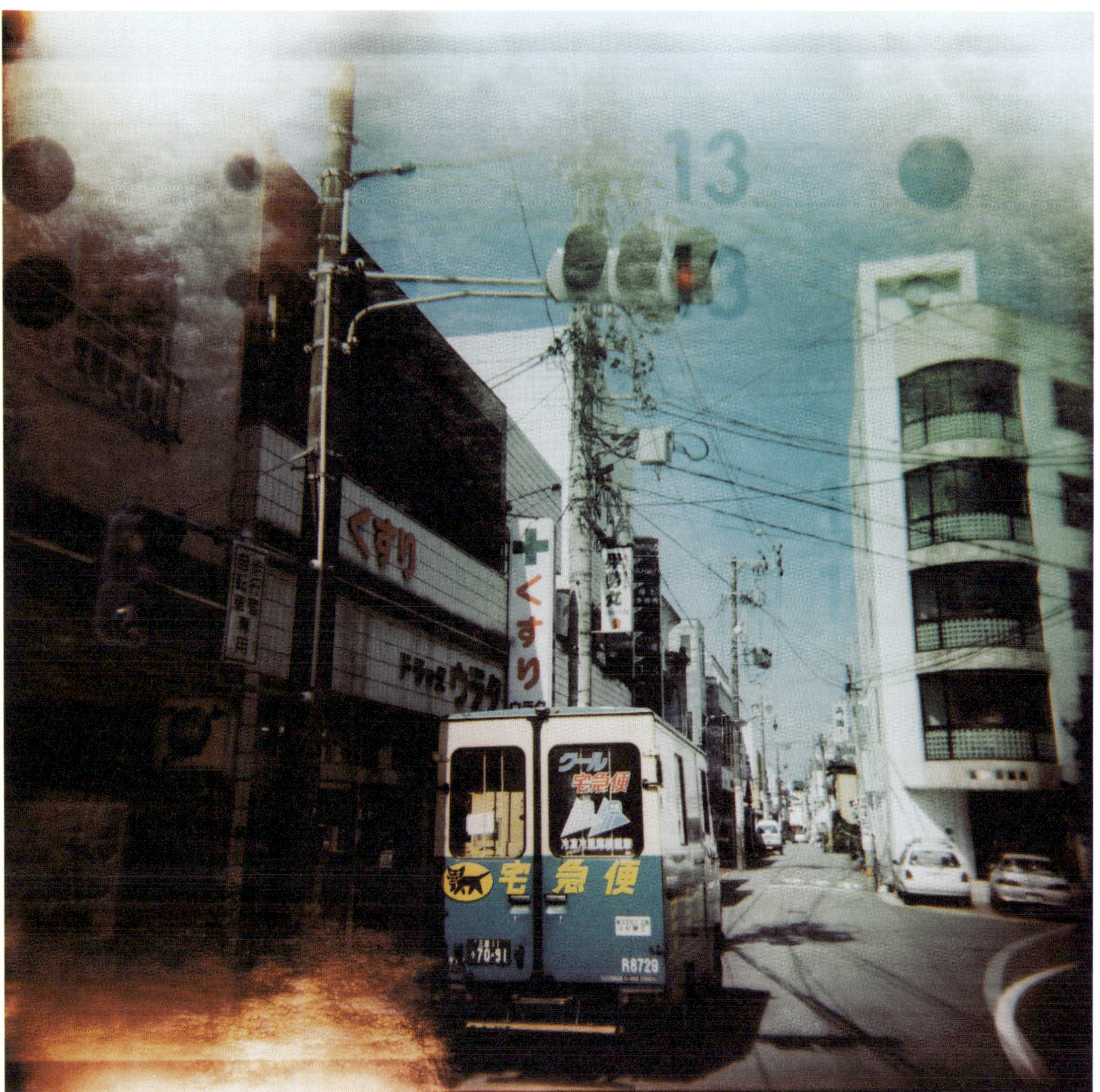
13
くすり
くすり
クール
宅急便
宅急便
R8729

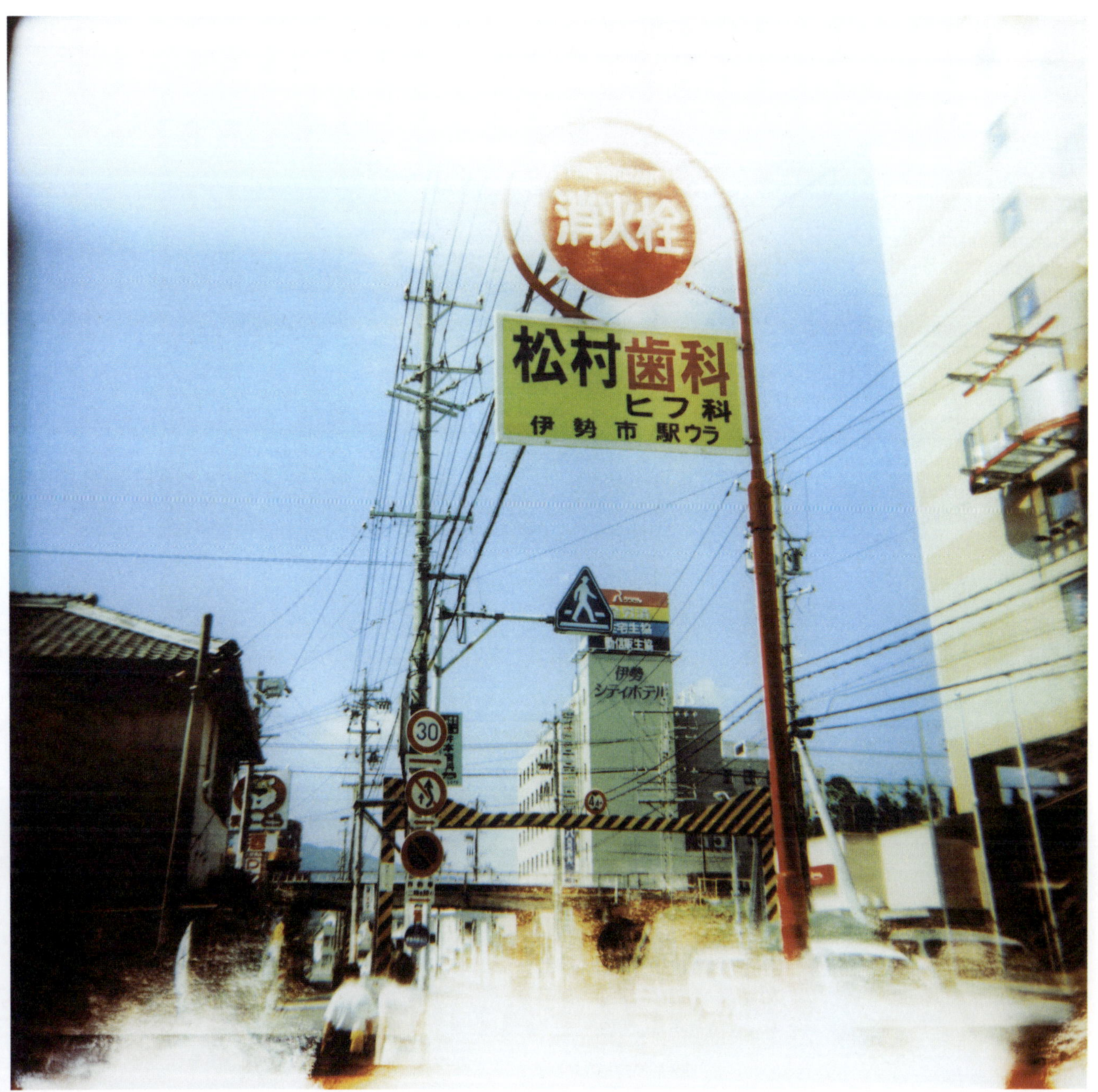
消火栓
松村歯科
ヒフ科
伊勢市駅ウラ
伊勢
シティホテル
30

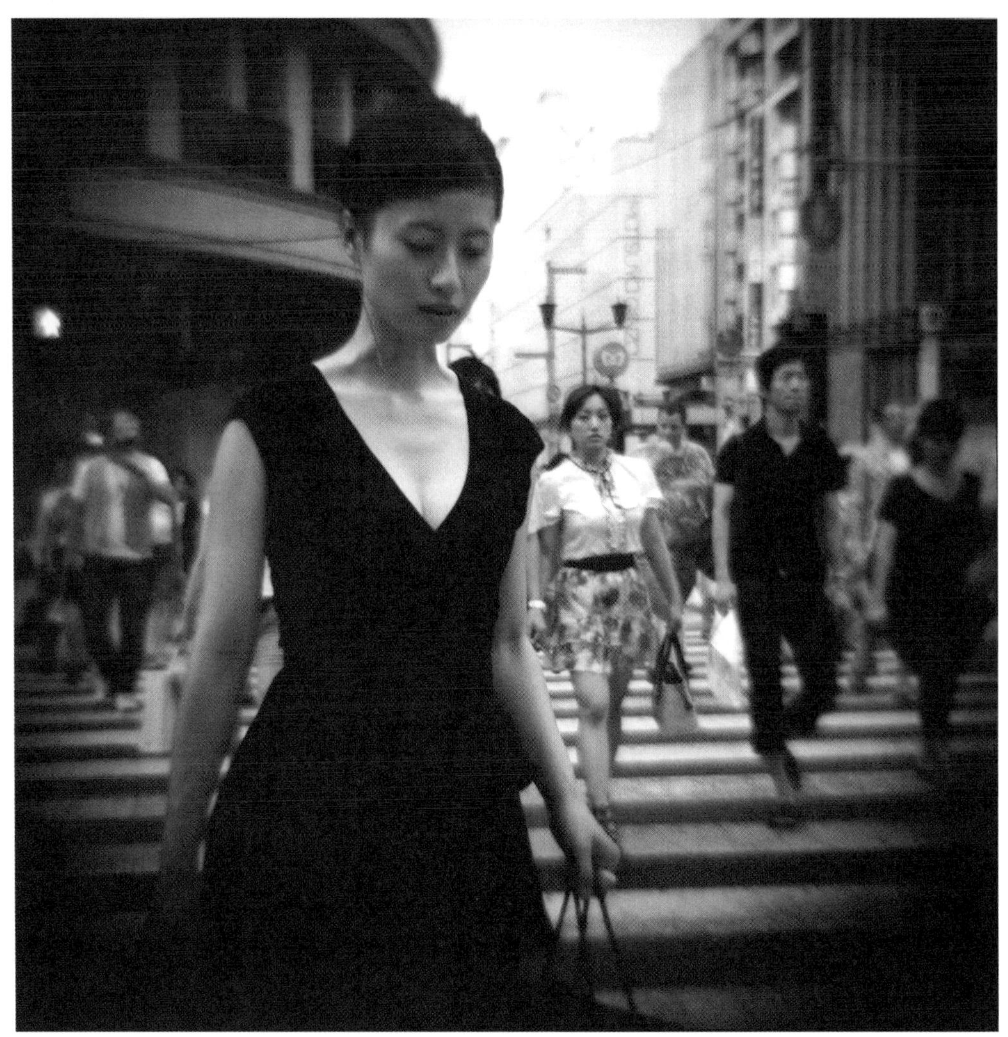

—— interview 04 ——

PAOLO PATRIZI

How do find Japan photographically, as a subject?
Initially it was all exciting because it was new, and there was a lot to see and document. I was getting commissions from European magazines, but they mainly want me to cover clichés about Japanese culture, which is fun for a while, but I thought it was more important to go a little bit deeper. That is also probably because not being able to communicate that well in Japanese, I always need some help with certain stories, so I lose on the intimacy of certain subjects, which is a shame.

What are some of the clichés?
Street fashion, sumo, the pop culture basically.

What appeals to you about working in Tokyo aesthetically?
It is mostly about people and certain situations. In terms of aesthetics, the cityscapes don't change that much, you go from modern to traditional, but within those areas that are considered more traditional, you go around the block there is a new house and it is beginning to get harder to find traditional things, and if they are there, they are known to everyone.

It seems that that Japan developed so fast, but the culture remained behind. Photographing people's thoughts is impossible so you need to balance that modern side with the real culture and that is a challenge.

It isn't the obvious choice for a photojournalist to use a toy. What made you want to pick it up?
It was a new thing, and I never tried it before and it was exciting to work with a camera that has no controls. Most of it is all down to luck; what comes out is a surprise. At first a Holga, and then I got a Diana; it is pretty much the same. The Diana lens is little softer than the plastic lens on the Holga.

In your series, you are shooting Ginza, which is one of the most exclusive suburbs in Tokyo, known as a high end, luxury shopping district. Why did you choose to shoot such luxury with such a low-tech camera?
Actually, I never thought about it that way – it was just a subject I decided to tackle and it turned into a story. It is connected to this period of recession, where the rich are still getting richer.

What is obvious is the high-end fashion stores, but what is interesting is the people that go there shopping – if you go there during the week you only see women, it is the ladies spending the money. And they are incredibly dressed and elegant, there is something about these Japanese women. There is this French word called allure which I cannot translate, but I think Japanese women are able to take it to another level. They are so incredibly elegant and beautiful, the way they carry themselves. I find that especially in Ginza because it is a certain age that I am focusing on, it is not like Shibuya where it is young fashion. I think they are 40s and above.

Do you feel Japan is conducive to film photography?
There are still a lot of photographers using film here. The shops still have very good stock of film, whereas in other countries like in Europe, most of the labs have disappeared and it is getting harder and harder to get film. People switched to digital and prefer it because you don't have expenses afterwards, after

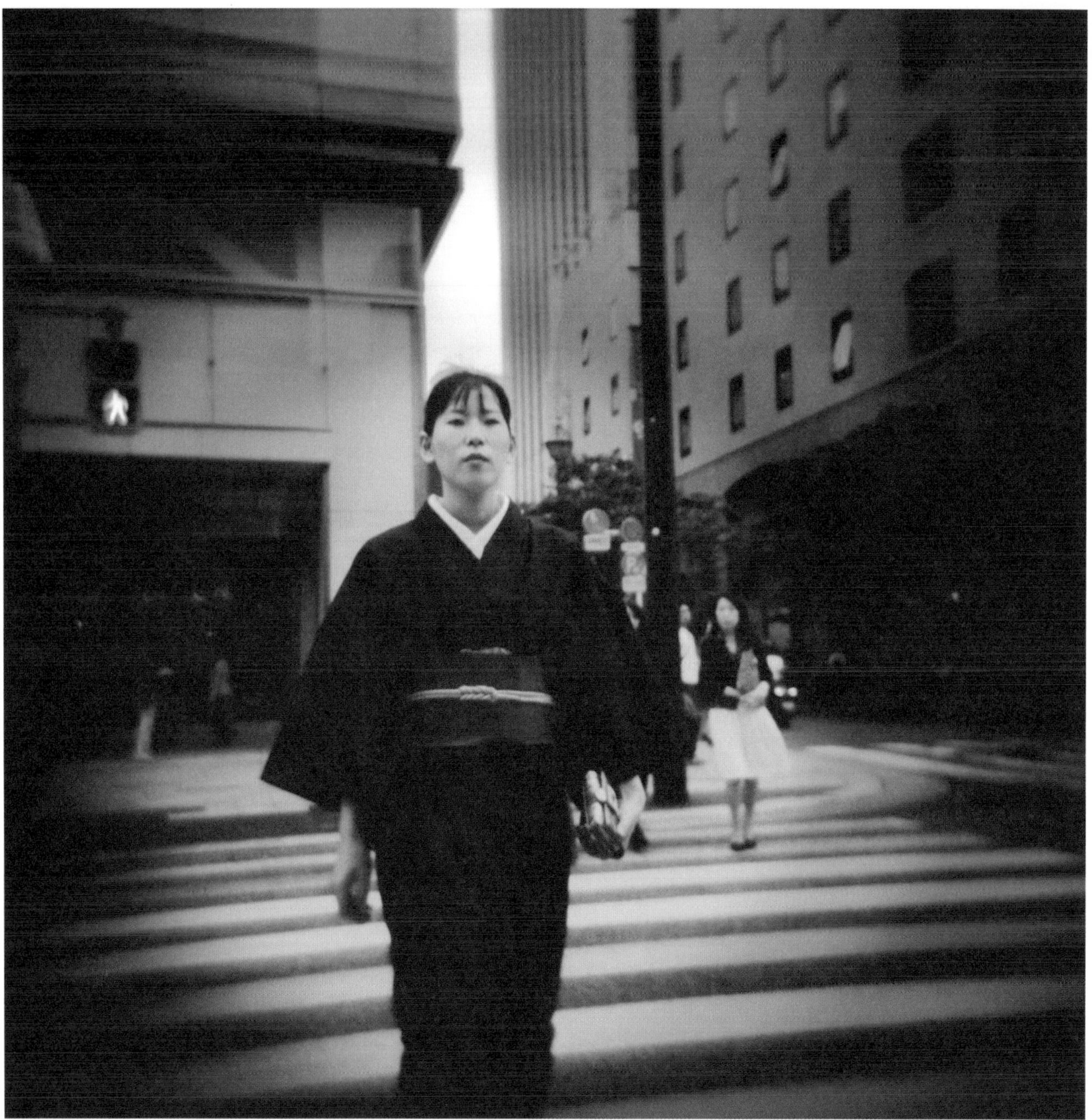

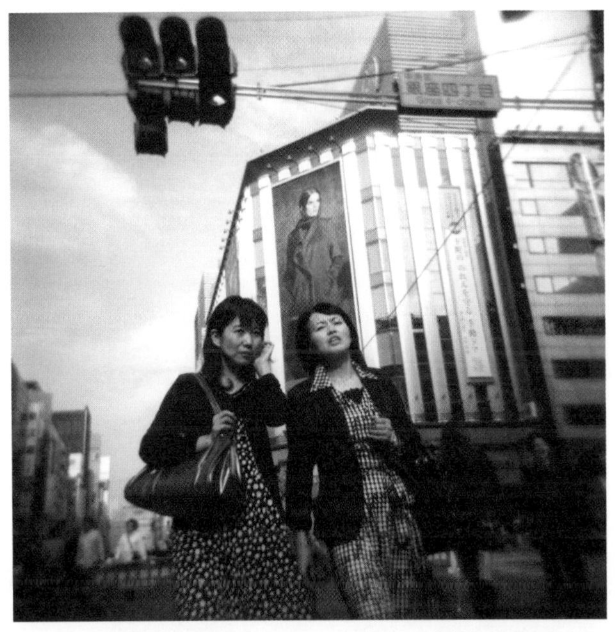

the initial purchase. There are some labs in Europe that develop RAW files for photographers and they do it in a very nice way, and that is probably why. There are a number of photographers in Japan who are very much influenced by the photography that was done in the 70s and they use black and white for that.

Was it refreshing to use a toy?

Yes, it was one of those moments that you get into this trance and go for it, until it is done, it is a special moment, and it happened with Holga.

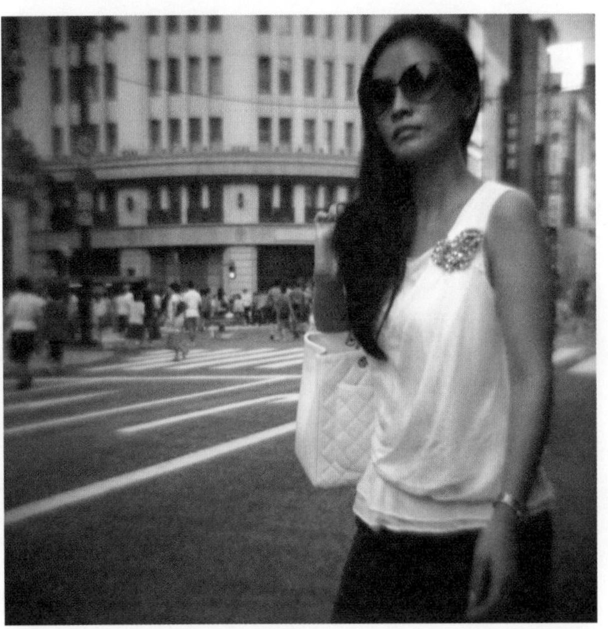

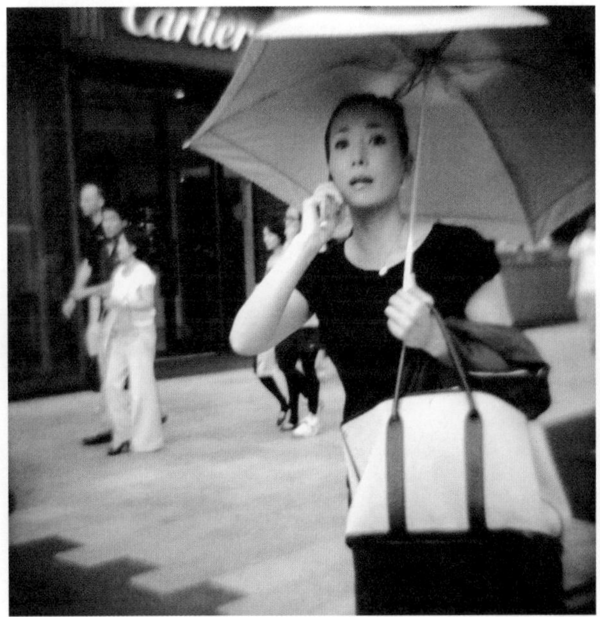

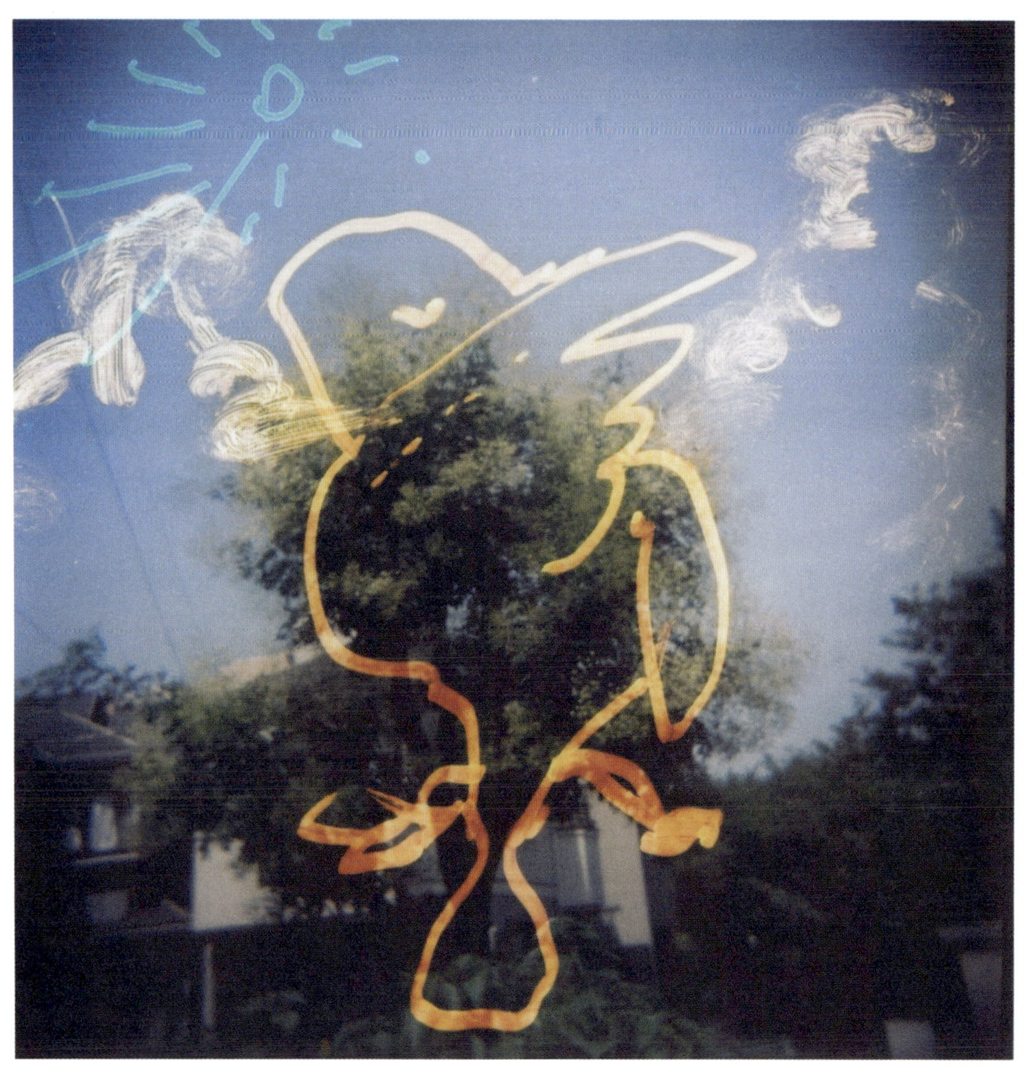

—— *interview 05* ——

REI SATO

Can you tell us how you became interested in toy cameras, and why?

I became interested around the time I released my photo collection *Sun* and it was my publisher, Power Shovel, who introduced me to them.

Which cameras do you use?

I have several varieties of toy cameras but the one I use the most is a Holga.

I had been shooting with a single lens reflex for as long as I could remember so at first, I was very unsure of how I should use it, but now I find that uncertainty interesting.

Plus it's quite light, so I can take it all over, which is more important than one would think.

What kind of subjects do you feel work best with toy camera photography?

I touched on this a bit in the second question but - it's difficult to gauge how the photo will turn out while shooting. This in turn forces me to think about what will appear clearly in the photo and what won't,what will be visible to the eye and what won't, what has form and what does not.

And this ends being the best theme for me when working with toy cameras.

The "everyday" is a popular topic for female photographers in Japan. How has the "ordinary life" played a role in your photography?

Rather than trying to shoot 'the everyday', I would say that I take photos as part of my everyday and doing so naturally encourages me to search for and take notice of the important things around me.

What are the challenges with working with toy cameras?

The fact that I don't have a clear idea of how the photo will turn out is part of the fun, so I wouldn't call that a challenge, but in pure mechanical terms, the film can become very loosely wound. I often find myself shooting something I really like and then fretting over whether the footage will get overexposed when I remove it from the camera.

(I suppose if I learned more about how to operate the camera, this would become less of a problem...)

Is there a link between your work as a Fine Artist and a photographer? i.e. are there things you can express with photography that you feel you can not with paint or other artistic mediums?

In my case, I draw and paint on top of my photos, which allows me two combine two separate worlds into one. I use the photo as a backdrop and then create images of a different taste over it, so even if that backdrop looks photo realistic, I feel the meaning is different.

What is going through your mind when you take photographs?

What is before me? What state is it in? How do I define this moment?

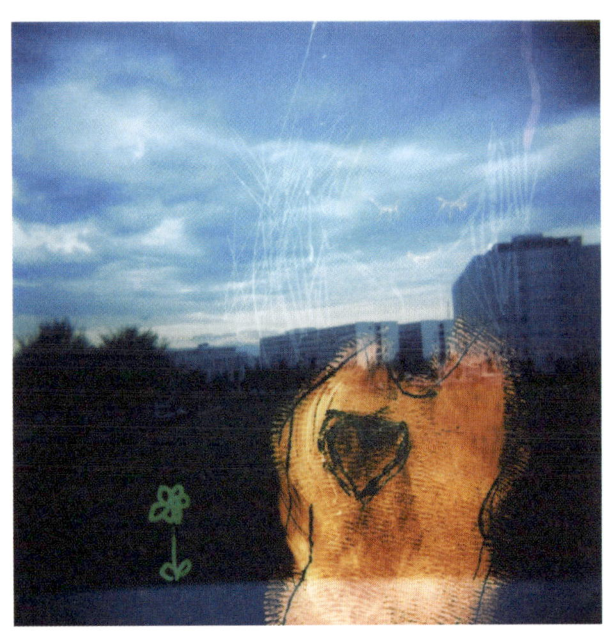

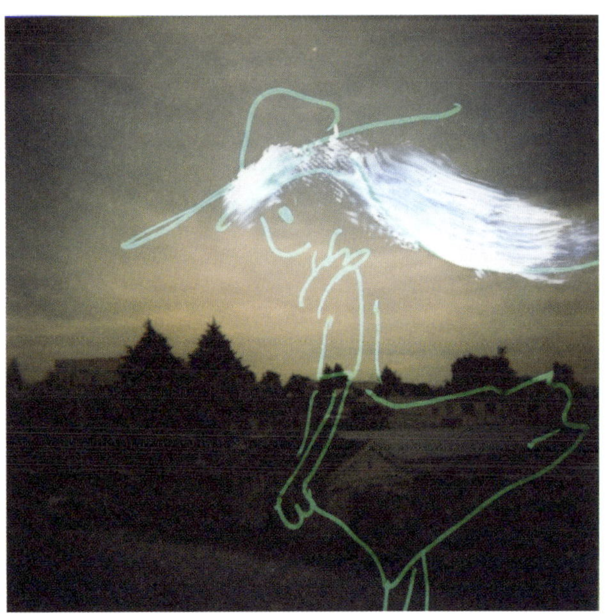

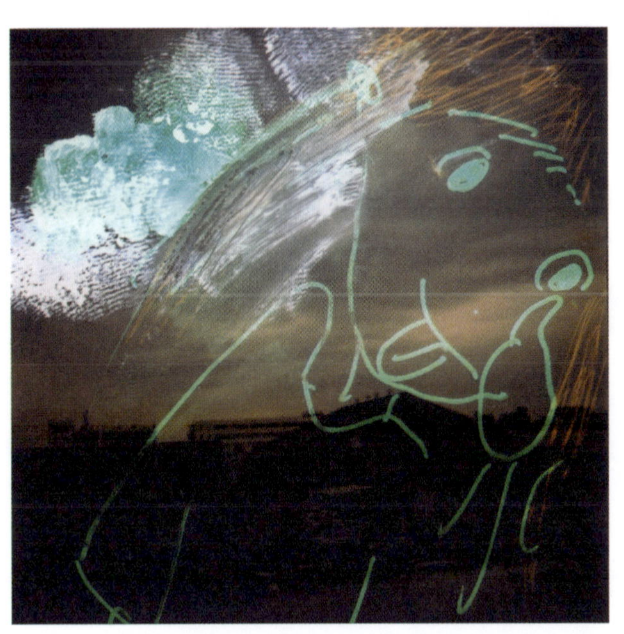

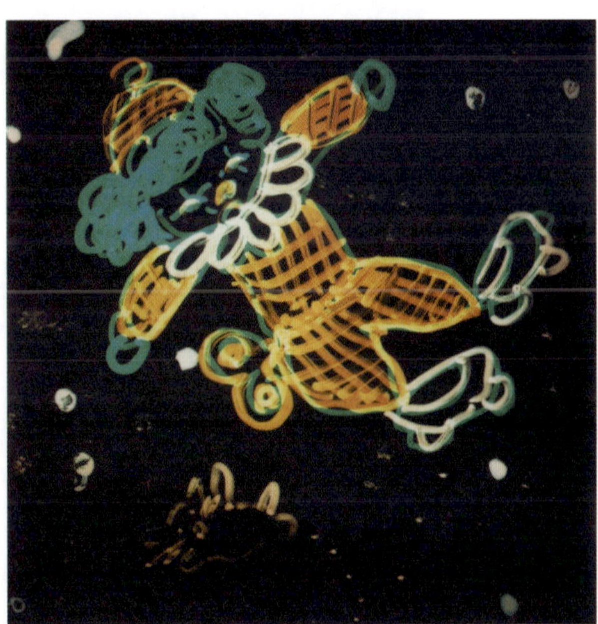

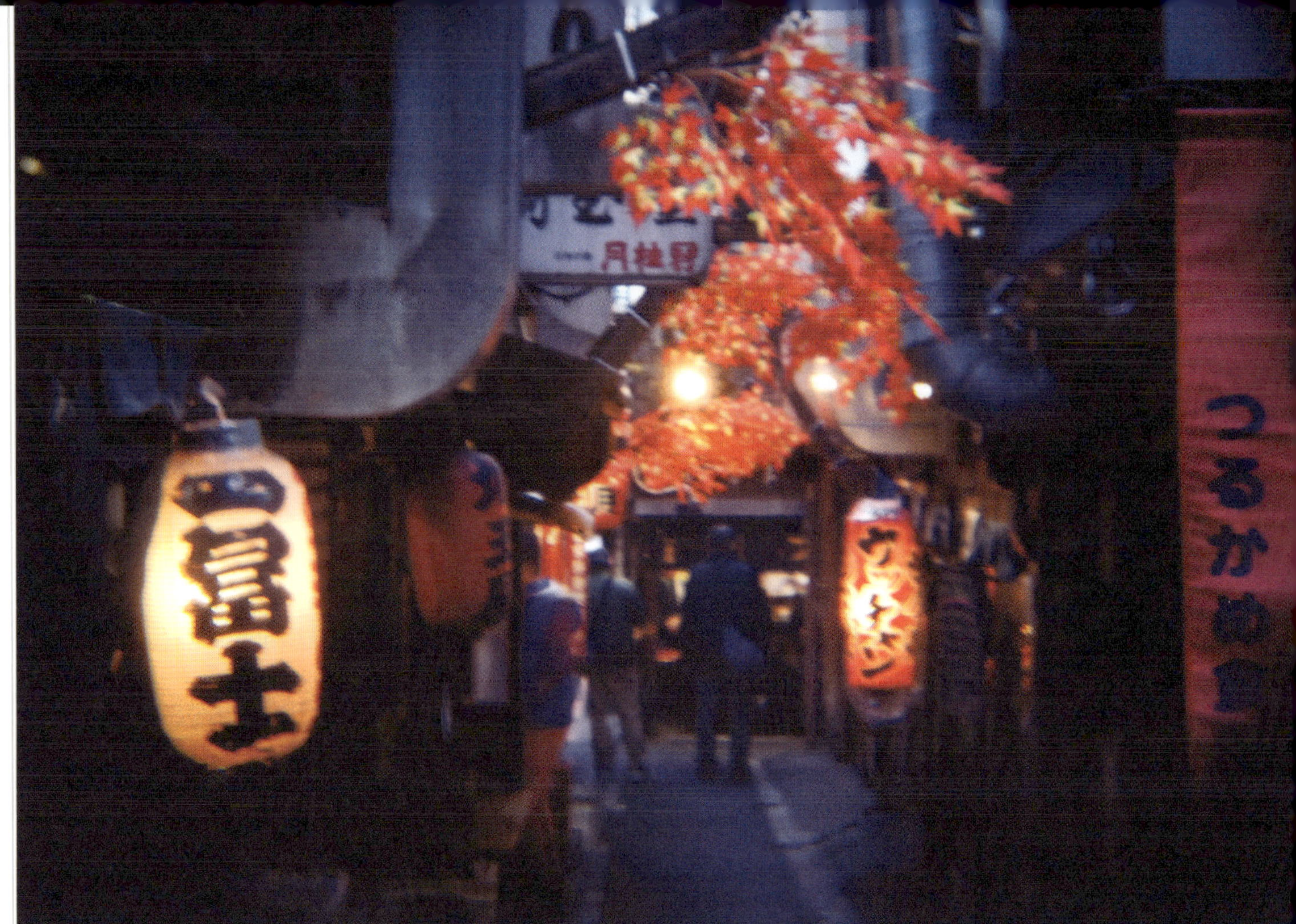

interview 07

ERIC RECHSTEINER

What kind of things did you shoot with the Holga lens – what part of Tokyo?
Shibuya, Shinjuku, mostly small details of the huge city. That's where I live and can walk around easily with a camera...

What was the appeal of using the Holga lens and how did the images differ to using a traditional Holga?
The main appeal is of course the ease of use. No need to buy film, no need to process. It is easy to check and correct the exposure on a digital camera, and thus easier to get a satisfying result quickly. Then the difference with the traditional Holga is the usual difference between film and digital.

Was it the first time to use a Holga?
No, I've used and owned a Holga in the past, and did at that time mostly intimate portraits.

You are usually doing reportage, how does your mindset differ when you dont have to do subject driven work?
To me it is roughly the same mindset, whatever I am shooting. When it is not a subject driven work, then I'll focus more on the colors, the frame, and the light.

Why would such imperfect technology have any relevance when cameras can produce such a hyper real image?
Well, that's exactly the point. To me the imperfection of a Holga lens brings back to the time when photographers were using only film to shoot. At that time, even with good technical skills you have to deal with the uncertainty of the process. You were never 100% certain of what would come out, and this unpredictability was also part of the magic of the photographic act.

Nowadays, with the newest electronic viewfinders, you can see on your screen the images you're going to take even before having pressed the shutter button! So a Holga lens is fun to use because largely unpredictable.

What is the appeal of Tokyo photographically?
For a new-comer Tokyo is just like Aladdin's cave, marvels everywhere! But for someone like me who has spent a major part of his life in the city, it's getting more and more a search for lost time and sweet memories.

Due to the decline in film production and availability, Holga met with the challenges of the digital age by producing a series of digital lenses for SLRs. They have a wide range for many models, as well as fun color filters, fisheyes, and prism filters that were seen in late 60s photography.

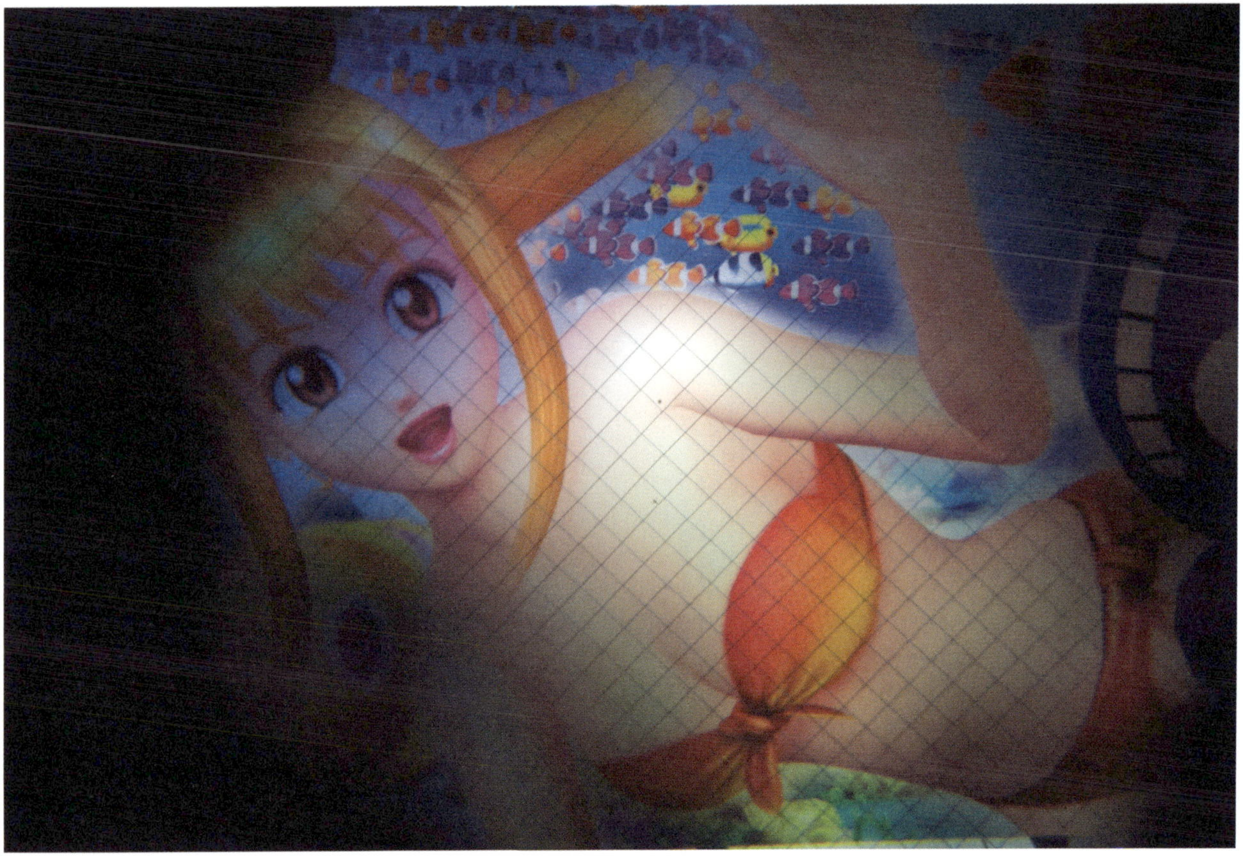

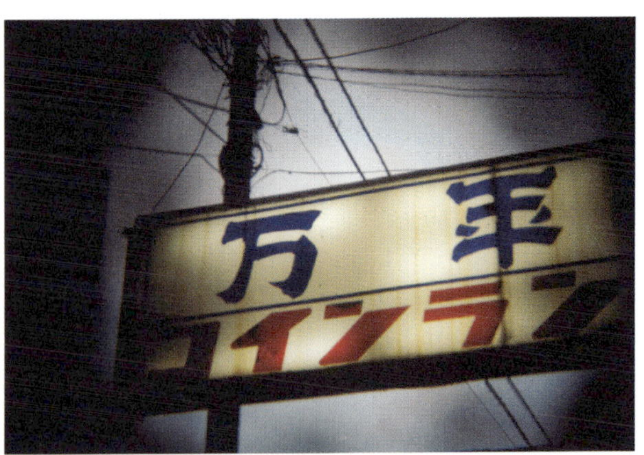
万年
インラ

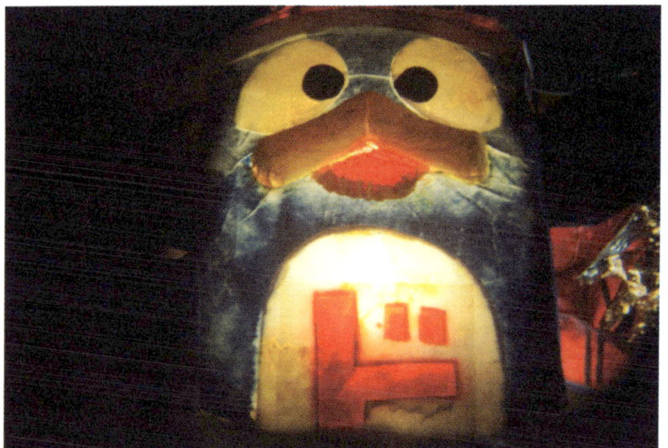
ド

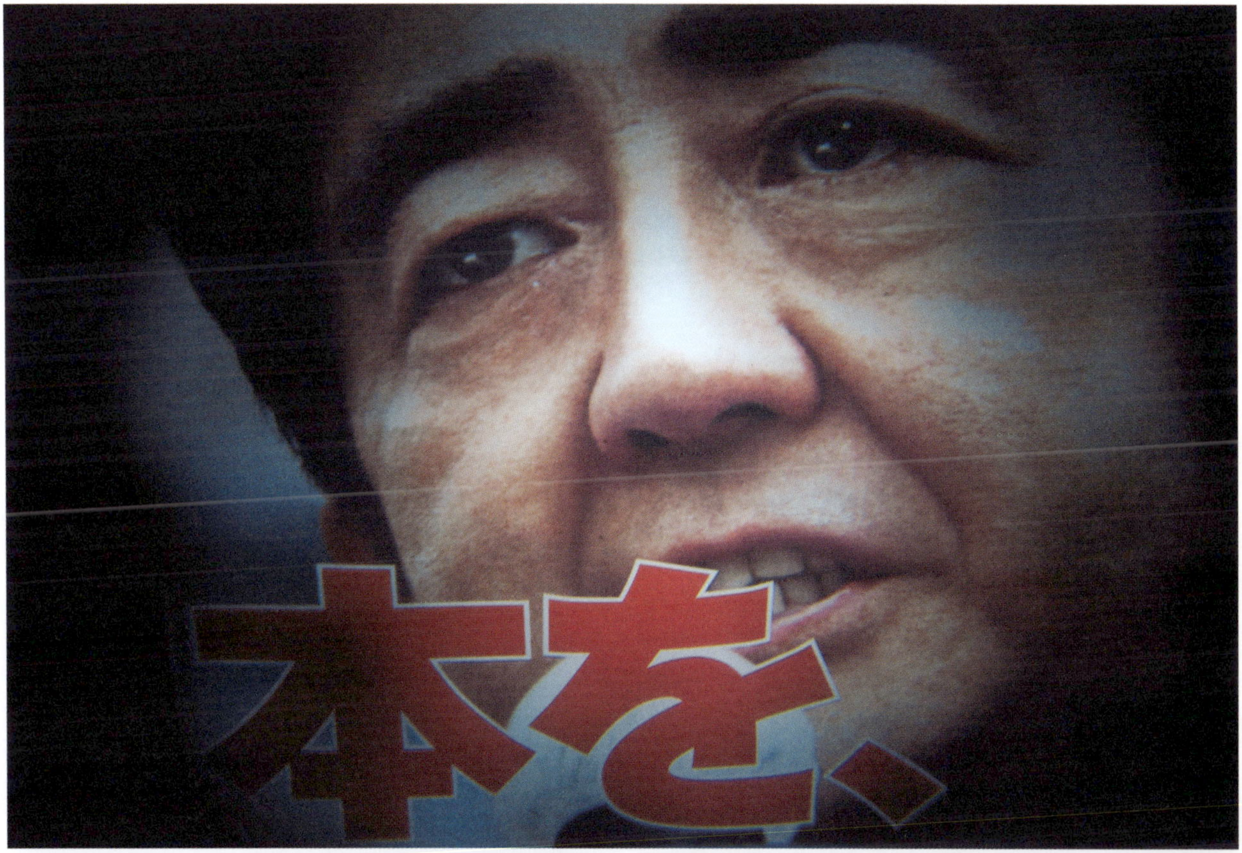

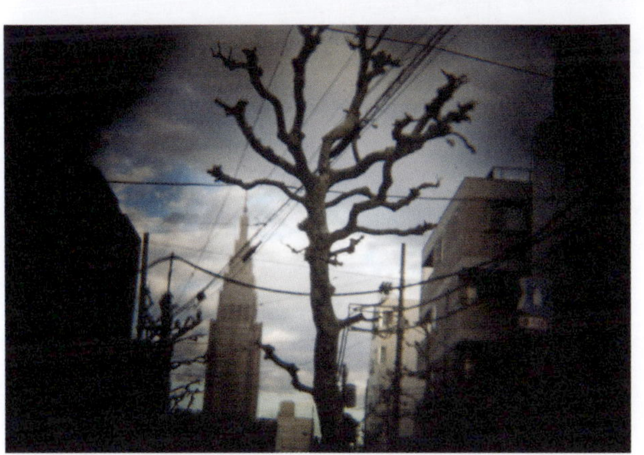

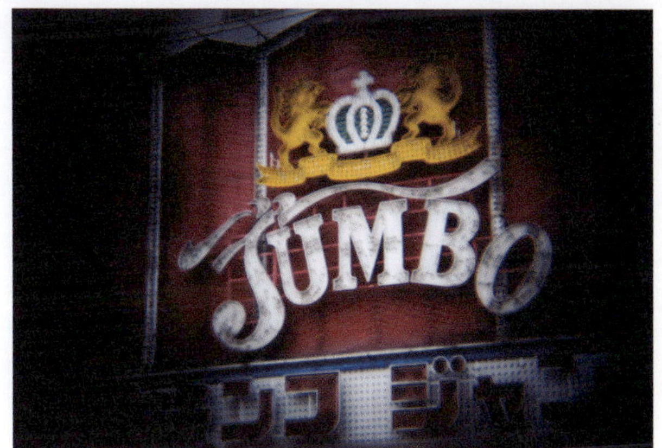
JUMBO

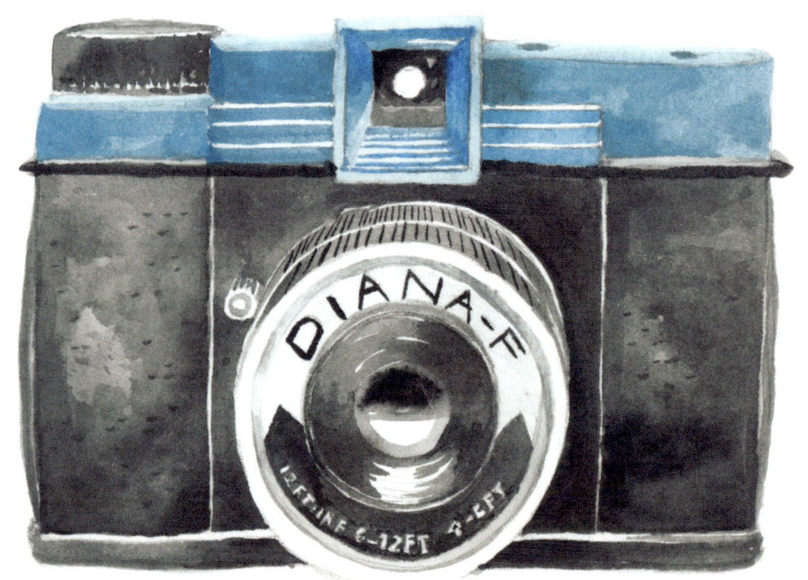
DIANA-F

DIANA

The Diana is a plastic camera with a meniscus lens, which uses 120 roll film and 35 mm film. It is a rudimentary toy, created in the 60s by the Hong Kong company Great Wall Plastics Factory, and was discontinued by the 70s. With a mechanical advance and a basic viewfinder, the camera was intended as a giveaway for children and as such, the inexpensive construction often lends itself to light leaks and problems with the film spool. The camera is known for creating soft, dreamy, low-contrast photographs due to the lens.

While the Diana has been discontinued, Lomography have produced the Diana +, Diana F+ and Diana mini based on Great Wall Plastics Factory's product. The Lomography product produces trademark soft photos produced by the plastic lens, often with vignettes. There are three settings: sunny (f/11), partly sunny (f/16) and cloudy (f/22). This 120 roll film camera has a removable lens. The F+ also allows for a flash attachment, which is indispensable for indoor shots.

The adorable mini weighs 235 grams and takes square format photographs on 35 mm film, and can also shoot in half frame mode.

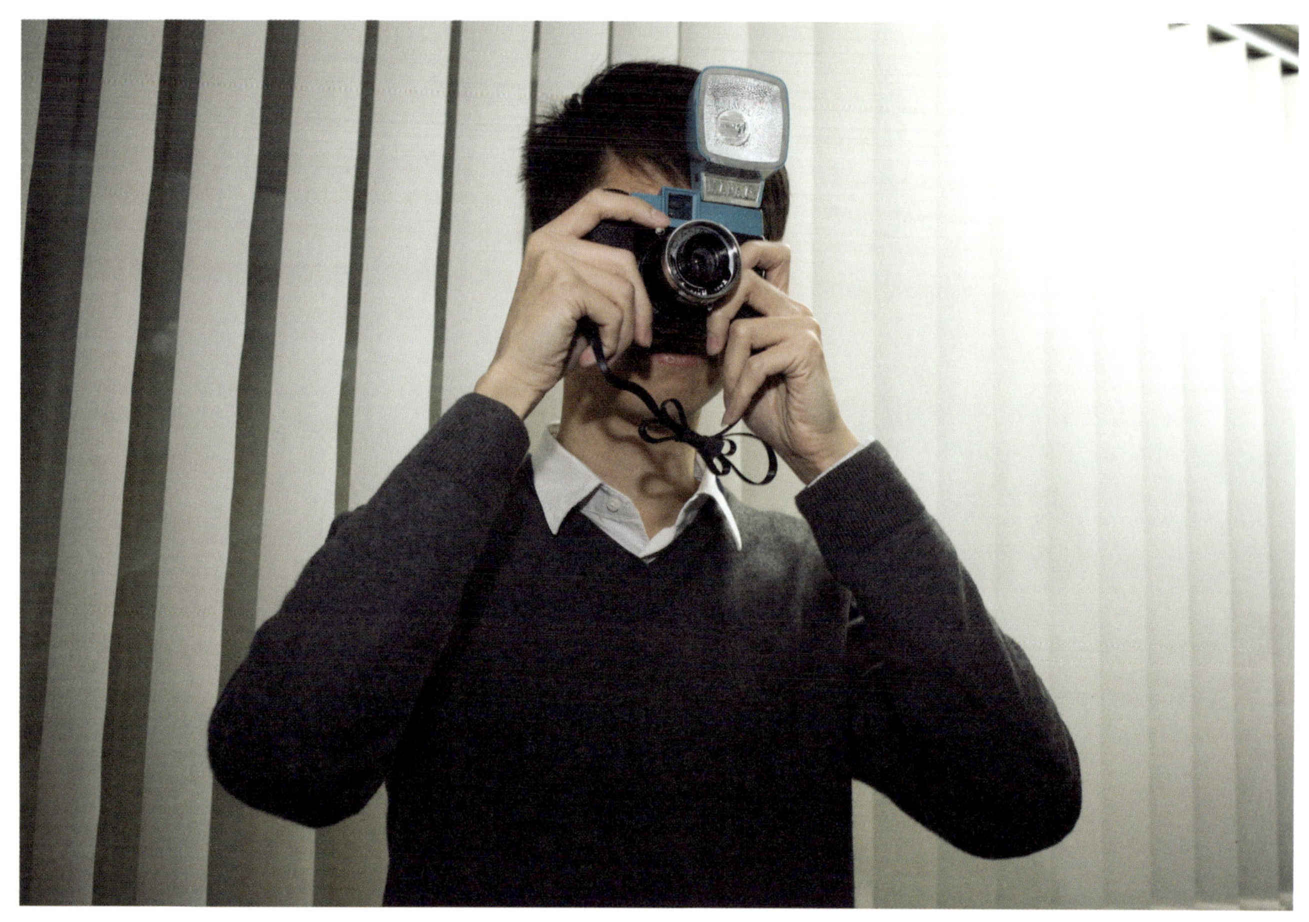

—— *interview 08* ——

EDDIE CHAN,

SALES AND MARKETING AT GREAT WALL OPTICAL PLASTIC WORKS

Can you tell us about the Diana?

Around 1960, we developed the Diana and we discontinued the product around the mid 70s. After that, Lomography reproduced this product, and used their own brand but not our patent because it had already expired, so they could develop this product again. So they launched it to the market and made a lot of money! We only made the patent for 20 years.

Are you surprised that it is such a cult camera?

Yes very surprised, we didn't realize that it could sell very well!

Why did you originally make it?

We intended it as a cheap plastic toy, and the first plastic camera on the market - during that time there were no plastic cameras on the market. All the parts are made in plastic, including the lens and case, so we were the first.

During this period, the boss wanted to develop this product for the toy market.

This product was originally intended to make sharp and clear pictures. But it uses a plastic lens which has distortion and the lens are sometimes out of focus, so the result is sometimes unexpected. That is why the dianas are quite funny for taking pictures, because you never know the result - but that was not our original intention! We wanted it to take clear and sharp pictures!

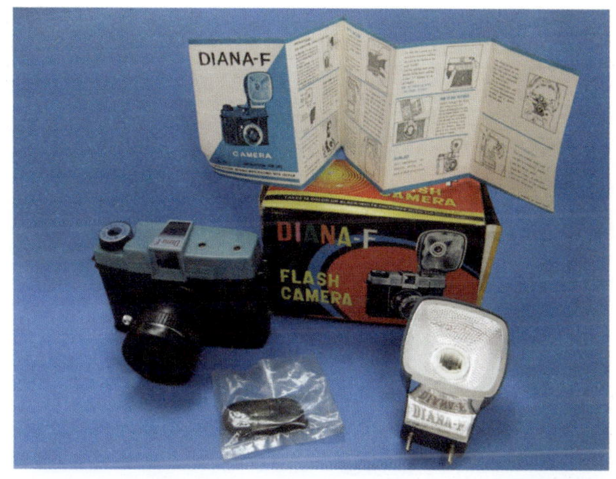

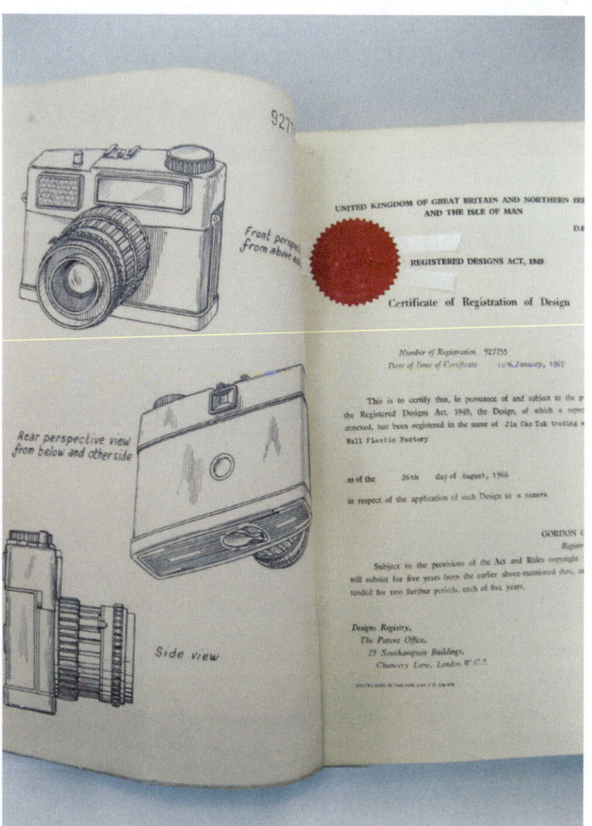

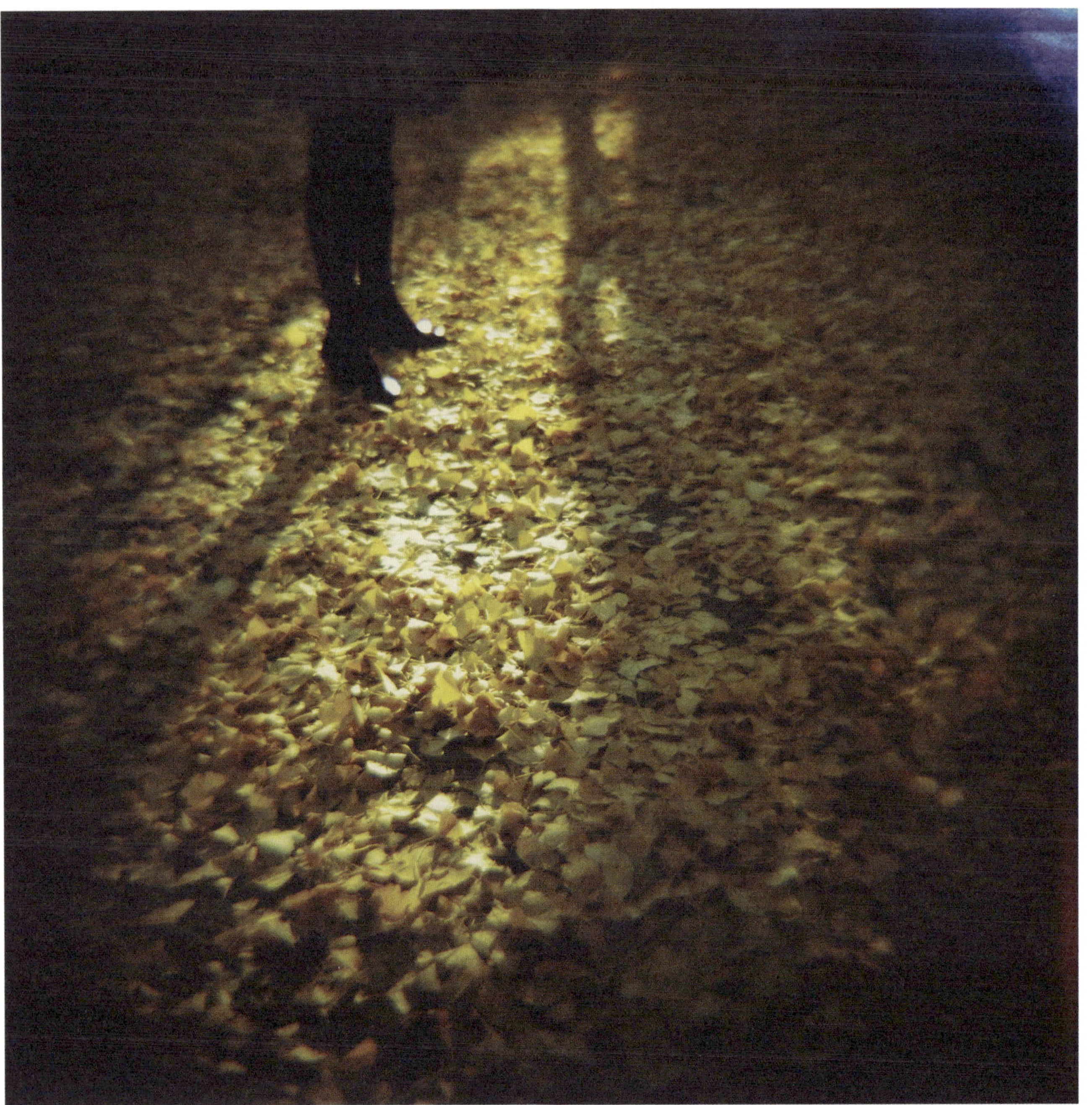

So it was for kids?

Yes for kids, and as a gift for customers. Because one of our customers was selling candy, and they packed this together with the candy, and they were selling it as a package.

Was it an export-only product?

Yes. we were making them in Hong Kong and during that period, our factories were based here, but they were for export. During this time in Hong Kong, the labor cost was still cheap, but it became very expensive, so most of the factories moved their bases to China.

We can't be sure exactly when this product was developed. Our company, Great Wall was established 1955, but according to some documents we found, it was before 1963 because we found some sales contracts from 1963. The price was 21.5 HKD per dozen, so the price was very cheap per dozen, and the retail price was about 50 cents in the US. A few years later some other plastic cameras came onto the market.

When was the peak?

Around 1960-70 and after that, the sales dropped because there were a lot of plastic cameras on the market, so the profits went down.

What were you making originally?

We were making plastic components and products, but not specifically one item, it was everything from plastic figures to cars, but it was all related to toys.

When you first developed the Diana, was it is a copy of a preexisting camera?

The Diana was designed by our boss, because he wanted to make a whole plastic camera so he did everything. They may have copied a metal case camera and changed it to plastic. But a plastic lens is different to a glass lens, the light transmission is different, so you can't just copy it as the calculation of the optics is different.

Have you reconsidered making it again?

It is really expensive to remake it, to do all the molds and redesign the optical structure because there are so many components. But actually, Lomography invested a lot of money to remake this model because I think they just copied the sample.

PHOTOS TAKEN WITH THE DIANA WHEN IT WAS FIRST PRODUCED.

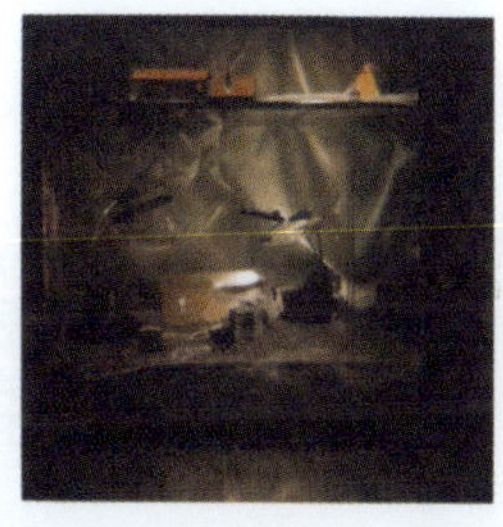

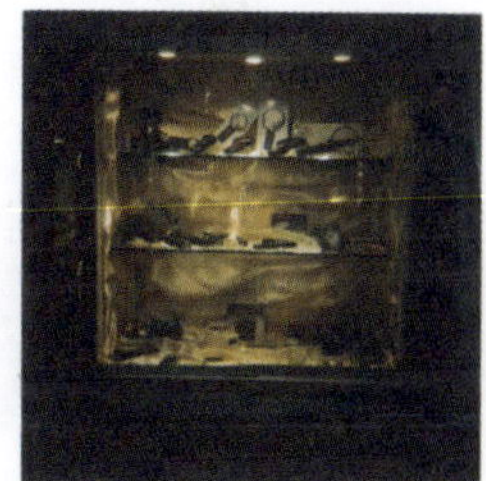

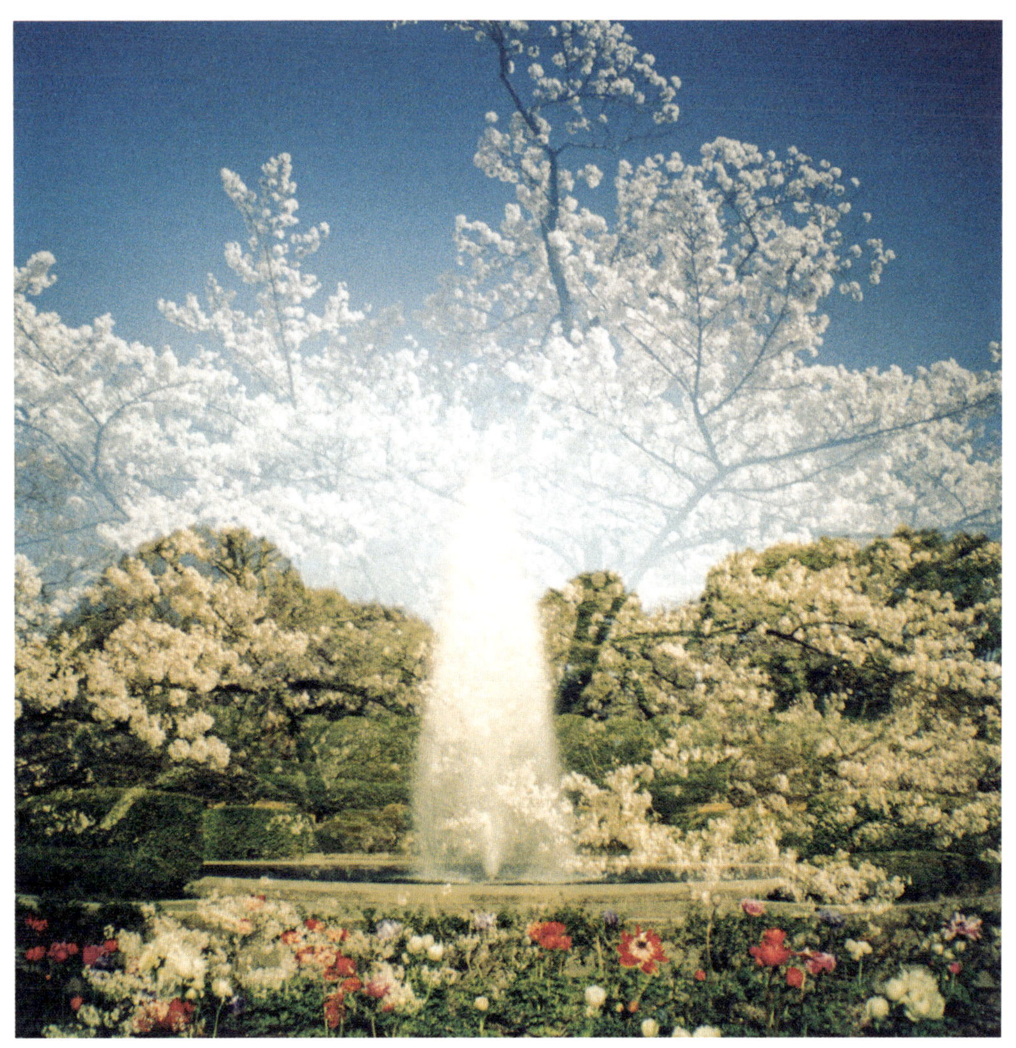

—— interview 09 ——

TAKESHI SUGA

I saw your bio and that you were working at NME doing journalism-style photos.

Yes. In London, I will start working at NME, I really love music such as British and American rock. I shoot digital for that. I want to get a balance (between work and personal shoots). I get a lot of inspiration from musicians such as Sigur Rós and indie music. When I take photos, it is the kind of music that lifts my spirits. I think that is what makes my work characteristic, that I get inspiration from music, rather than photographs. A lot of other photographers base their aspirations on photographers' work, for example Daido Moriyama. He is considered to be the pinnacle, and he inspires everyone to go into street photography.

Is there that kind of direct lineage in Japan still ?

Yes, in Japan, street photography is very popular and everyone is into monochrome. And for private autobiographical photographs, they look to Araki. For young people, maybe they are into Rinko Kawauchi. If I am influenced by music, I can keep a sense of originality in my work.

With your double exposures, do you have the composition in mind when you are taking them?

Yes, I am thinking while I am shooting. It is important is to imagine the imposed images in my mind.

Would you say your aesthetic sensibilities are shaped by your living abroad?

I think these sensibilities are shaped by me being in the UK for 4 years, even though I went after I became an adult. I think this kind of fantastical aesthetic has its roots in the western world. Of course, it isn't just a British thing, and this type of dreamy fantasy imagery can be found all over Europe based on things like folklore. Japan has folklores too, but it is different – we don't have stories like Alice in Wonderland! I also went to Wales for one year when I was in high school, but one year is short. After three years I could ascertain cultural differences. When I was in university, I was studying film, not to make them, but the theory, so I think that is also really influential.

Which directors do you like?

I really like films, such as those by Yasujiro Ozu, and Kenji Mizoguchi, Italian neorealism and Fellini. Also recent directors like Pedro Almadovar – people with their own visual style.

When you are taking photos what mood are you in?

Really high. A word I use a lot is "euphoria."

Do you develop these yourself?

Yes, well, I take the photos with film and then scan them and play with the colors in Adobe Lightroom and use an Epson inkjet printer. It is the best method for me. You can use a variety of different papers. I am using a type of washi (Japanese traditional paper) called kyokushi. It has a texture, which has sheen in places, and it matches the atmosphere of my work.

When did you start using a Diana mini?

2003. I got a toy camera book in which there was a list of cameras, and Diana mini seemed like the most fun. It is small, and this format was fascinating, to have the 35 mm and in square format.

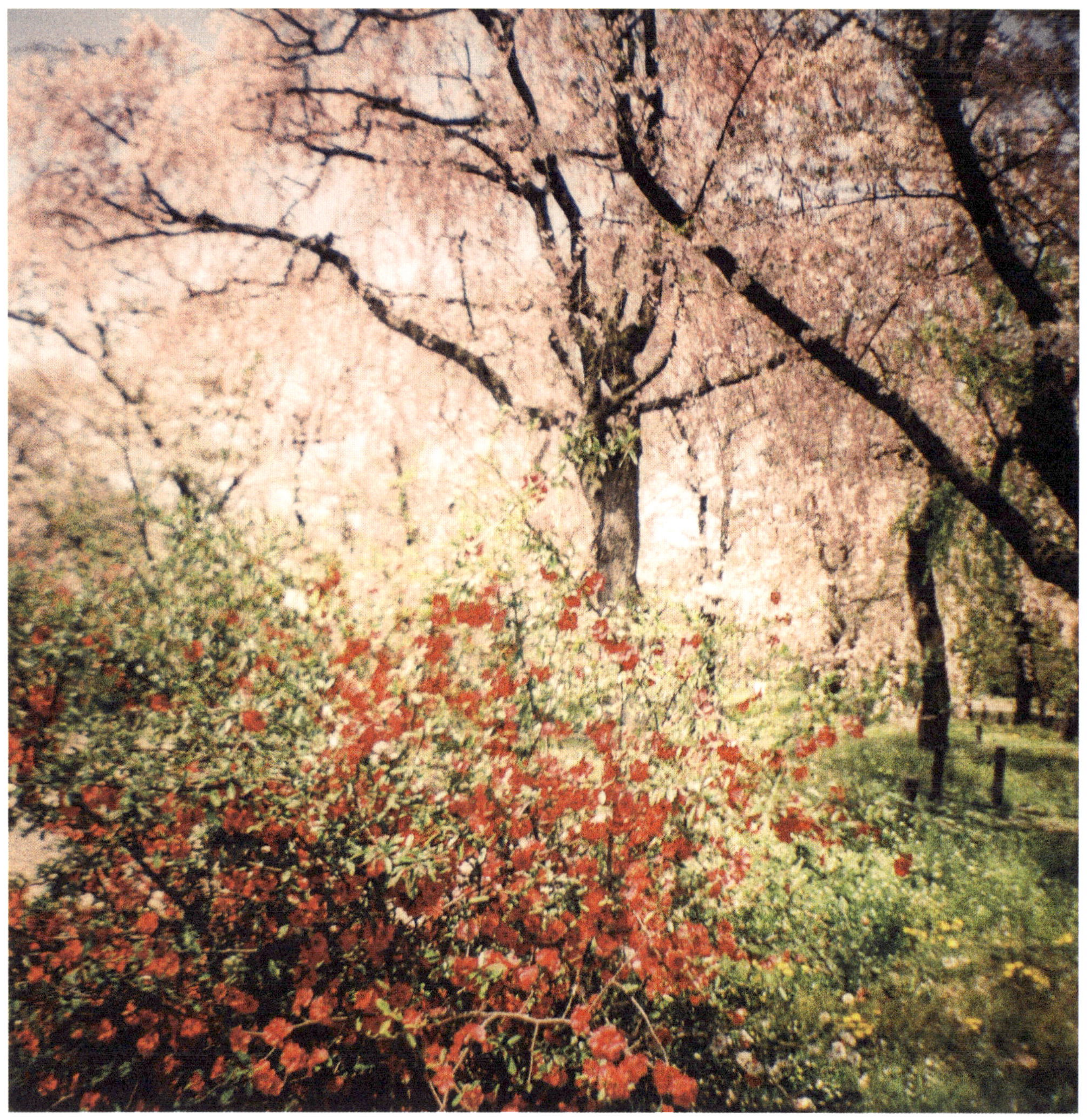

Did it take you a while to get used to it?
There were many coincidences when shooting it. When I first tried it, these accidents turned out nicely, so I continued using the Diana. I also have also run about ten workshops, both through Lomography and independently, using the Diana mini but it is also has a tendency to get duds, as it is easy to get blurry photos.

There are a lot of people who get blurry shots because the camera is so small, and so they don't continue using it, but if you use it 3 to 5 times, you get used to it, but a lot of people quit before then. It is not expensive, so at the workshop I always insist that even if they don't get good results the first time, they should keep trying.

Can you let us know about your Winter Wonderland series?
Before I went to Hokkaido I went to Fukui and was able to take photos there, and thought I could do this winter wonderland series, so I went specifically with that in mind, to go to places where I felt I could find a "winter wonderland."
I took spontaneous photos, I like taking them, and they are the characteristic of my work. I have photos from a train in Hokkaido with frosted-over glass, near Kushiro and Tomamu, and of my hotel window and curtain, and glaciers from the boat.

Of course, I was taking a lot of photos from the train, so I was getting a lot of duds. I am going to the UK, so I won't be able to continue, but I will be looking for things I can only find there.

I am particularly interested in piers; they are still existent in the UK. We don't have them here. I think it is a really particular atmosphere, and for the British, there is a sense of nostalgia, as they would go with their parents. It suits my previous work, and I am not British, to go to see it from a Japanese perspective.

When do you use a Contax, and when do you use a Diana?
I don't really separate them, for example, when I was shooting cherries, I took both, and shot the same thing with both cameras.
I think the difference is when I want a square frame, but in terms of situations, I always take both.

For your personal work is it predominantly landscapes?
I occasionally take portraits; I was taking my friends' more flippantly previously, but my demands got higher and it is harder to shoot friends. It's not like my friends are professional models, so I can't demand things from them, but I think I will shoot a lot more in London as there are a lot of people who aren't shy to be shot over there.

What is the most fascinating thing about toys at the end of the day?
Basically they are fun to use, hold and also the appearance is characteristic. Of course it isn't like the better it looks, the better it is, but ultimately you are trying to express your individuality, and I think what kind of camera you are using is a part of that. So even if there is someone really good holding a huge SLR Canon, I would be more curious about the person holding a Diana.

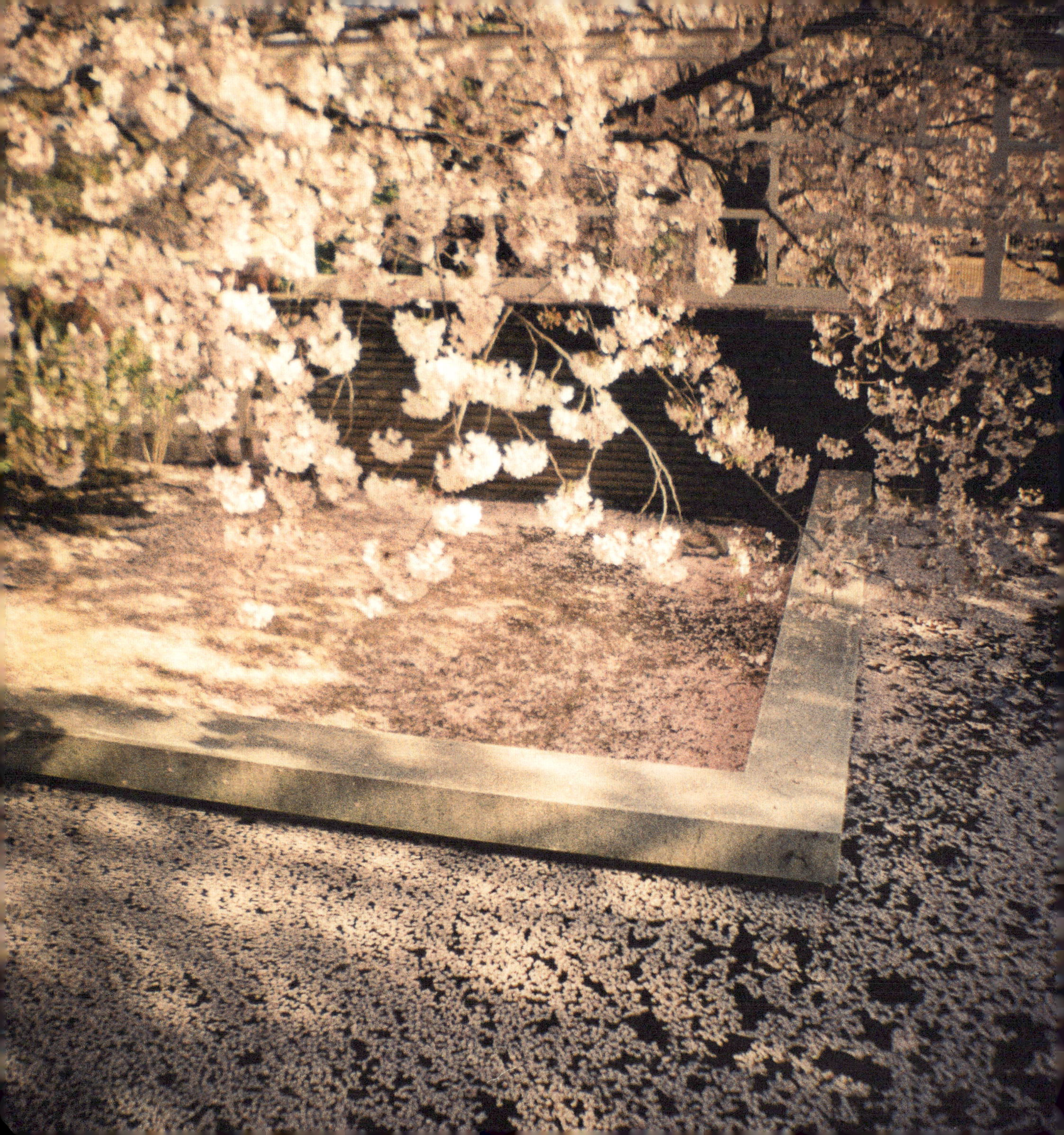

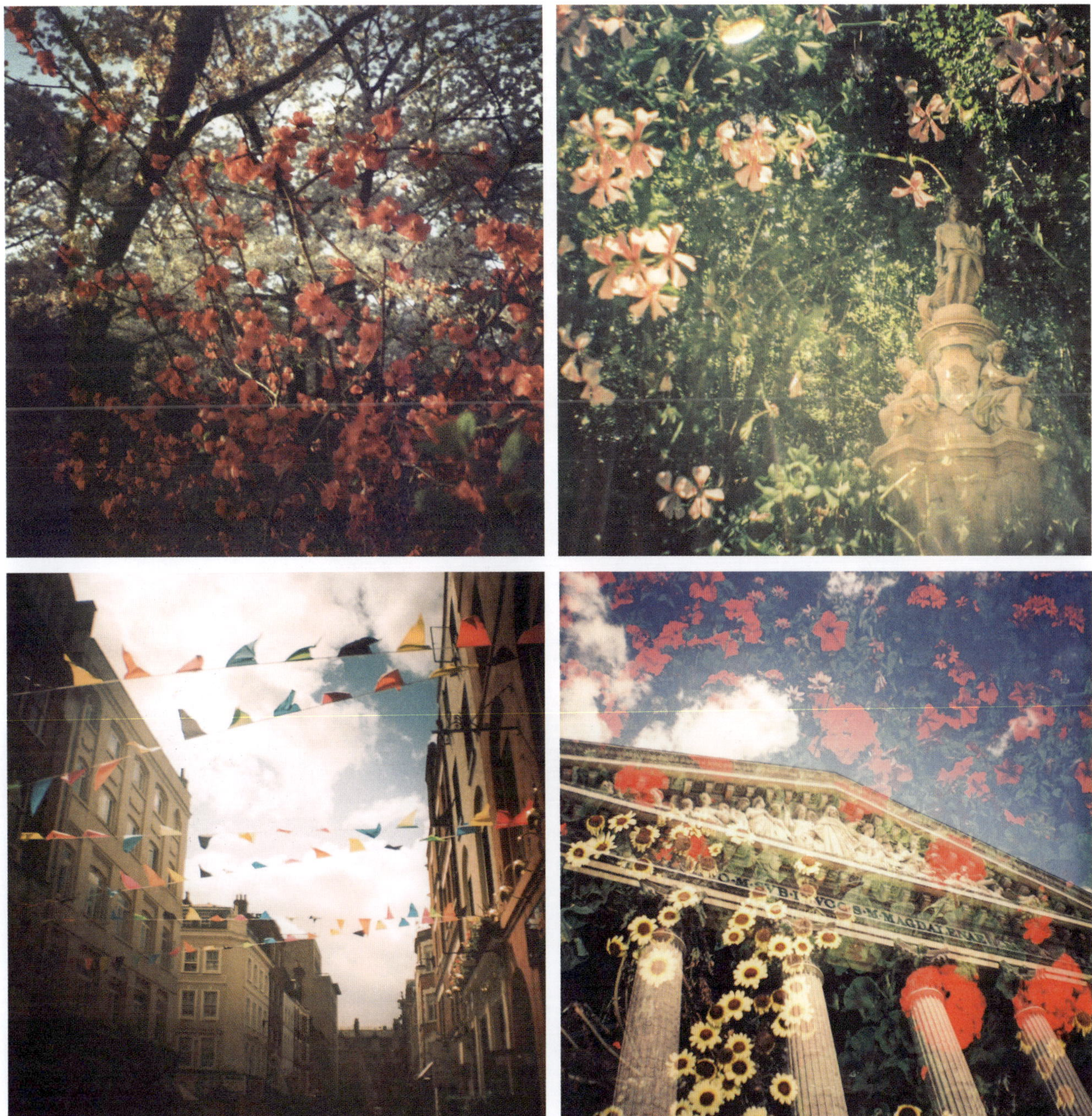
O·M·SVB·I VOC S·M·MAGDALENAE

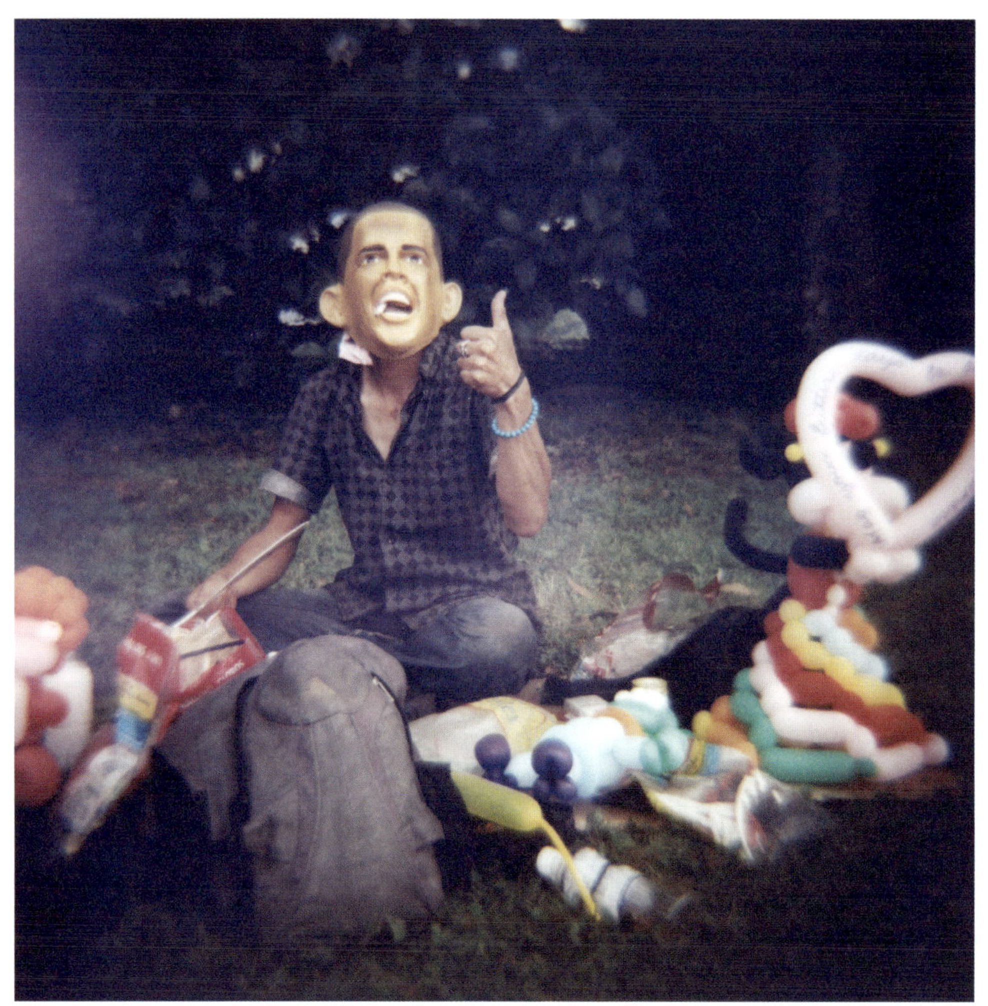

—— interview 10 ——

SEAN LOTMAN

How did you end up in Japan?
I wanted to get out of the States, and I ended up in Japan. I was thinking here or Latin America, and I thought I would have more opportunities to travel here. I lived in Tokyo for 6 or 7 years, I was often travelling and was living in Ebisu and moved to Kyoto 2 years ago.
My wife took over the family business, which is a 15th century soba restaurant. We planned on moving eventually but with Tepco and Fukushima, it accelerated the move.

Your photographs have a beautiful texture!
I only work with film, and I buy paper from New York, and the chemicals as well. I do all my prints in the dark room. I like the Diana a lot. I like to shoot serious stuff, a lot of photos on (toy camera) websites are kind of silly, like selfies. But I am trying to make something like a painting, like 19th century romantic, and impressionistic paintings. I want them to feel timeless, I want people to feel that you could see these at the Louvre. I love paintings and I grew up going to museums - not so much galleries, but museums. When I shoot 35, I always cross-process my images. Both are high-risk techniques.

But you don't get the really blown out colors?
No, no! I try to take out all those blown out colors, I'm more into a hyper reality than an unreality. I think cross process can sometimes look ugly, unreal, too bright, whereas in the darkroom I am taking out the greens and blues, so it looks like a normal photograph, just a little heightened and it works really well. I hate most cross-processed images.

Does using a Diana suit you as a travel photographer?
Yes, it has been for a long time, in Turkey it was the only camera I was using. I don't know if I am a street photographer or a travel photographer, I call myself a surreal humanist.

You also write haiku, do you see any parallels between poetry and photography?
Yes, I companion haiku with the image. I have been a writer for 15 years and a photographer for 5. I think it helps to be a sensitive person. Seeing the world, what is beautiful and remarkable around me. If you are a writer, you are looking at details, so you already get a sense of what is not a cliché.

With writing, you are trying to avoid clichés. You have to make anything you are doing as personal as possible, not universal, and in that way you can create something that no one has seen before. That is the most important thing. Too many magazines and people try to win everyone, it is like advocating a template, rather than a signature.

This is a great way to present travel images, as I feel with a lot of travel images, they could be anyone's. They are all about the hotel, or about finding yourself, it is really challenging to write a good travel story - not about writing 'I went here and there' - I'm looking at the photos and trying to create a narrative.

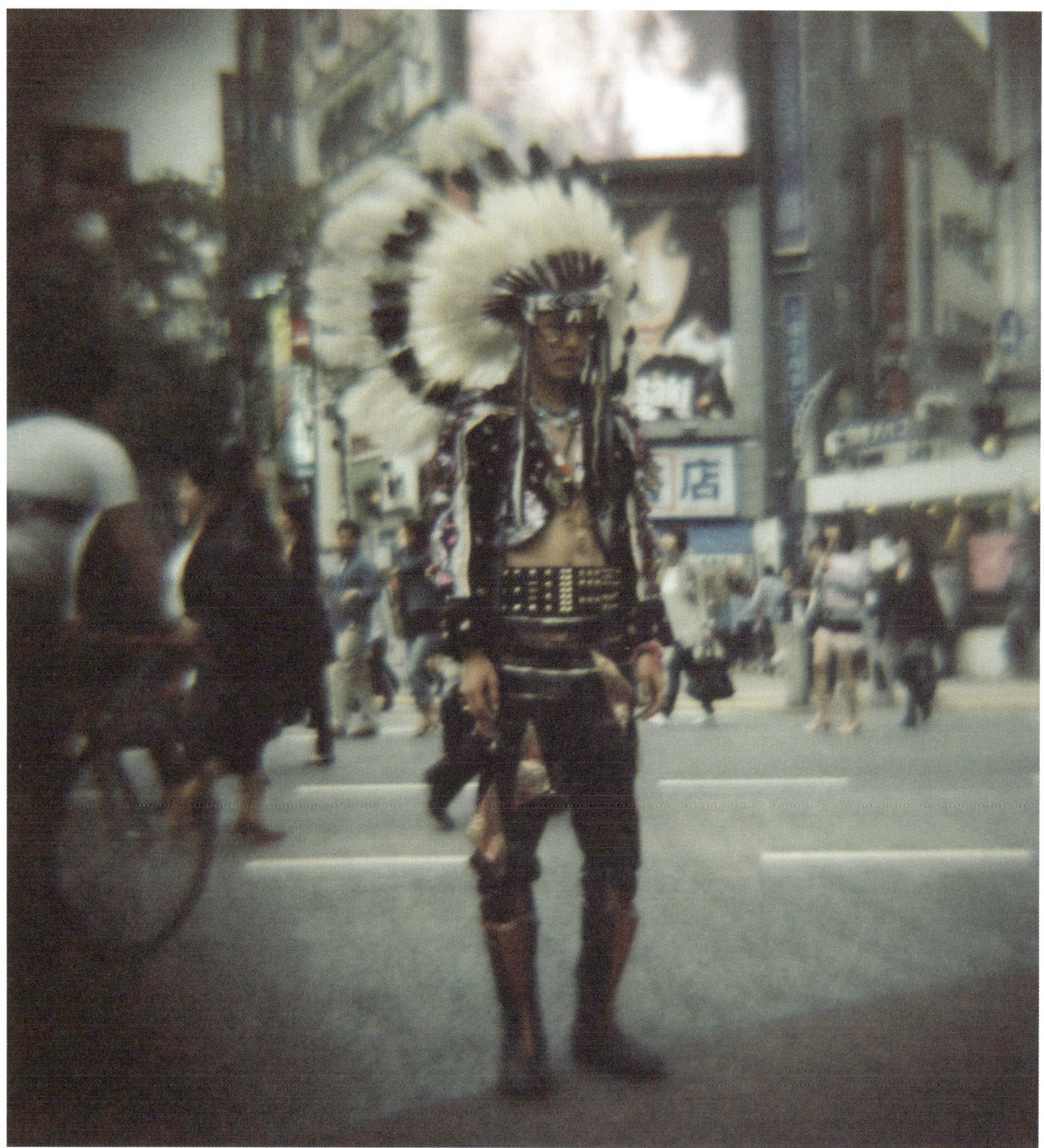
店

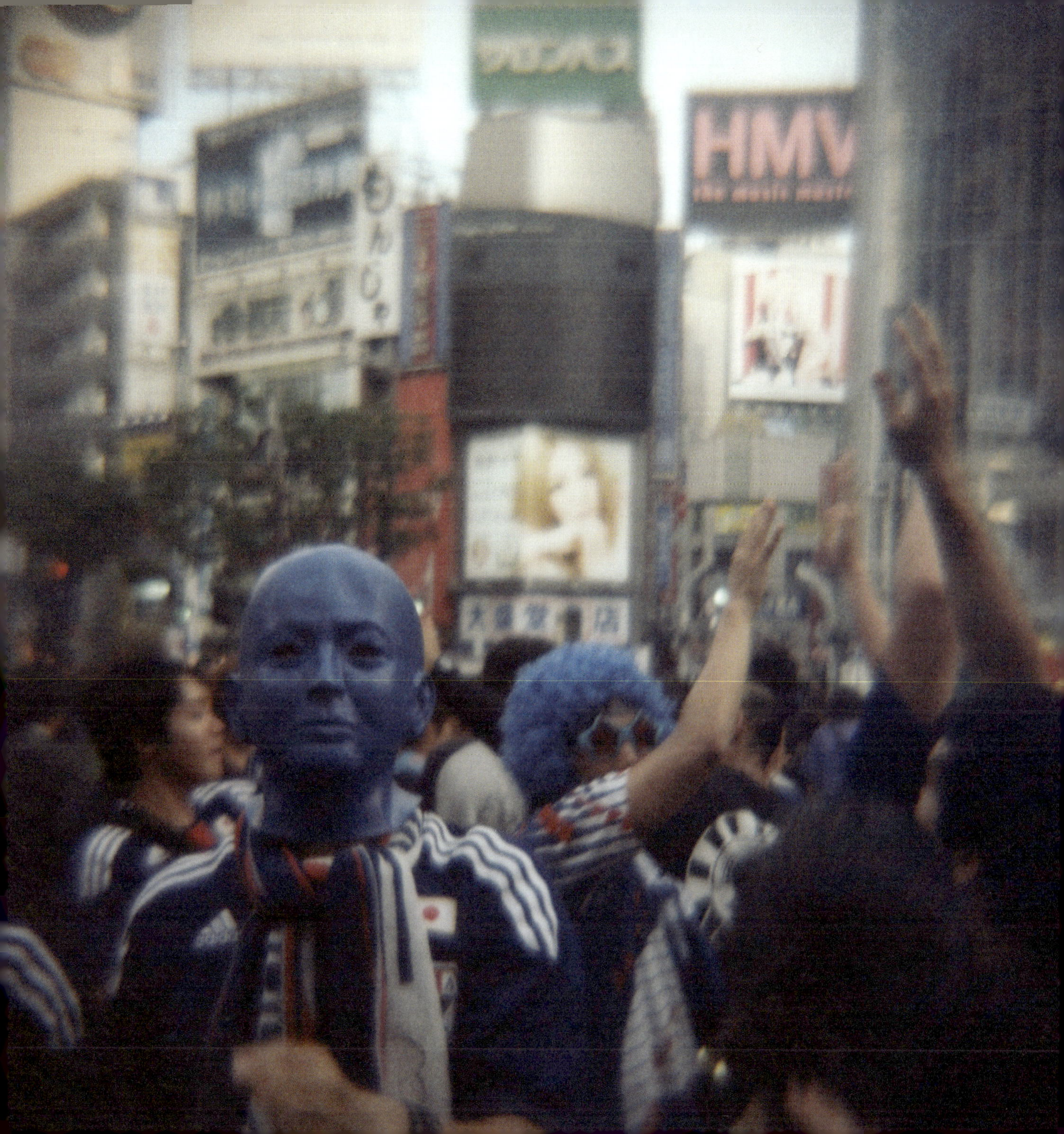
HMV

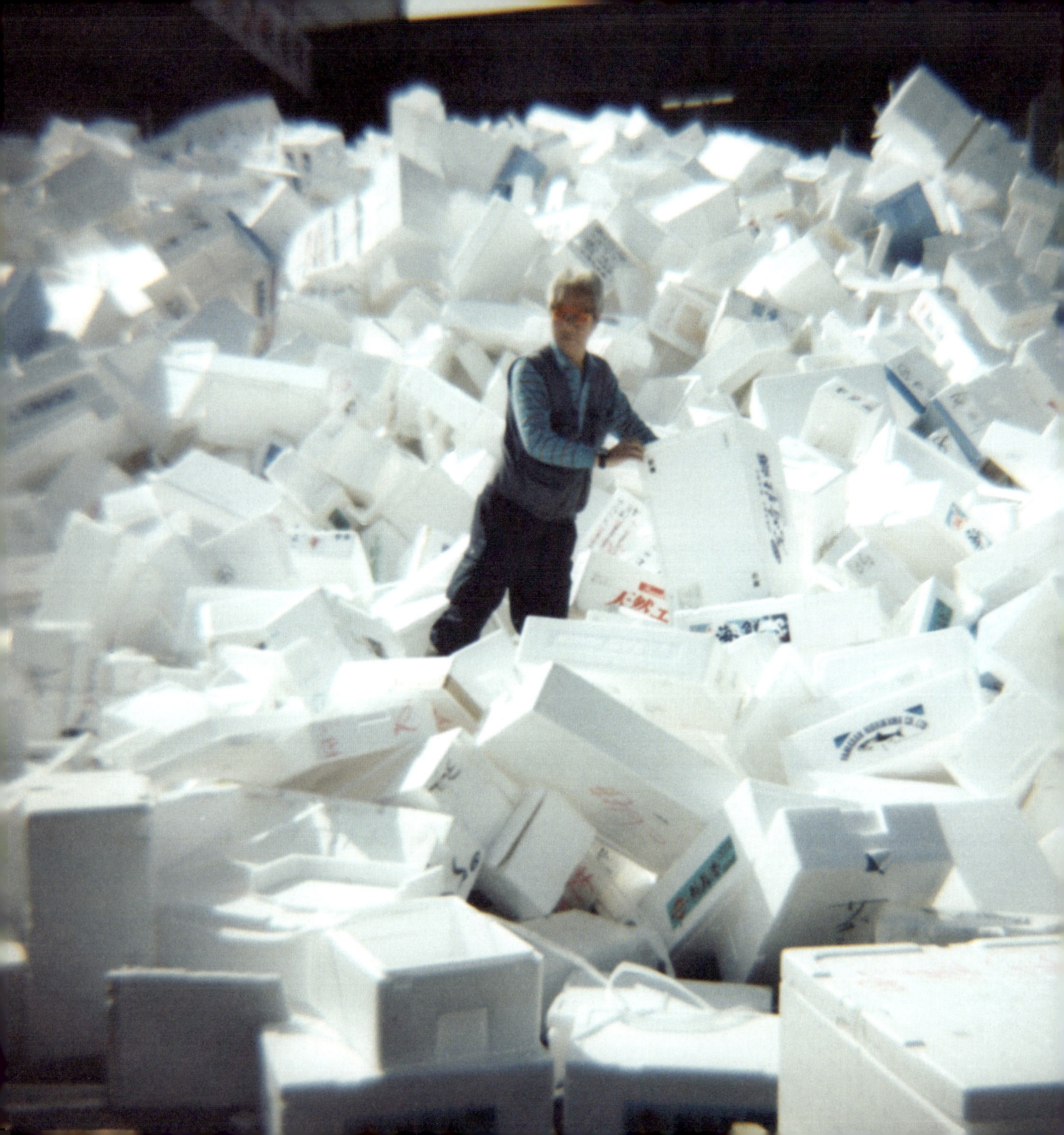

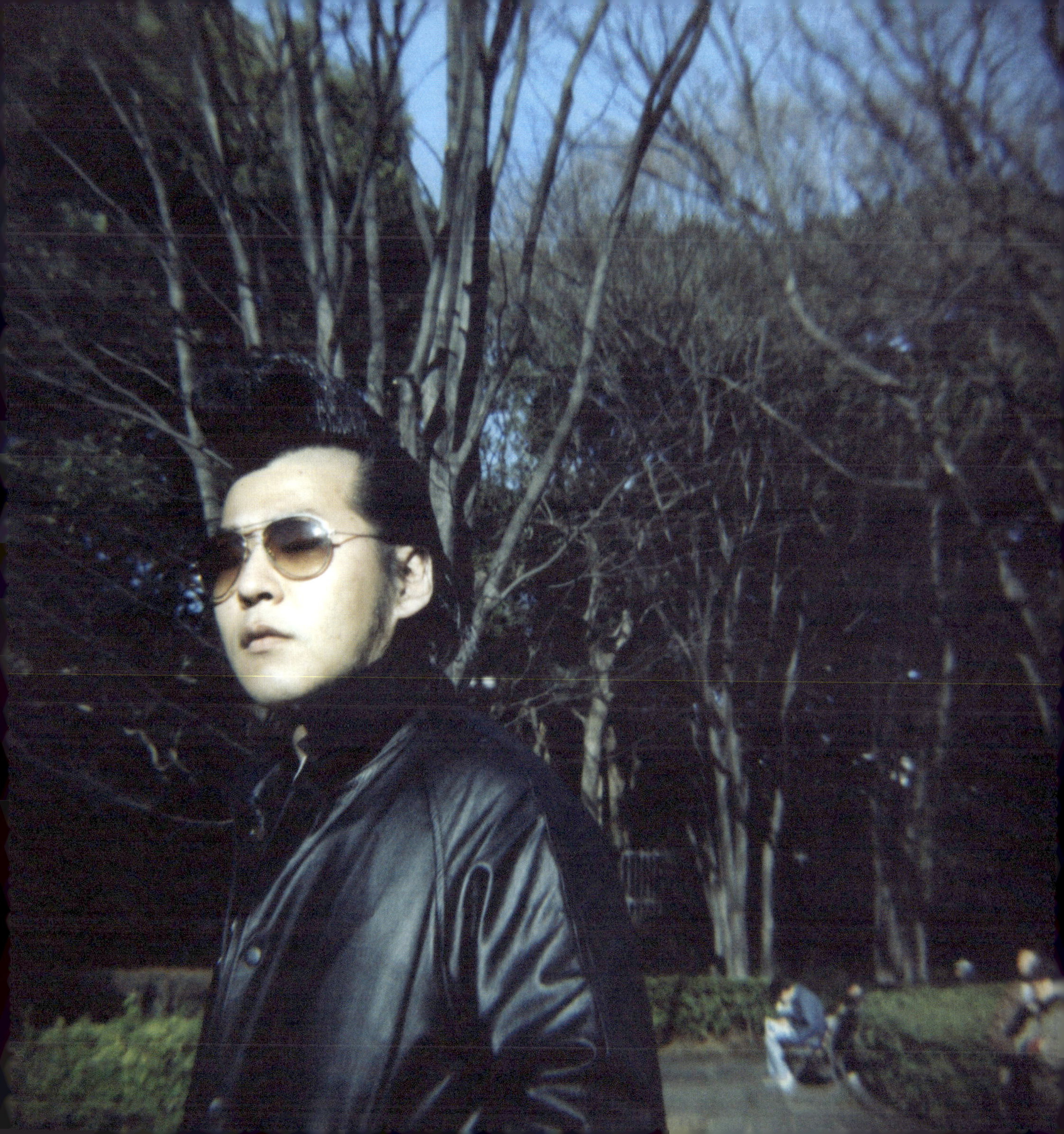

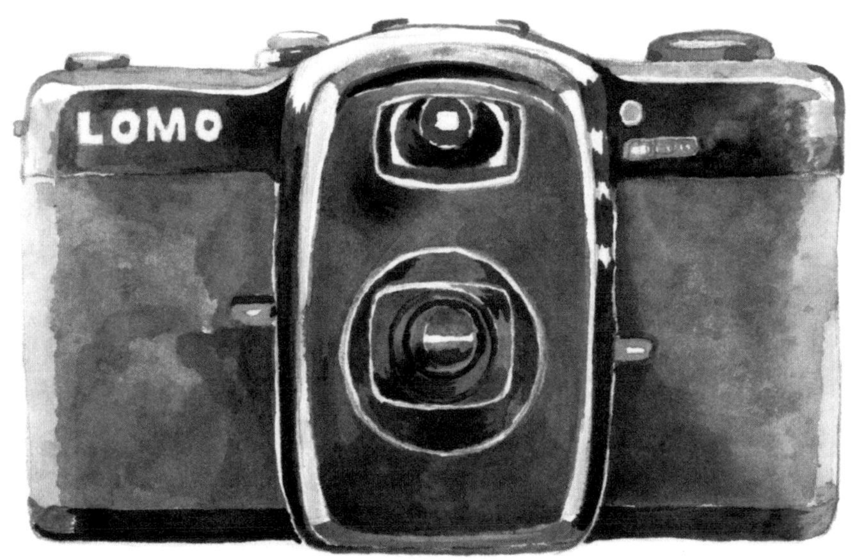
LOMO

LOMO LC-A

LOMO (Leningrad Optical Mechanical Association) is an optical instrument maker based in St, Petersburg that makes, amongst other optical instruments, legendary cameras that are often credited with starting the toy camera craze. The LOMO LC-A is a fixed-lens compact camera with manual film loading, winding and rewinding. The lens is a zone focus system, at 0.8m, 1.5, 3 or infinity. The Lomography LOMO LC A+ is based on the Russian LOMO LC-A, but the plus has new additions and improved ISO settings, and a cable release. It is compact, robust and takes 135 mm film, and has a 32 mm, f/2.8 Minitar lens with an f2.8-f16 aperture. There are film ISO setting for 800 and 1600. The multiple exposure function allows the photographer to shoot multiple exposures on one frame, which creates interesting images. There is also a "splitzer" accessory (see Jorge Sato and Hodachrome's portfolio) that allows you to cover part of the lens as well. The optical viewfinder is above the lens. There is a focus lever next to the lens at 0.8m, 1.5m, 3m, and infinity. This camera works especially well in bright light and produces quality contrast-rich photos, and often vignettes for a characteristic aesthetic. The LOMO LC-Wide has a Minigon wide-angle glass lens and can take square and half frame photos.

Lubitel is the name of LOMO's twin lens reflex cameras, which was inspired by the Voigtlander Brilliant camera from the 30s. It was the first Soviet twin reflex lens camera and while it is bundled in the toy category, it uses 120 medium format film and has a glass lens so the image quality is often superb.

Lomography also have their version, the LUBITEL UNIVERSAL 166+. The twin lens camera comes with the ability to shoot on 120 and 135 roll film, (which can be rewound at any time). It can shoot the 6x6, as well as the 6x 4.5 format, using a mask. There is also a flash hot shoe attachment and zone focusing modes at 0.8, 1.5, 3 and infinity. The camera also has a 100 % coverage pop-up viewfinder with a flat glass, which is great for hip level shooting.

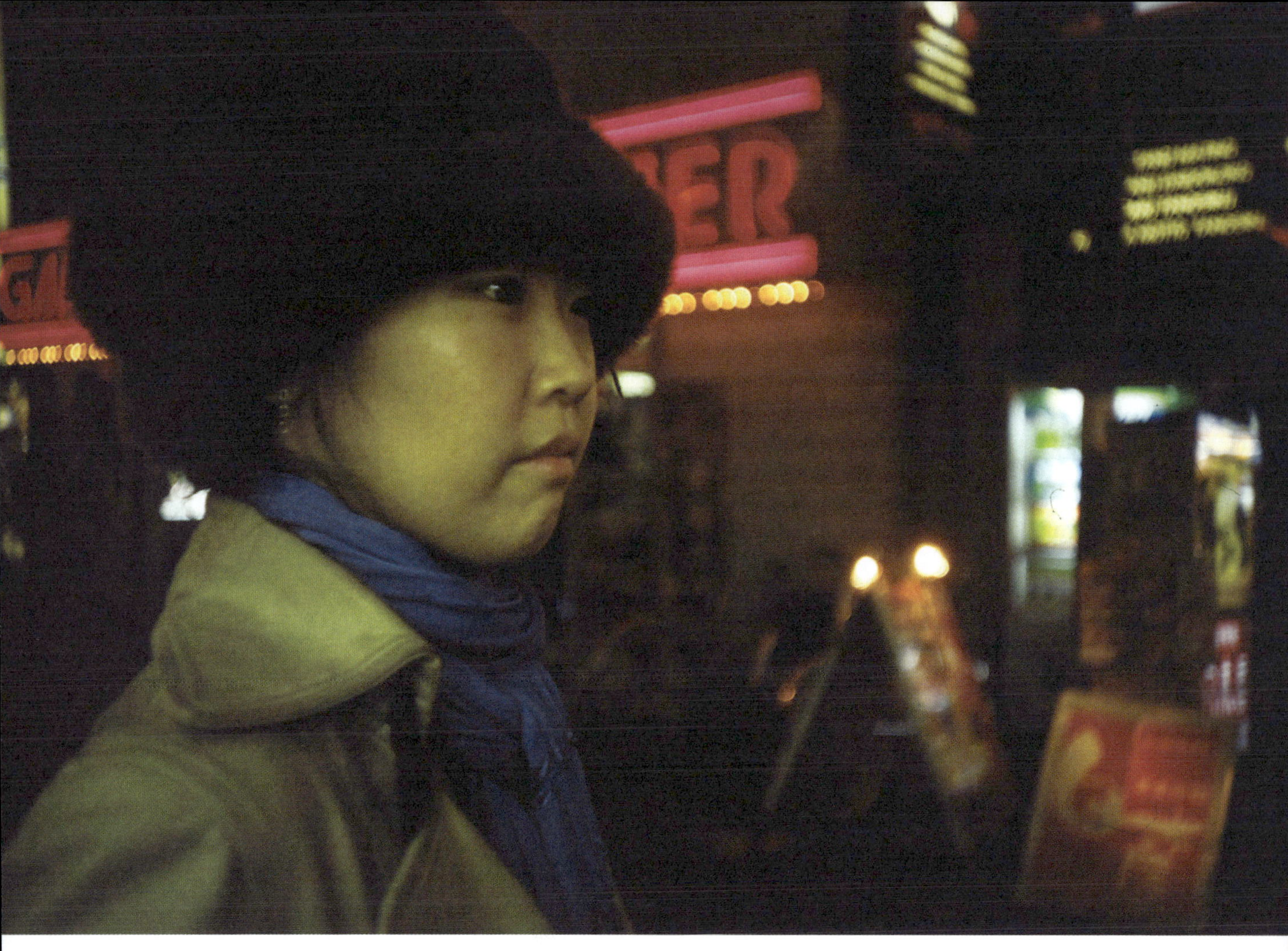

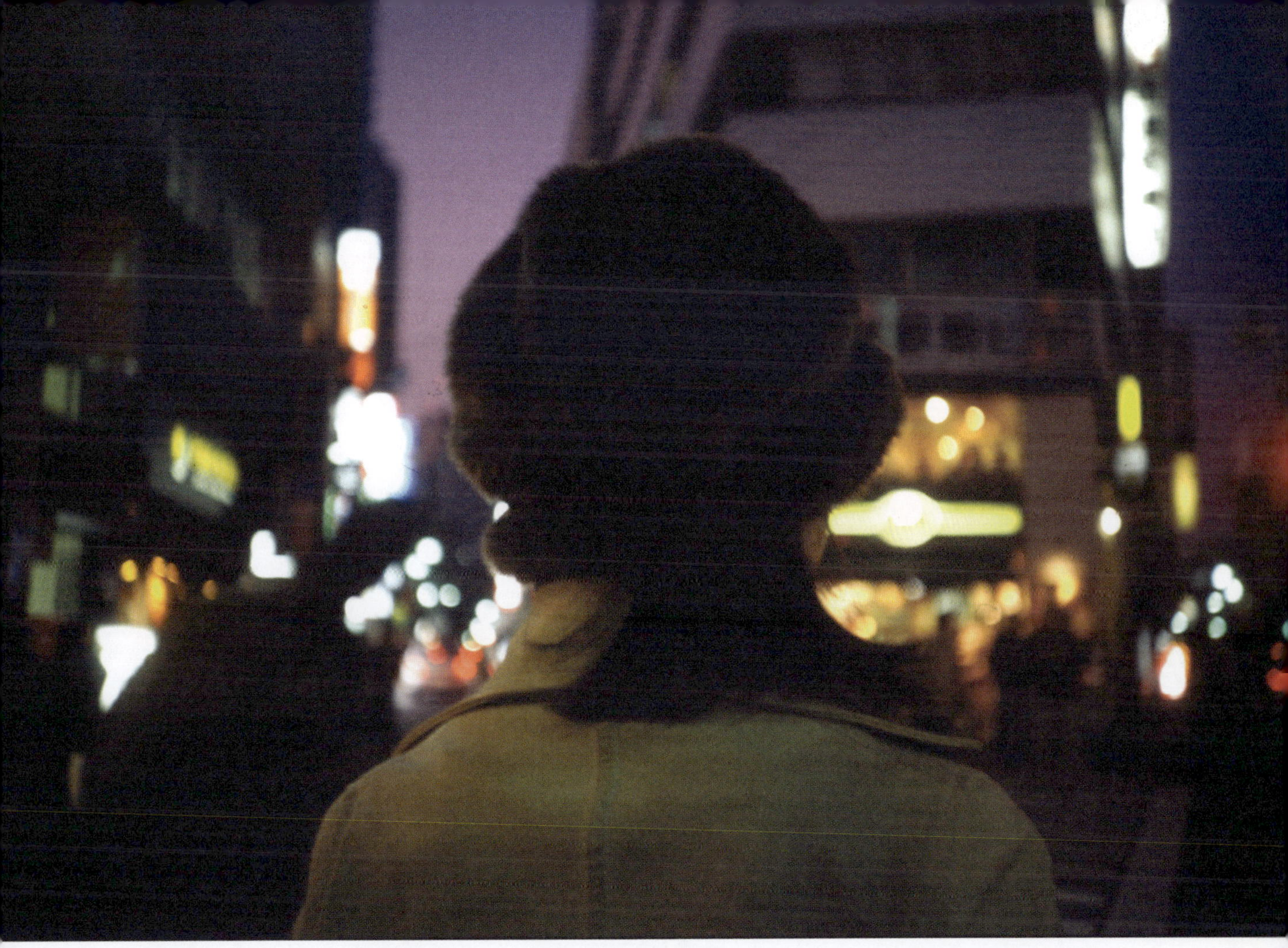

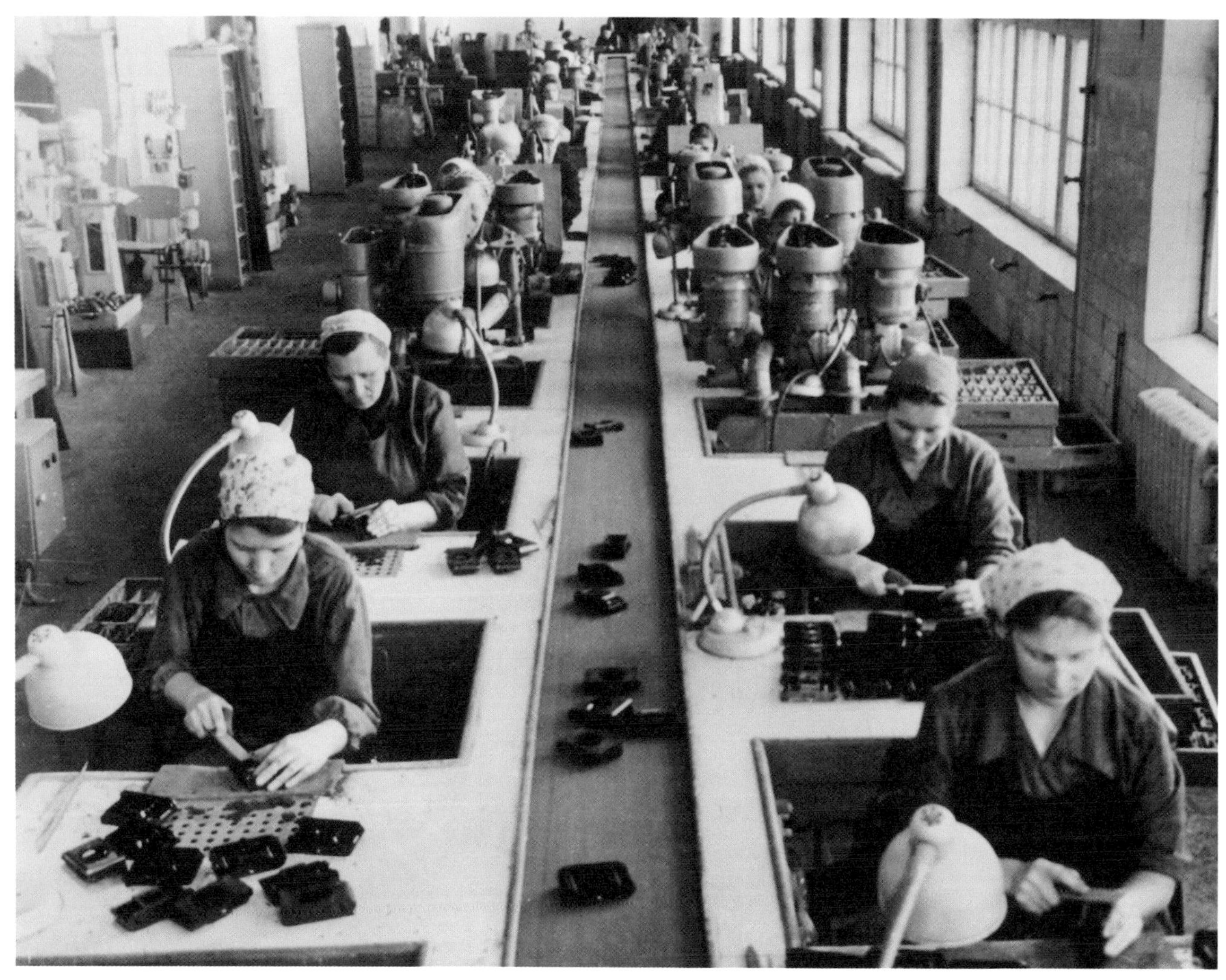

CAMERA ASSEMBLY LINE, 1955.

—— *interview 11* ——

LAZAR ZALMANOV,

ASSISTANT DIRECTOR - GENERAL, LOMO

Can you tell us how LOMO was established and what your initial products were?
LOMO was founded 4th of February 1914. It was the first optical plant in Russia. Until 1914, the Russian army was using German-made optical devices. Since it was clear that the war between Germany and Russia was inevitable (First World War in 1914), a group of military engineers, industrialists and bankers initiated the creation of our own optical industry. In order to equip themselves, the Russian army and the navy optical devices division began to create the first optical factory in the form of a joint stock company. Not surprisingly, its first products were military products: sights, telescope, sighting devices for checking lines, detonator tubes, rangefinders and others.

In 1918, the factory was nationalized and in 1921 it was renamed "State Optical Plant" (GOZ). Then, it was called "State Optical and Mechanical Plant" (GOMZ), amongst other names. And in 1962, after the merger of the three plants (Gomza, "Progress" and "Kinap"), there was a large optical-mechanical association, which was renamed the "Leningrad Optical - Mechanical Association (LOMO)" in 1965. In 1993, there was an auctioning of the company and since then it has been called "Open Joint Stock Company "LOMO. "
Today, LOMO is the assignee of all three former independent plants. Thus, the first optical LOMO factory in Russia traces its history back to 1914, i.e. 100 years.

When did you make the first cameras, and who were they intended for?
The first Soviet film camera was set up in 1925 at the "GOZ," and was called "Photo- GOZ." It was developed by the designer of the plant, P.F. Polykov. This camera had not gone into production, but it was very important for all subsequent developments with our cameras. In 1928-29 we designed a wooden tripod camera "13x18 " for photo studios and photo shops. It was a small-scale production that began in 1933. However, the first Russian camera, which started the country's massive passion for photography, was the "Fotokor number 1," the production of which began at the "GOZ "in 1930. It was a camera for amateur photographers. During the period from 1930 to 1941, we produced over 1,000,000 pieces of this camera.

Can you tell us about the industry at the time? Is it correct that you made the first camera in Russia?
It's correct. It is our company that created the first camera in the country.

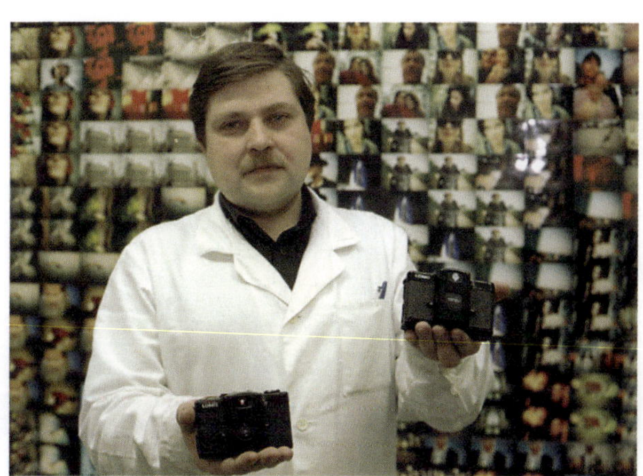

LOMO cameras also created the Krasnogorsk Optical and Mechanical Plant, in the Moscow region during their early camera production, around 1947 to1949.

In 1960, we also created the Belarusian Optical and Mechanical Association (BELOMO) in Minsk, the "Arsenal" Kyiv in1960 and a factory in Kharkov in 1960 for the early production of cameras.

Was the first camera based on a preexisting camera, or an original design?

The prototype (model) for the camera "Fotokor number 1," a folding plate camera with a frame size 9x12, was from the firm "Zeiss Ikon" (Germany). The design was our own, but during the beginning of production, the chamber used shutters purchased from Germany's "Kompur" and "Vario". Since 1932, the chambers has used our own shutters.

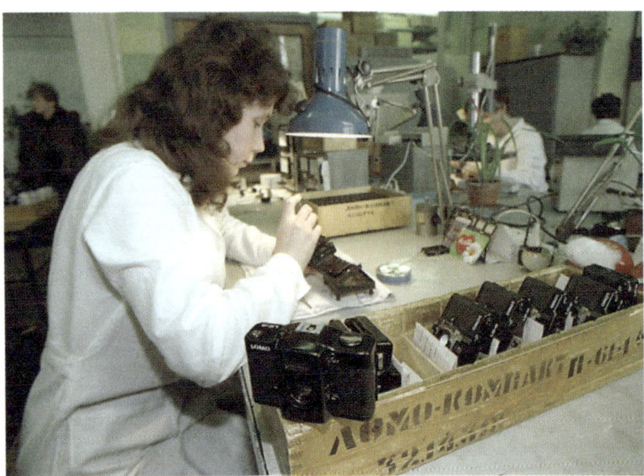

Who developed the optical technology?

The lens for the camera "Fotokor number 1" was developed by V.S. Ignatowski, who later became a professor at the Leningrad Institute of Fine Mechanics and Optics.

What have been some of your other cameras and optical products?

From 1930 until 2004, LOMO (then called "GOZ") made more camera types regularly. During this time, we created more than 140 camera models, 100 of which were for mass production. Over the last century, for other areas of civil engineering, we produced microscopes in the mid 30s, astronomical instruments in the late 20s, medical equipment in the mid 50s, laser systems in the mid 50s and cinema equipment in 1918 (such as the first Soviet film projector "Rus").

When were "regular" people able to buy your cameras, and how did the company change as it went public?

The present mass (or rather large-scale) production at LOMO began in the mid 70s, when we produced the camera "Smena-8M". From 1970 to 1995, we produced more than 19 million cameras.

As for publicity, everything is complicated. LOMO was originally created for the production of military equipment. Today, the most important products of the company is for military and space applications. This imposes certain restrictions on the company to distribute information related to state secrets. LOMO became a public company after the 1993 privatization occurred, and is now 100% private. Today, LOMO is the only fully private optical company in Russia, and there are more than 15,000 shareholders. This necessitated the creation of a specific corporate culture. In addition, publicity has become necessary for LOMO for another reason. The early 90s were the years of the so-called "perestroika".

In economic and managerial terms, this meant termination of the "planned economy" and the transition to work in the free market. Prior to these global changes, state industrial enterprises, including LOMO, did not sell their products on the domestic and world markets. They performed only targets coming from ministries, or from centralized foreign trade companies, and we would ship the product in response to incoming requests.

After the start of market relations, LOMO and other industrial companies had to take care about what products to produce, how to produce it, to whom and at what price to sell it. Under the circumstances of the time, there was no money for government orders in the state budget, but the vast majority of the time LOMO products were intended specifically for budgetary organizations. There was not the money nor the population for which the LOMO cameras were produced.
Asides from this, the Russian market was opened up to international manufacturers of photographic equipment and stores filled with cheap Chinese "compacts". We had to find ways to promote the name LOMO in world markets, and for the company to develop new marketing techniques, one of which was publicity.

Can you tell us about the Lubitel and the LOMO LC-A?
For the Lubitel, the idea was to create a mirror medium format film camera at LOMO's "GOMZ" factory, in 1947, and at the same time under the leadership of designer I.G. Shapiro, a prototype camera called the Komsomolets, which was not made in large quantities because of the shutter's quality problems.
In 1949, A. A.Vorozhbit developed a new shutter called "ZT" which helped in the production of the new Lubitel camera. Since 1950, this camera has been available for export to Sweden, and was first called "Amator", and after a little modernization in 1951, it was named the "Atlantic".

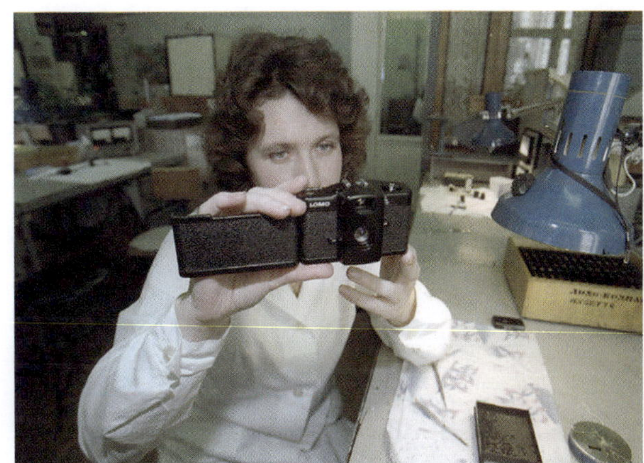

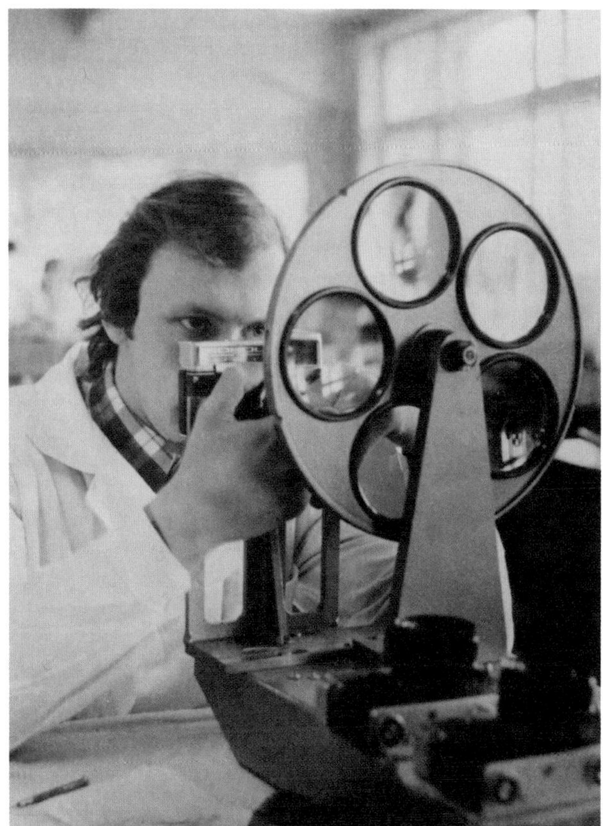

TESTING 'SOKOL' CAMERAS. 1970S.

For the camera "LOMO Compact automatic," the idea of creating the first Soviet camera with automatic exposure was born after Soviet experts visited the largest international exhibitions in Cologne (Germany) in 1980. The prototype (model) to create the LC-A was the Japanese automatic camera "Cosina CX- 2." The first six prototypes camera "LOMO Compact Machine " appeared in the spring of 1982. In early 1983, the first industrial lot was produced, and in June 1983 we began mass production of this camera.

Were you surprised that LOMO products gained such a cult following? And how did that come about?

This simple question can be answered very briefly: yes. LOMO was surprised at the rapid growth in interest and popularity of the "Lomo Compact". Especially after the end of the 90s, there were numerous groups of tourists coming to LOMO during the ongoing Lomographic Society tours "in the homeland of the "LOMO Compact," sometimes reaching up to 60-80 people. They enthusiastically visited the assembly shop, and some tourists here eliminated minor faults. Lomography development has also led to a surge of interest in the LOMO in the media, both Russian and foreign. We constantly appeared in many newspapers and magazines and on television. In addition, after the start of the Lomographic Embassy in Russia, many employees were involved in unusual LOMO competitions that were held in St. Petersburg.

When did you sell the most cameras?

The biggest sales occurred in the period from 1997 to 2000, when we delivered 3500 to 6000 cameras to Vienna per year.

Do you still make them?

Production of all LOMO camera models ended in 1992, except

for the “LOMO Compact, “ which was terminated in November 2004 due to large losses. In 2005, LOMO and Lomographic Society International have signed an agreement to outsource the production of the cameras rights for the “LOMO Compact” and “Lubitel” to China. Serial production began there in 2006, when a camera that has been a bit simplified was produced under the name “Lomo Compact auto plus” and ”Lubitel plus.” Prior to 2011, LOMO continued to deliver Minitar lenses for the LOMO Compact to Lomographic Society International.

I want to clarify that the cessation of the production of the “LOMO Compact” camera was due solely to economic circumstances. The fact was that during the ten years of cooperation with the Lomographic Society, this camera was the most unprofitable amongst all products produced at the plant. Nevertheless, the popularity of the Lomography camera promotes our name LOMO around the world. During those years in Russia there was no funding nor state orders, and only the export of various products could enable LOMO earn and grow. However, in 2004 production losses from the camera exceeded all limits. Therefore, the joint decision to move the production to China was a very reasonable solution.

Is there anything interesting you can tell us about how they are produced?

For the entire period during which cameras were produced at LOMO, production was done by hand. Since 1994, all “LOMO Compact” cameras were made only to order by the Lomographic Society International exclusively.

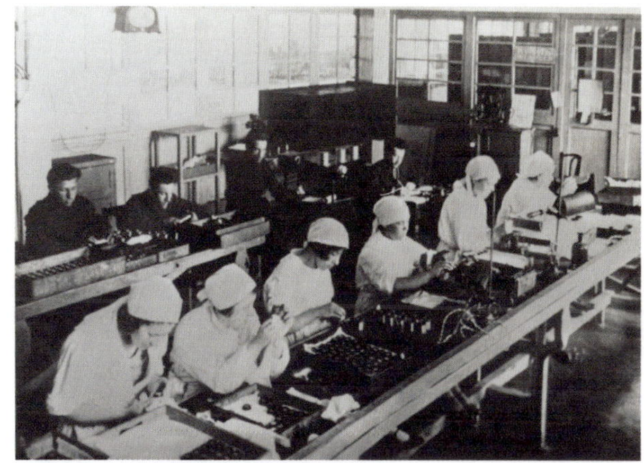

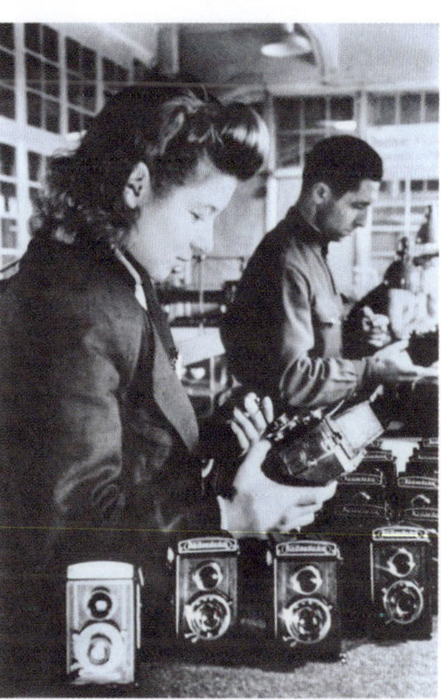

ASSEMBLY OF ‘KOMSOMOLETS’ CAMERAS. 1946.

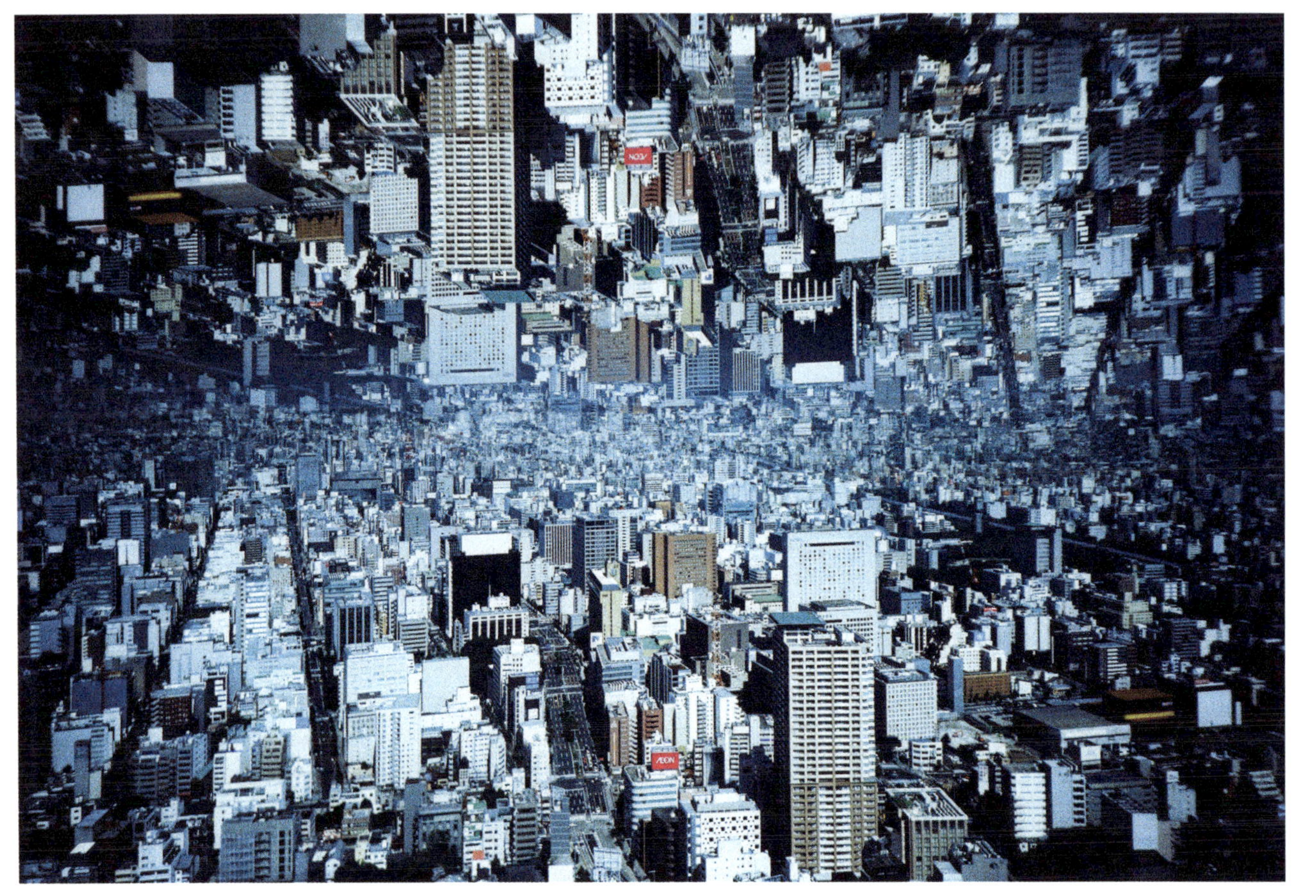

—— interview 12 ——

HODACHROME

When did you first come across a toy camera?

In the beginning, it was an introduction from a friend. It was the LCA made by LOMO, not the LCA plus. And I bought that - that was the start.

Before that I was using a film SLR, about 7 years ago.

What was appealing about the LCA?

I think the individualism, the contrast is high, the colors are brilliant and there is vignetting. If you say "toy camera", you do associate it with vignetting and particularly this camera produces strong vignettes. It is easy to use, as the aperture is large so it isn't too shaky, but you need to be careful.

Were you able to get decent photos from it from the first time you used it?

No. If you compare it to an SLR it isn't that easy, and it was a continuation of failures. In the beginning, I was using SLRs as the main, and the LCA as the sub only 30% of the time, and it was just for fun. Gradually, this became my main tool, and it became more fascinating.

I started to use multiple exposures three years in, and it was since then that I began to see the beauty of that camera and started to focus on it.

Your multiple exposures are amazingly precise, how do you do that?

I think of it in my head and through experience you get used it, and become acquainted with the idiosyncrasies of the camera.

Because you are used to the "personality" of the camera now, is that why you stick with the LCA?

Yes. I still get a lot of duds, but with my multiple exposures, if you get used to them you can get good results.

Can you tell us about the process?

For a straight multiple exposure shot, I shoot the top half and the bottom half once each. And I use a "splitzer," an accessory from Lomography. Firstly, I set it and it covers half the lens and the top half is visible and black, and when you shoot it again, you use the mx function and you can take a photo simultaneously. Then you turn the splitzer and the camera upside down, and the bottom half is taken and the previously black half is shot cleanly. I also shoot at an angle as well, and you can also take multiple exposures many times.

Another technique I use, is called the EBS. There is a front and backside of the film usually, but when you reverse it, you get the backside and according to that, you get a red tinge on the images. And when you use that, you can take EBS images. The first time you take the photo normally with the top half, and

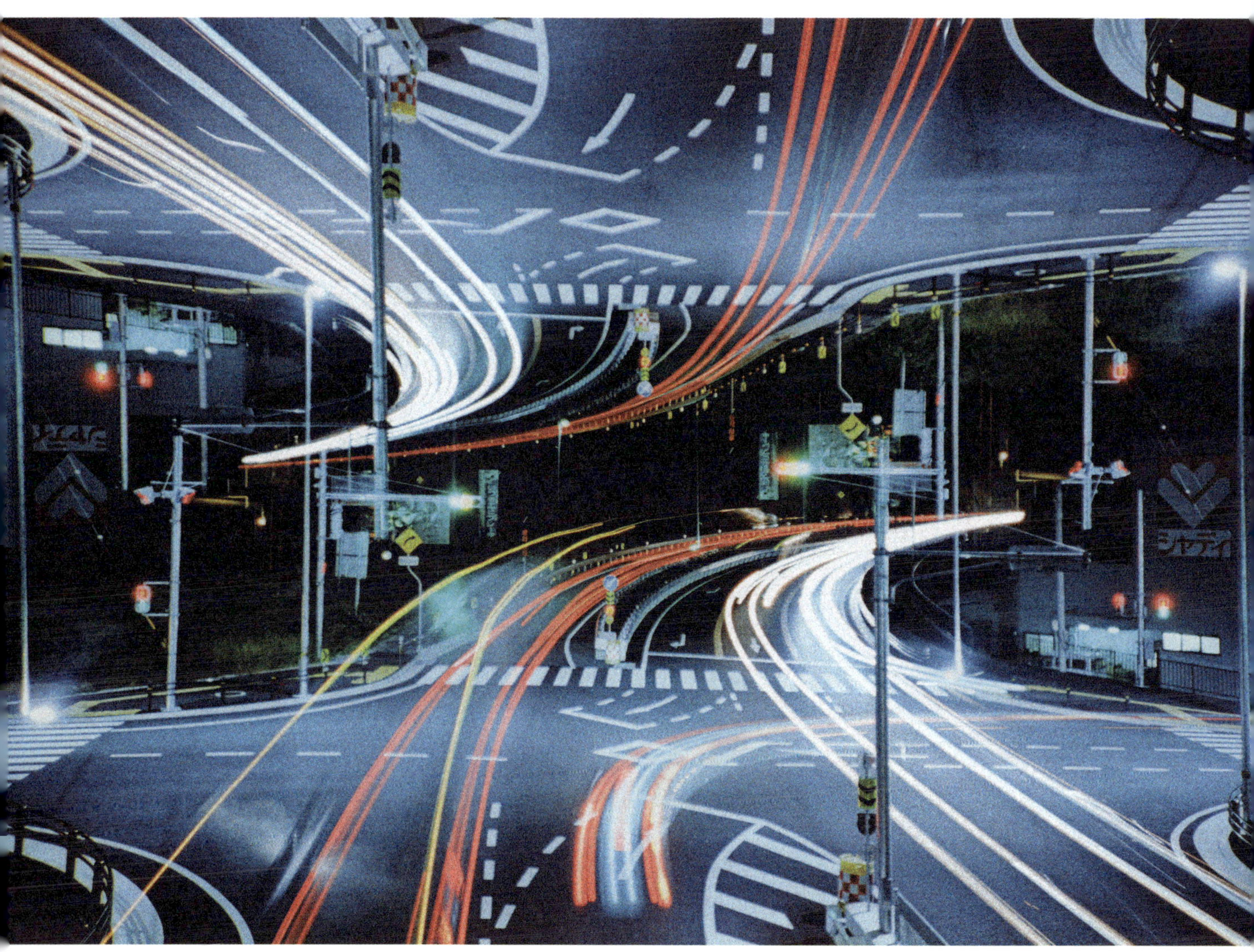

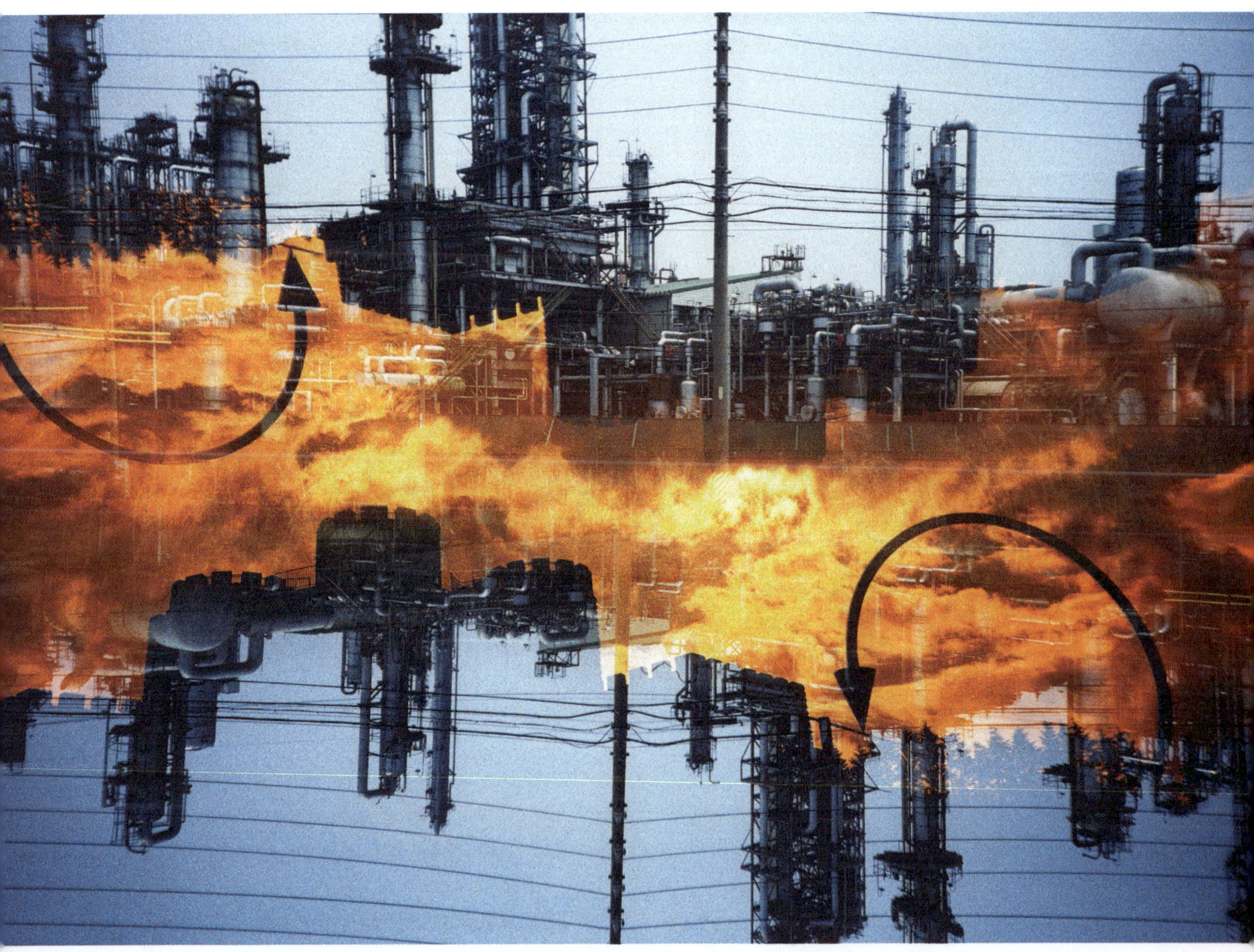

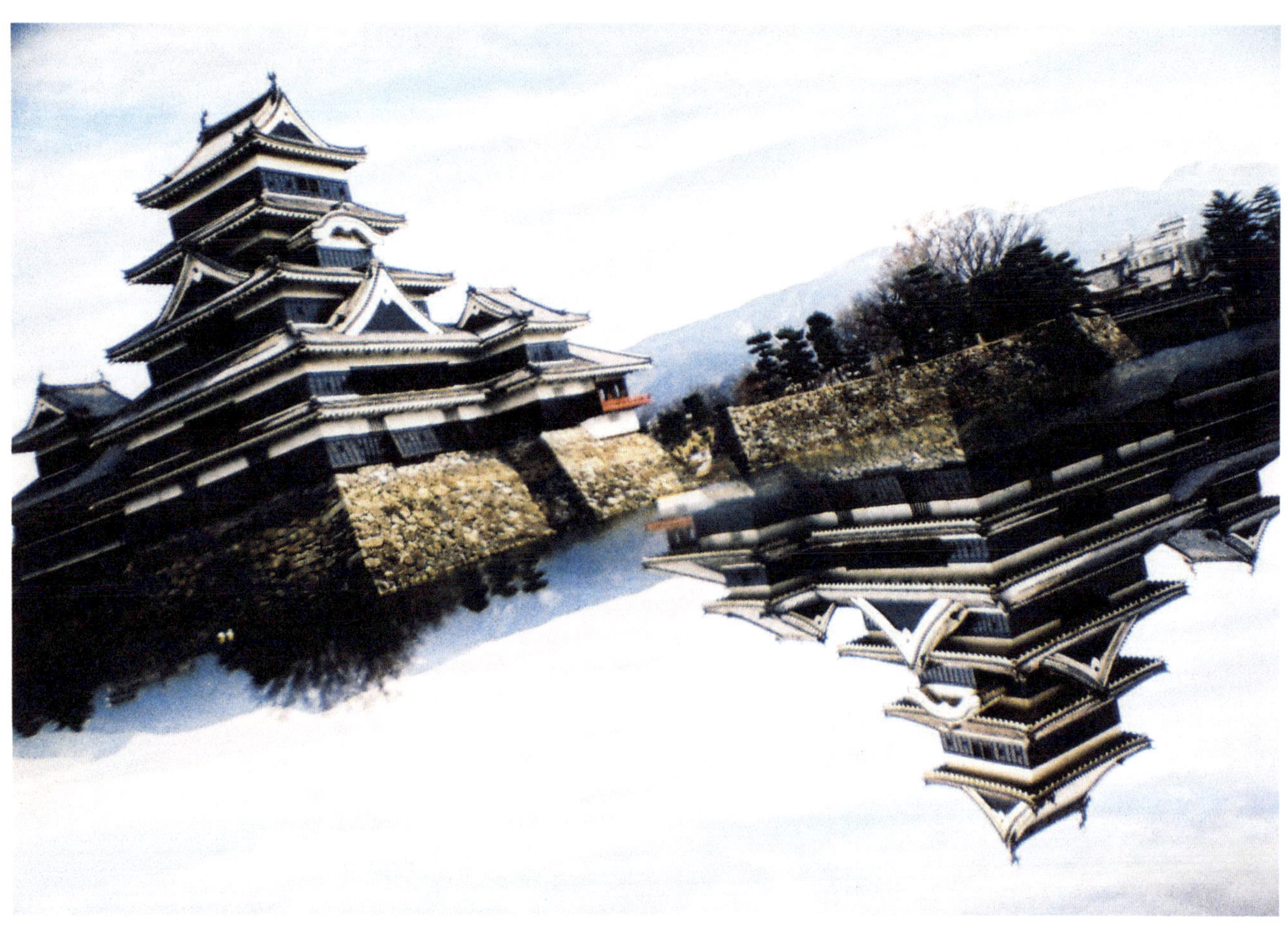

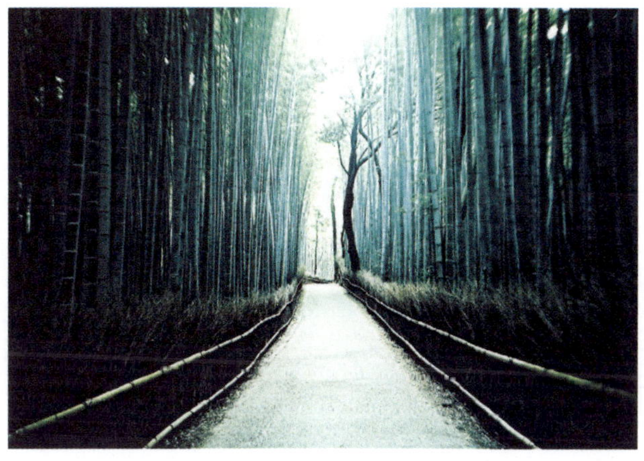

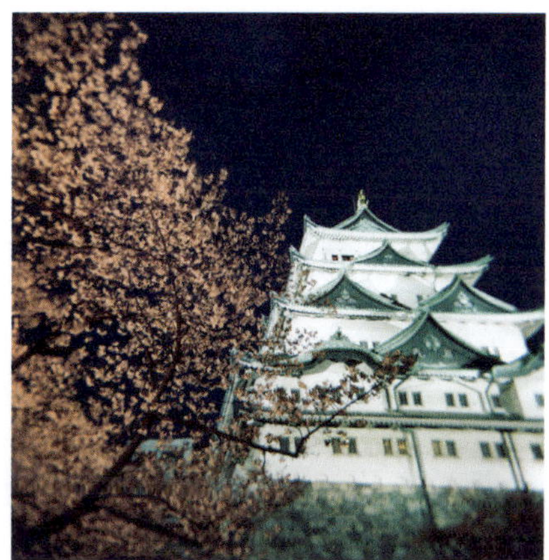

then I reverse the film. So then I take the other half, which has a red touch, if you explain it very simply.

Is it because you can experiment with film, that you enjoy toy cameras?

Yes. It is the digital era, so conversely, there is value in film. Having said that, I like digital as well, there are things that you can only take with a digital camera.

One of the themes in my work is nature. And when it is really beautiful, I think it is best just to show the beauty as is. I use a lot of strange colors and layers so when it is beautiful I think it is best not use these techniques.

How do you find these locations, do you look them up beforehand and get an idea, or do you walk along and something catches your eye?

Both; if I have a destination and a theme in mind I might find something on the way there. Nature isn't always beautiful. If I go to take shots of flowers and it is too early or the petals have fallen, or it is raining - in those instances, I can use interesting methods to create interesting photos in any situation.

I love cities as well, and they are really ideal for multiple exposures, doing things like superimposing factories and cities with flowers.

What kind of architecture do you like in Japan?

Temples and castles. They are particular to Japan, in that they have a design and color way that is only in Japan, they are quite elegant and not loud.

Are there any challenges when taking photos in Japan in particular?

The electricity lines - they are so messy! When I went to Australia, I could really sense something was different and it was the lack of lines. It is really hard to avoid them when you take photos.

I really choose the weather according to the film and the development method, like some are for sunny days, and some are for cloudy days. It is a characteristic of film. The weather is really important, so I am always looking at the sky, and the movement of the clouds.

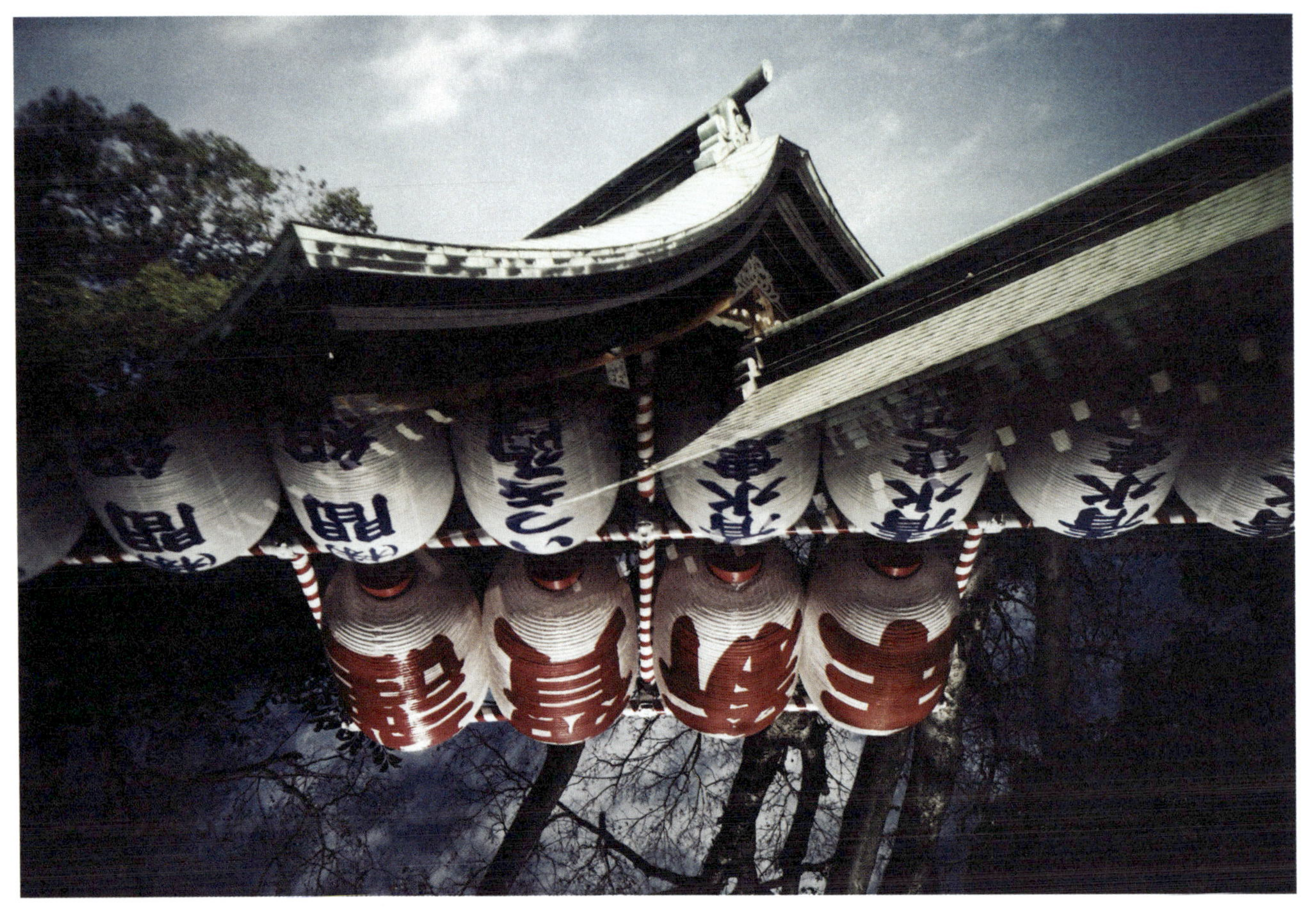

— interview 13 —

JORGE SATO

Can you tell me about your background as a photographer?
I'm a self-taught photographer. I graduated in advertising at Escola Superior de Propaganda e Marketing. At that time, my goal was to work in the creative area of a great advertising agency, and to get this job I had to study several aesthetic references and work a lot nonstop. Making the portfolio, I learned about design, art direction and photography. Fortunately, I had some amazing tutors guiding and helping me to evolve.

When did you first come across lo-fi photography? It is a totally different direction to advertising!
When I got the job, I felt it was like a dream coming true, but after some months I realized it was not my real dream job, I was missing being outdoors and taking photos. I quit and spent some time thinking about life. Then I decided to become a photographer. I had an elementary photography portfolio and started looking for a job as an assistant.

My new goal was to find a unique visual language and approach through artistic photography, and I started working for a famous fine art photographer (Claudio Edinger) in Brazil. It was supposed to be a 1 month internship, but I worked there for 3 years. I learned about art galleries, labs, managing film rolls and how to produce an essay, from the concept to the exhibition. Edinger used to shoot just using large format 4x5 film. This is why I started shooting film. When you slow down, you think and imagine much more, the process becomes deeper and more introspective.

When I decided to come back to film, I must confess I was afraid of those old manual cameras, it was a new world to explore. Lo-Fi cameras were chosen to smooth the transition between digital and analog, and I really appreciate the concept of being free, experimental and creative where the technique was not the main goal. It is like life: we can't control everything all the time.

What aesthetic possibilities do toy cameras afford?
After years shooting with lots of lo-fi cameras, I realized it was possible to create my unique visual approach that I mentioned in the beginning using plastic cameras. It is funny because the lo-fi was supposed to be a "transition," and turned out to be my main artistic goal and signature.

My creative process fits perfectly to the aesthetic possibilities of lo-fi and I didn't plan that, it just happened. Instead of documenting the places using the traditional photographic aesthetics, I enjoy creating new worlds, rebuilding and mixing locations and objects to achieve undiscovered places. Painting is one of the most important references that guides me, especially Romanticism from the end of the 18th century. Film can deliver a similar aesthetic (related to textures, depth and colors)

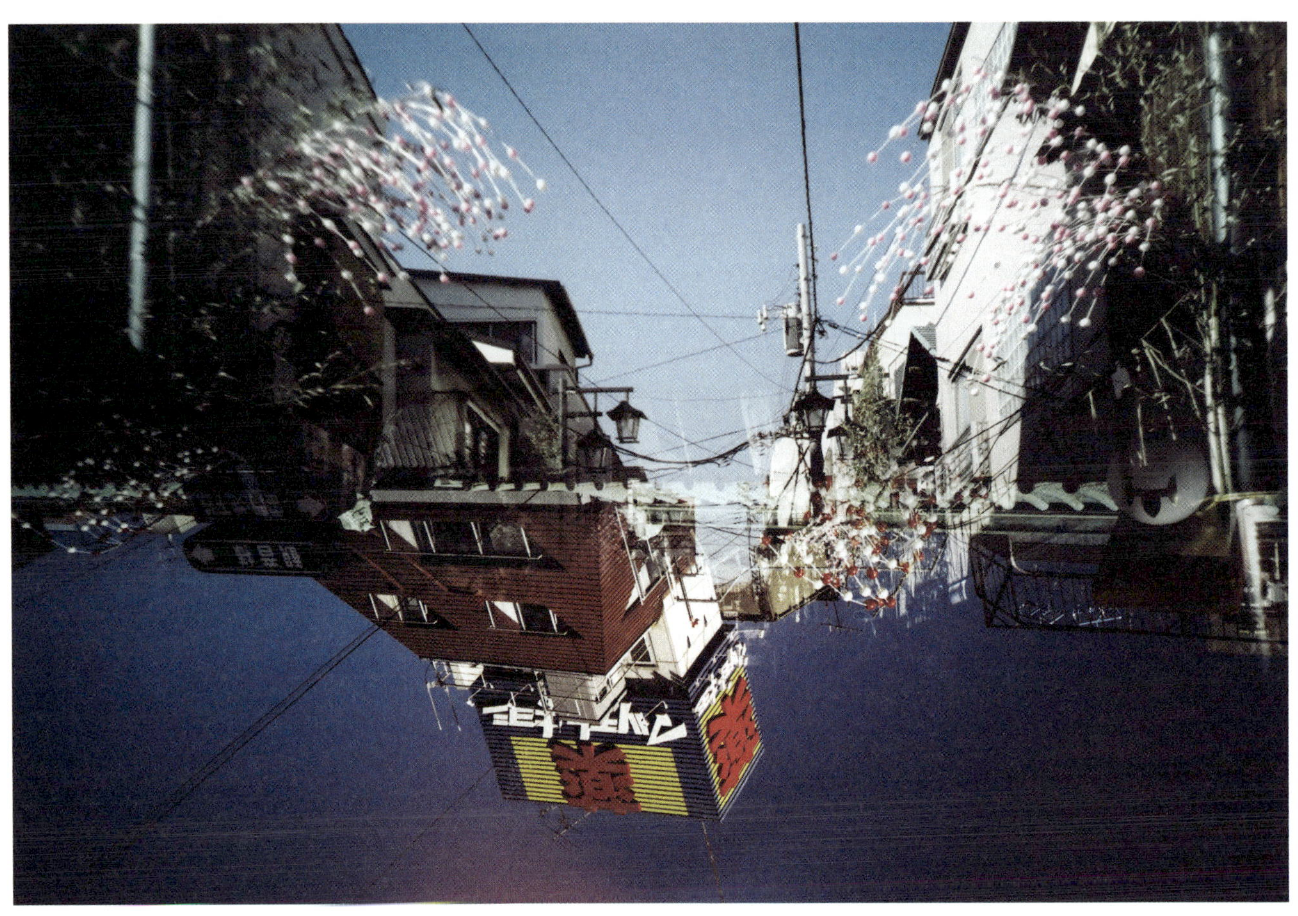

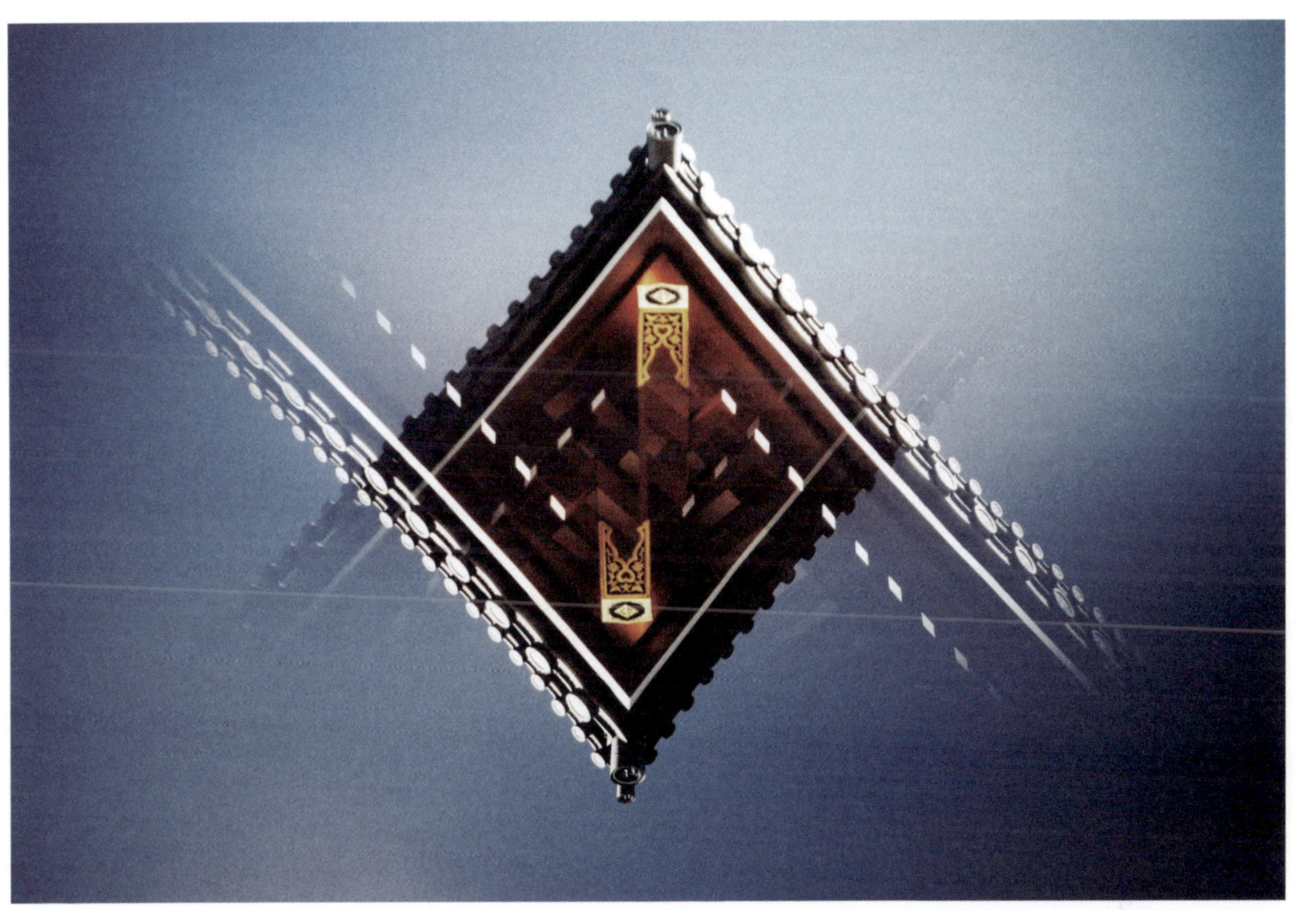

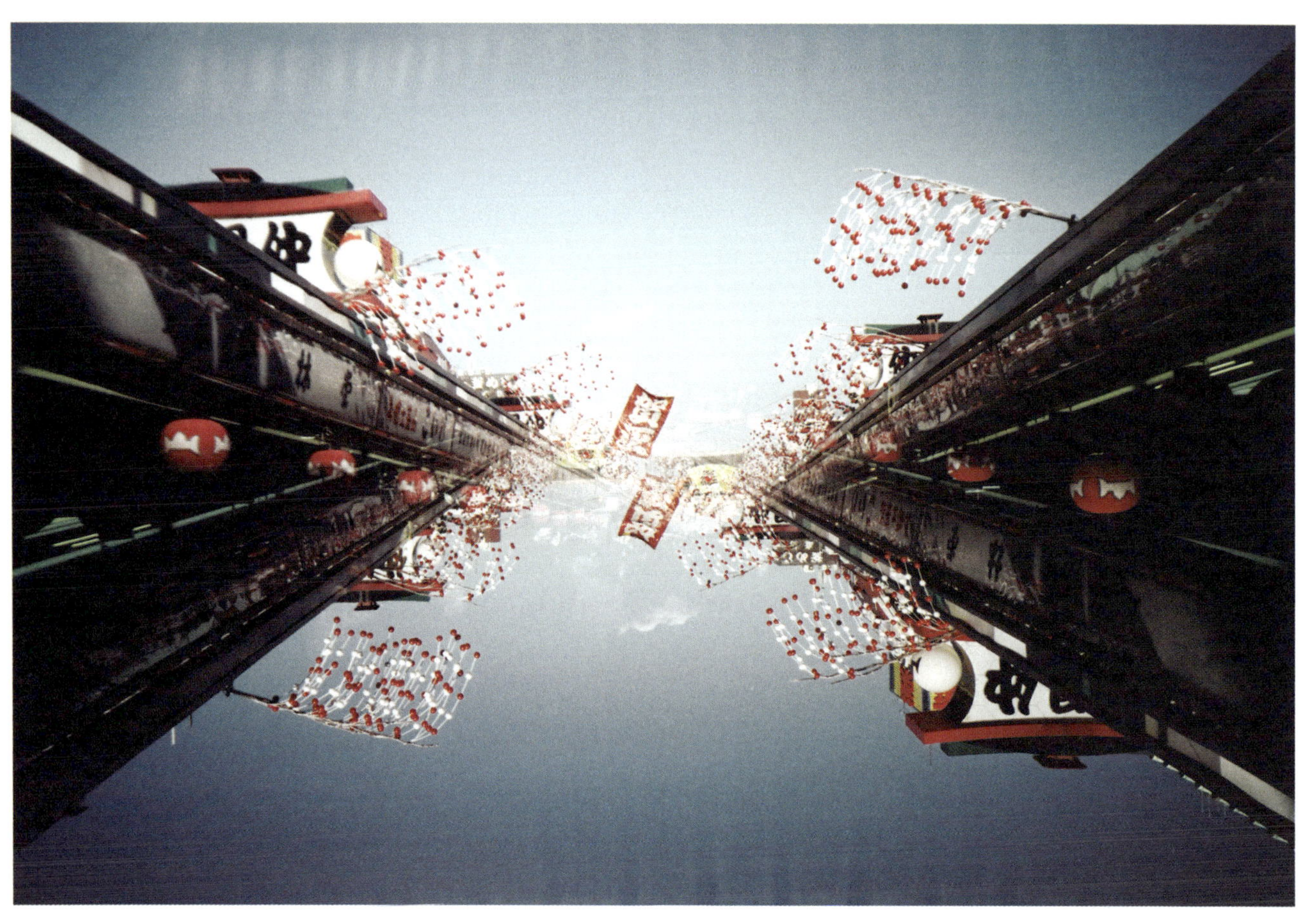

I can't and I don't want to have full control of the multiple exposures. I do believe you can achieve wonderful results through the unpredictability. This is why I love the lo-fi cameras.

I think there is a positive conflict in my work: sometimes I want to control more and other moments I want to let it go. I never know how to balance the "formula," and this is inspiring.

My favorite camera is Lomo LCA+ because it's more reliable and stable than other lo-fi cameras without being bigger or heavier. This camera has a light meter which means you can use it indoors or in a low light situation. You can set the ISO which is perfect for multiple exposures and especially because of the "Splitzer" accessory that I use all the time.

Is there a particular advantage in using toys in terms of the process when you shoot as well?
Oh yes, lo-fi cameras are usually quite small and light, this is wonderful for street photography and for your back. They're not intimidating which means you can shoot spontaneous photos easily. Even in terms of safety, lo-fi cameras are amazing since you don't to have to worry about carrying expensive gear in your backpack and drawing people's attention to your belongings. Sometimes people even feel sorry for you.

Can you tell us about shooting in Tokyo, and what challenges it presented to you?
Oh! Shooting in Tokyo is just amazing. As a fan of sci-fi movies, Tokyo reminds me of those futuristic cities I've always wanted to get to know. I wish I could have stayed more; I spent just four days there. There are so many interesting and beautiful places to be photographed, that this was my biggest challenge: how to do so much in a short time?

What was interesting about the city (photographically), i.e what aspects of the city appealed to you specifically about Tokyo? I see you have a nice juxtaposition of the traditional downtown and the modern architecture.
For sure, it is the coexistence of the traditional buildings and culture such as the wonderful temples with the modern ones. I really like this contrast. This absolutely fuels the imagination to rebuild and create realities. I usually don't take lots of photos at night, but in Tokyo it would be impossible. So many shining, colorful and lovely lights everywhere. I had to make an exception.

Can you tell us about the subjects that appeal to you (no matter where you are)?
I really enjoy architecture both modern and traditional, monuments, local culture, landscapes, and cityscapes. I would say I do a kind of documentary photography, with some surrealism and oneiric narrative. I believe photography is not just about

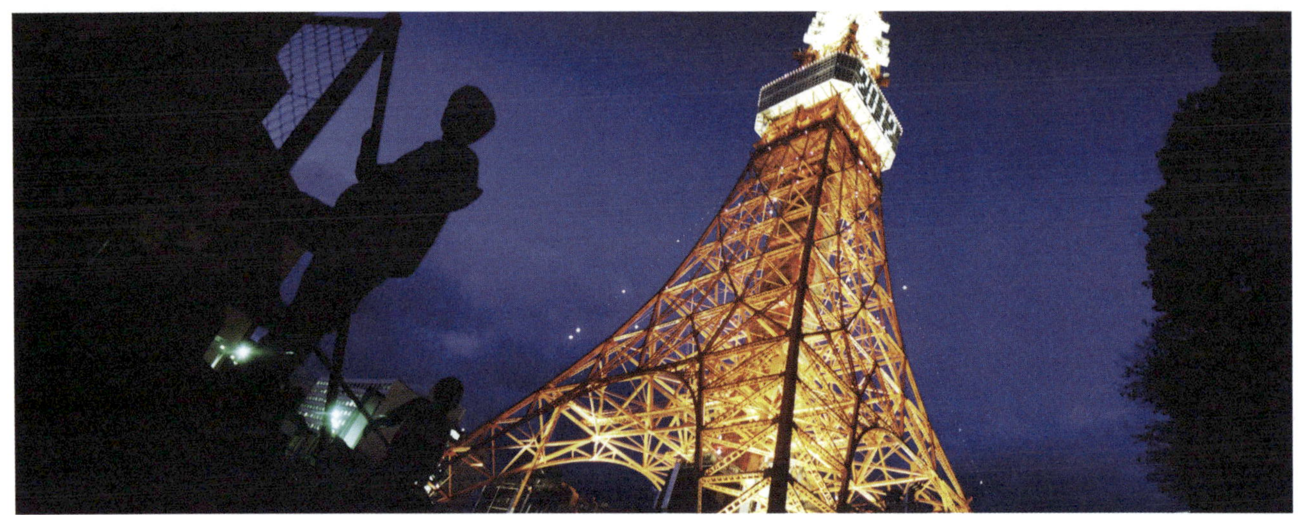

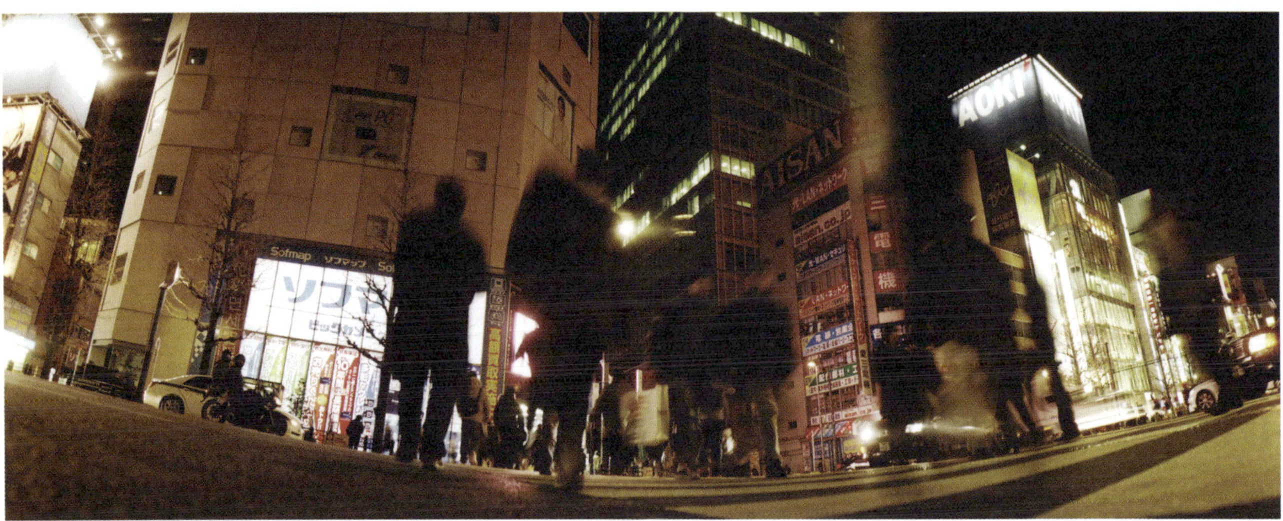
Sofmap ソフマップ
AOKI

beauty. The images should touch your soul and convey an emotion.

Nowadays I've been traveling through Brazil to shoot a project which I've been doing for about three years called Olhográfico. It is a tribute to the Brazilian architect Oscar Niemeyer. The visual approach is based on a futuristic, mysterious and sidereal aesthetics using lo-fi cameras. There was an exhibition about this work last year in São Paulo and Tripolli Art Gallery (which represents my work) is planning a huge exhibition in some cities in Brazil and maybe abroad starting next year.

For next year, I have two plans in my mind: go to Tibet and Nepal in order to take photos of the local culture especially its spirituality using lo-fi aesthetics and a concept to achieve a unique essay.

The other plan is much more difficult but I'll keep trying: shooting in Antarctica because going there is highly related to a Romantic concept which I really admire: the Sublime, mastered by the painter Caspar David Friedrich. I believe it is possible to redeem that deep emotion through lo-fi aesthetics.

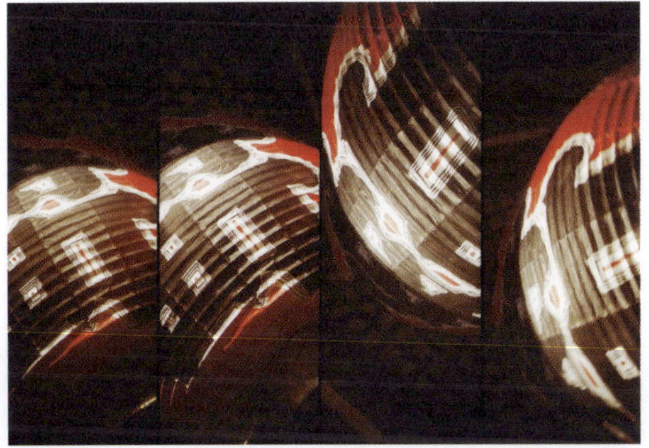

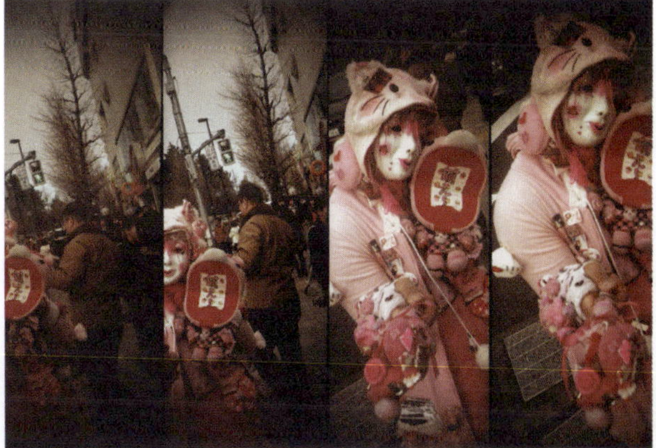

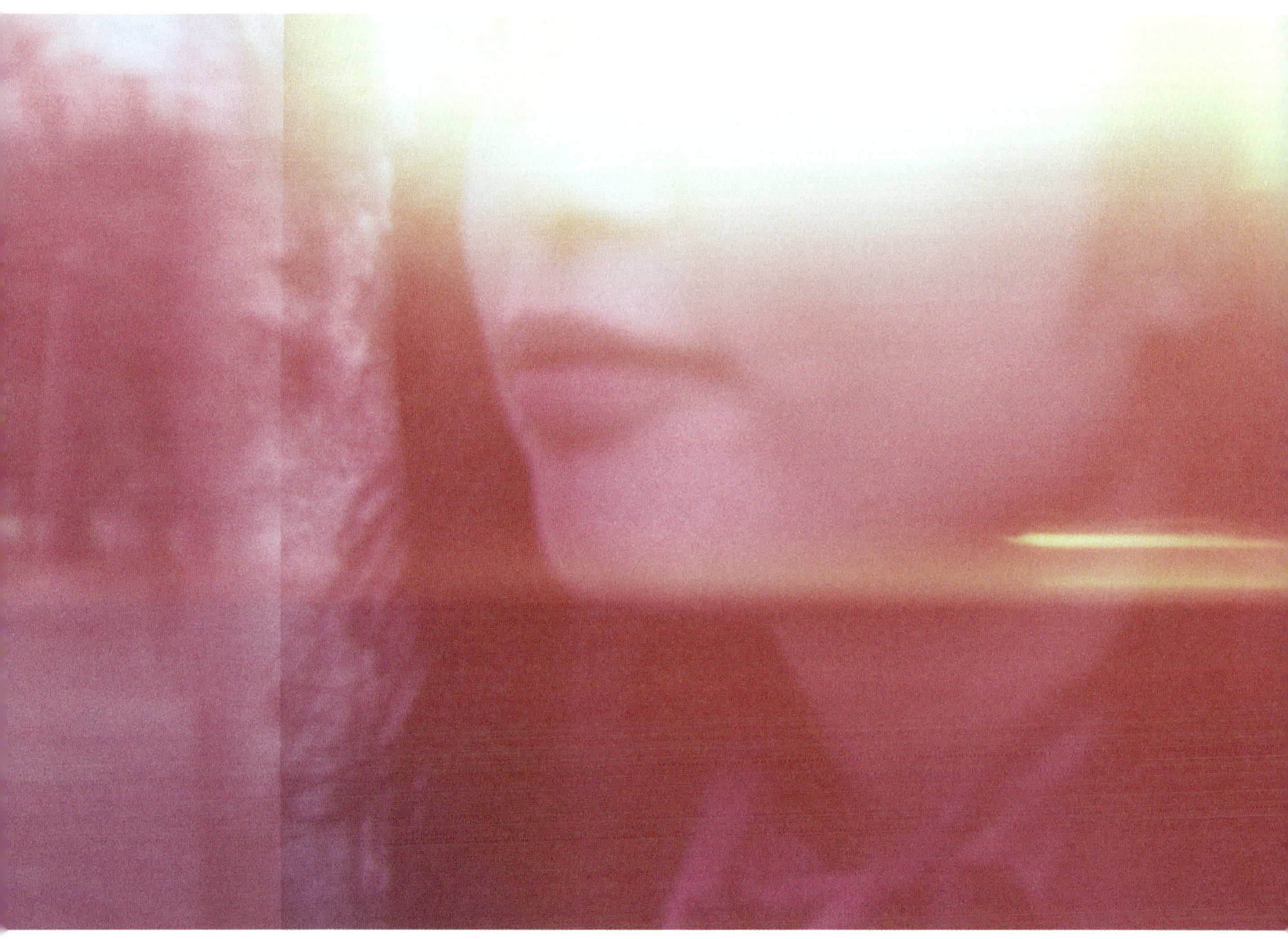

—— *interview 14* ——

REMO CAMEROTA

Can you tell us about your background as a photographer?
I started taking photographs when I was very young, and I was lucky enough to play with all my family's cameras. My uncle was a cinema enthusiast and he had a movie camera and he would shoot home movies. We would use that a lot when I was a kid.
I got my first toy camera when I was about 7 or 8: it had blue plastic so it was either a Diana or a Diana rip-off. I remember my photos were always on the interesting, dark side. Lots of shadows and symmetry. I went through a lot of my old photos recently for a conference talk, and I can see a correlation between what I used to do when I was young, and now.

You are well known for your book Graffiti Japan, can you describe that project?
I always wanted to go to Japan and I knew Japan had a cool graffiti scene and there were no books about graffiti in Japan around 2005. The book project changed my whole life, even though it was a tiny little project.
This opportunity came to go to Japan, and I was like, 'Ok I will go there and have some fun, and I won't make a lot of money out of it, but I will take photos and make the best book I can.' I went over, and I spent about two months there, and of course, I started meeting all the artists and hanging out with them. I fell in love with Japan, as a country, which was not surprising I suppose.

I made some great friends in Japan, so I went back again and I met my wife to be there and that was it, I ended up living and working in japan for the next 6 years and that was all because of the book Graffiti Japan, that took me there in the first place and changed my life. While I was shooting Graffiti Japan, we would come across drain covers in different parts of Japan that were painted.
My book (Drain spotting) had enough strength to change the face of Singapore and Hong Kong, because they saw this book and they contacted me. They held competitions in both Singapore and Hong Kong to get people to create manhole covers for their towns. I got a chance to illustrate and create one for Hong Kong, which was awesome. So this little book that you make, you don't think anything of it, and you are just doing it for the love of it, and you want people to know about these funny little quirky subject matters, and really they have the power to change the face of a whole city.

Did you prearrange meetings for Graffiti Japan, or was it on the fly?
It was on the fly, I didn't even know if there was a huge graffiti scene there, I just knew there was some great work there. So when I proposed the idea, I went online and I found all these artists and I contacted them. Though they couldn't speak English that well, they knew I wanted to come and photograph their work and put it in a book. They were excited as it had never happened before. I got in touch with one guy called SUIKO and he was really cool, he is one of the best in Japan and he was in Hiroshima. He invited me there, and I went there first and he took me all over and showed me secret locations, such as farmhouses in the middle of nowhere.

Yeah it's not really obvious where they are in Japan, it's not like Vienna where you get off the train and it's in your face.
That's right. You really need a tour guide. There used to be a two-kilometer wall in Yokohama that was in a train station

called the “Graffiti Wall of Fame”, and that was one of the main places. Everyone in Japan that was painting at the time painted there. Unfortunately, it is gone now, but I was lucky enough to make sure I photographed the whole wall. Also, along the train lines on Yokohama, Ebisu and Shibuya, but if you want to see some great stuff you need to meet the artists and they have to take you to these locations that no one ever sees such as warehouses they have broken into, or under tunnels. I felt quite special to get to know the artists, I got to stay with them.

What was the reason they gave you such great access? Is it because you are an artist yourself?

I think so, I think that is one of the main reasons, and they enjoyed my work as well and I would paint with them. At that time, my work was not as extensive as theirs, but they accepted me and they also saw my enthusiasm. They were intrigued that someone from a western culture would want to go to Japan, and seek out these guys and document them. They had no idea that anyone had any interest in it except for themselves and they are very different to western graffiti artists in that they do not go out and seek fame. Of course, in the west everyone wants to get that Banksy fame or whatever, but in Japan they don’t care. Some of

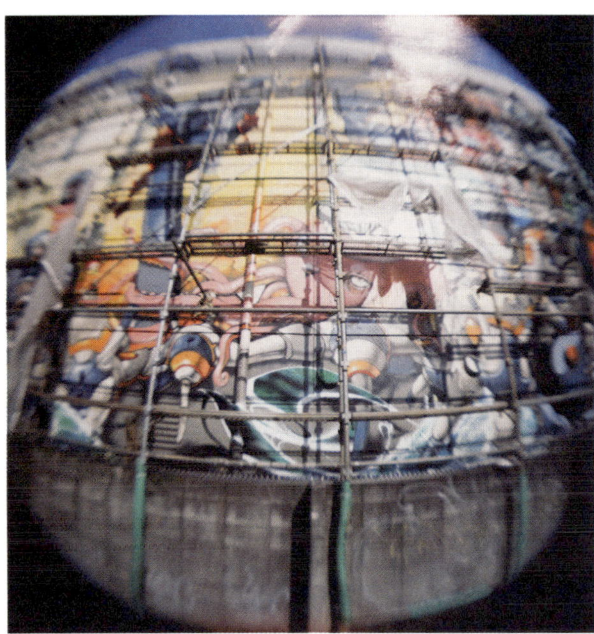

the best artists in Japan were construction workers and I would say to them, 'You can make a living by painting and doing that everyday and they would just shrug their shoulders and say, 'I like to do this for fun, but I don't want to do it for a job.' Yet, some of the best work I have ever seen comes from these construction worker guys that just do it on the weekends.

And, onto toy cameras, you use a wide range of them, when did that all start?

People that know me, know that I walk around with maybe four or five cameras at a time, which did my back in, including an iPhone, a digital, even a Polaroid and a toy. Sometimes four and five, but I really enjoy shooting with a toy camera because it gives you a texture and aesthetic that you can't get with anything else. Even if you are good at Photoshop, which I am, I can make any of my photographs look like I took them with a toy camera, but you still don't get that quality that you do through that lens.

And a lot of it is you don't know what you are going to get anyways. You don't know it will turn out, but a lot of it has to do with shooting point and shoot, and not thinking about it. The problem with digital cameras is that you are always thinking about that shot and making it better, so you don't get the spontaneity in a digital shot because you don't get a window to look at, whereas with these toy cameras you don't.

So many things can go wrong with the toy cameras, including dropping them and having the back open up, which has happened to me on the streets of New York, in London and Japan - and it is always a bummer, but then you get the photographs back and there will be one that is really good and a streak of light through another, which actually made something cool happen to the image. So these mistakes and these inadequacies in the toy camera enable you to take some great photos sometimes.

You grew up using toys – is it nostalgia as well?

Yeah totally! That exactly has a lot to do with it and I love the design of them all, all of them are fabulous. They are plastic and light, when I do choose just to take the toy camera, it feels like I'm not carrying anything and it is fantastic compared to heavy lenses and all that kind of thing. They are always a talking feature with anybody when you pull them out and for me, I always get greats shots out of my rolls every time I use the toy camera.

In Japan, I could just walk to the film-developing place. Japan lends itself to using toy or film cameras in general. I realized that film is cheap there and you have these cameras everywhere and I started collecting all these toy cameras, and not just toys but film as well. So I have about 50 and I try to use them all. We find some from Oxford like the Kodak brownies, which are from like the turn of the century, and then we go to the markets in the US and they have loads of these American-made cameras, and Japan is great for finding cameras. I own a lot of cameras but with toy cameras you can get a special aesthetic you cannot with anything else.

What do you use the most?

Holga and Diana. The Holga is more reliable, I feel pretty safe with the Holga that every shot will turn out. With the Diana a couple of shots don't turn out or the lighting isn't right, as

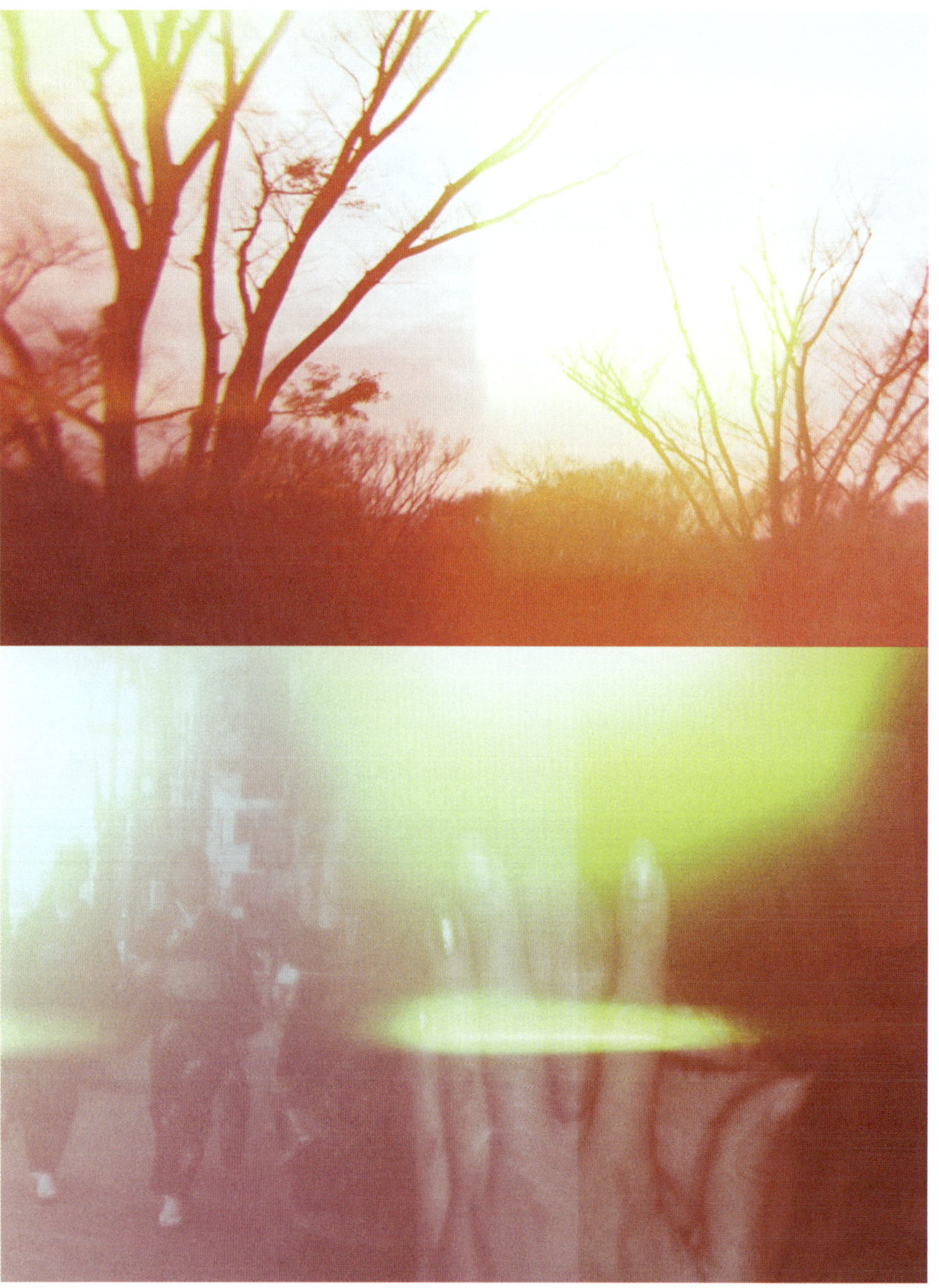

the Diana has a few extra buttons that you forget to move, or sometimes your finger pushes the button to the wrong setting and puts it on pinhole.

I don't have just one Holga and I don't think anyone who uses these cameras have had just one, they have a few and they have a favorite. And then your favorite breaks and you say, 'Oh no, what am I going to do?', you try to replace it and then you are like, 'the photos are not the same as this one, why are they not the same?

What situation lends to using a toy specifically?
When you go out on photo shoot, that is a decision I am going to make. Often, I would bring both to make sure I am covered, and often I would just end up using the toy camera but there are some scenarios you would not shoot toy cameras and that would be sports and fast moving things, although you might get some nice effects, but you won't get a precise shot of a sportsman or a horse running.

They are more art-based cameras and they lend themselves to still landscapes or street work, where you can get nice movement between movement and experiments like double and triple exposures, so they are really an artist's camera, and that is what they are used for by people around the world. They can be used commercially as well, like record covers; there have been some famous album covers with Holga cameras and campaign work.

Does the dynamic change between yourself and the subject when using a toy?
Most people are curious, and there might be disbelief that you will get a good shot but the dynamic doesn't really change when I'm working with a subject - most people know that I am an artist so they already take for granted that I am crazy, so using a toy camera doesn't really make them feel any different towards me, but it might with other people. I create these weird and wonderful worlds and people understand that I will use anything to get that.

Is there a relationship between toy cameras and a love of film?
The toy cameras really use the film that is out there, and there is a beautiful relationship between the two. It makes film accessible to a lot of people because the cameras are cheap, anyone can buy them, especially students in uni trying to experiment.

It doesn't seem like such a burden to buy some film and get them developed because everything is kind of relatively cheap. When you are using film in a toy scenario, the affordability and accessibility makes it work really well, and you get to experiment with different film, which you can't do with a digital camera. So you get to try different things. Lomography are very good, they keep putting out colored films and all sorts of black and white films, you keep learning the process of film developing forever and it really never stops, whereas digital, it is not fine art, you can learn everything you can.

With film there are always surprises with it, and that is what the relationship with the toy camera brings out - when you use the toy camera you get the surprise with the film and the toy camera, it is a really fun relationship.

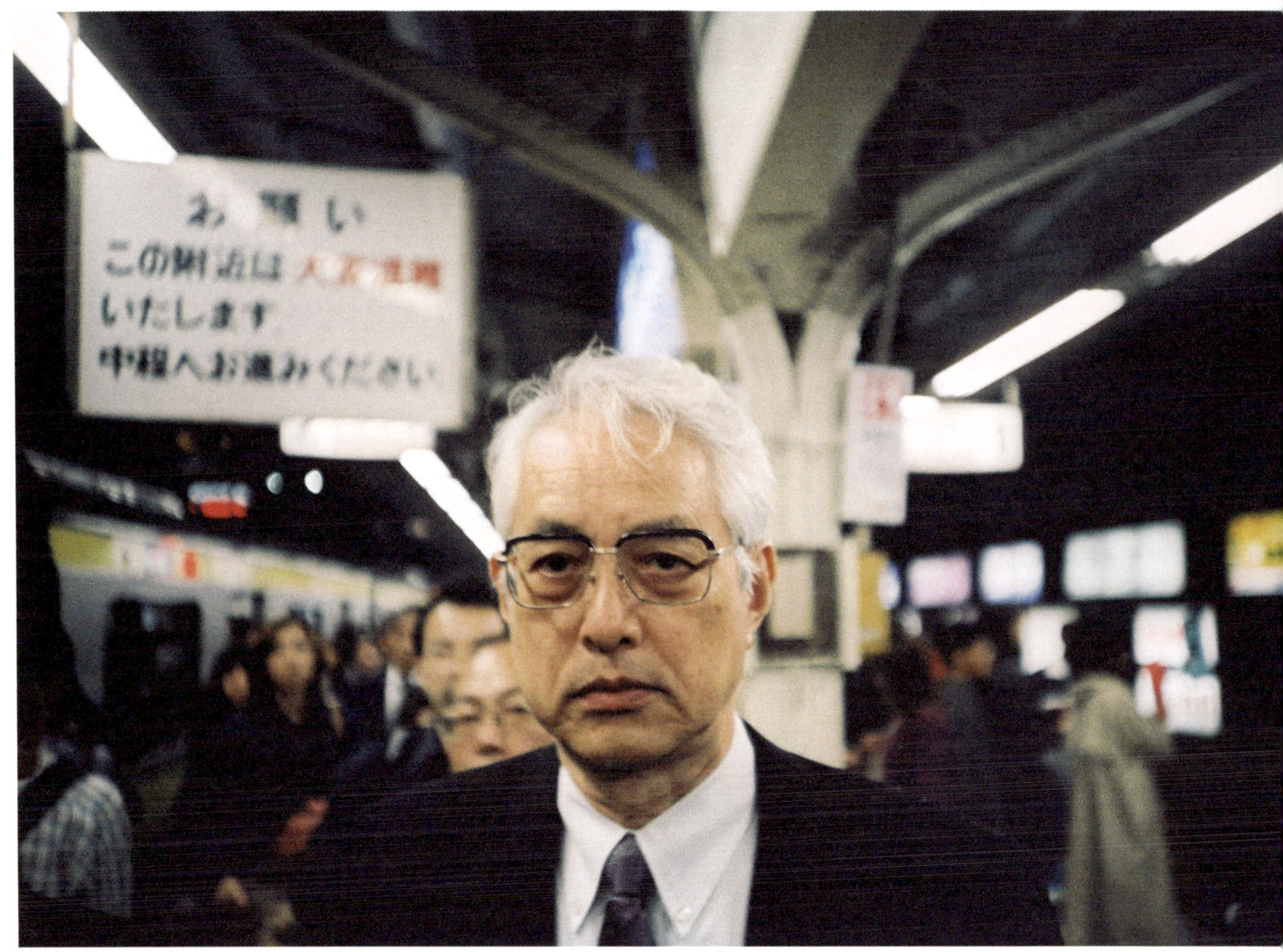

—— interview 15 ——

KEVIN MEREDITH

When did you first come across a toy camera?

The camera that I love to use the most, and that I think is essential to the toy camera craze, is the LOMO LC-A. It is technically not a toy camera, but it is lumped in with them because it is a Lomography product. I first heard about this camera in 1997, but it was like, "Wow!". My friend got one, and eventually I got one too. But at the time, digital compact cameras didn't exist and other autofocus compact cameras were really expensive, like way out of the reach of a student, so this LOMO LC-A for 90 pounds was just incredible. Back then, Lomography only sold the LOMO LC-A and action sampler, and then soon after that, they added the Holga and then it went from there with more cameras.

What are your long-term projects; you seem to do a mix of portraiture and reportage?

I became well-known for taking photographs of my full English breakfasts before that "taking photographs of your food with Instagram kind of cliché". I always used to take a lot of photographs of just people's feet, and that developed into full montage portraits, and then the Brighton swimming club. But generally, I just carry a camera everywhere I go and just snap things. Now that I have a child, I don't go away as much and when I am with her, I am busy playing with her and not thinking about photography as much.

I saw that you used to shoot a lot of raves. With this kind of embedded subculture journalism, it always interests me what the dynamic between the photographer and the subject is.

When I was doing that I was really young, like 18, so I wasn't thinking about any grand scale. I was a raver, and I loved that culture, so I was documenting it for magazines. I know people that have documented subcultures way better than I did; I hadn't fully matured as a photographer back then, but it was fantastic. Most people are off their faces, so they were happy to have their photo taken. I don't know if it is the same now, as obviously back then all the images were going into an obscure magazine which most people wouldn't see, whereas now it is easy for the images to go viral.

But if you are involved in the culture, does it help you take more personal photographs?

For me, if you are not personally involved in something it is quite difficult to break the ice, and you have to spend a lot of time and embed yourself in that culture. So as a photographer, if they are comfortable with who you are, they ignore you when you are taking photographs, so that is a good thing if you are part of that culture.

Has the culture of instantly sharing everything affected your photography?

Absolutely, because photography used to be something just for me, and I would actually have these really nice Muji photo albums, that were like little books that I used to carry in my bag. This is before Flickr and social media, so the only way you could actually get to see the photos is if I showed them this book, and then all that changed with Flickr. It was really weird, because you would put stuff online and it would go out of its

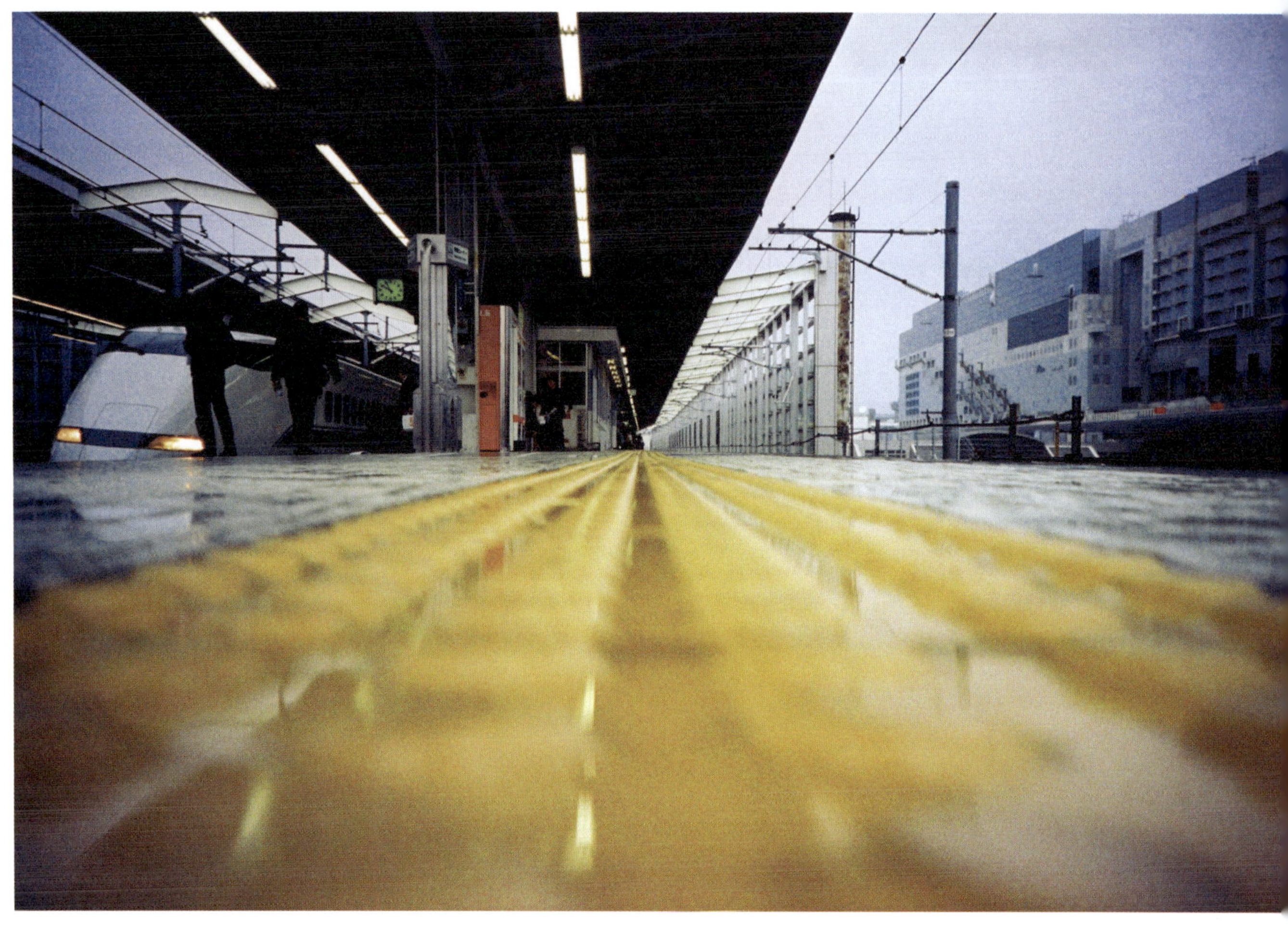

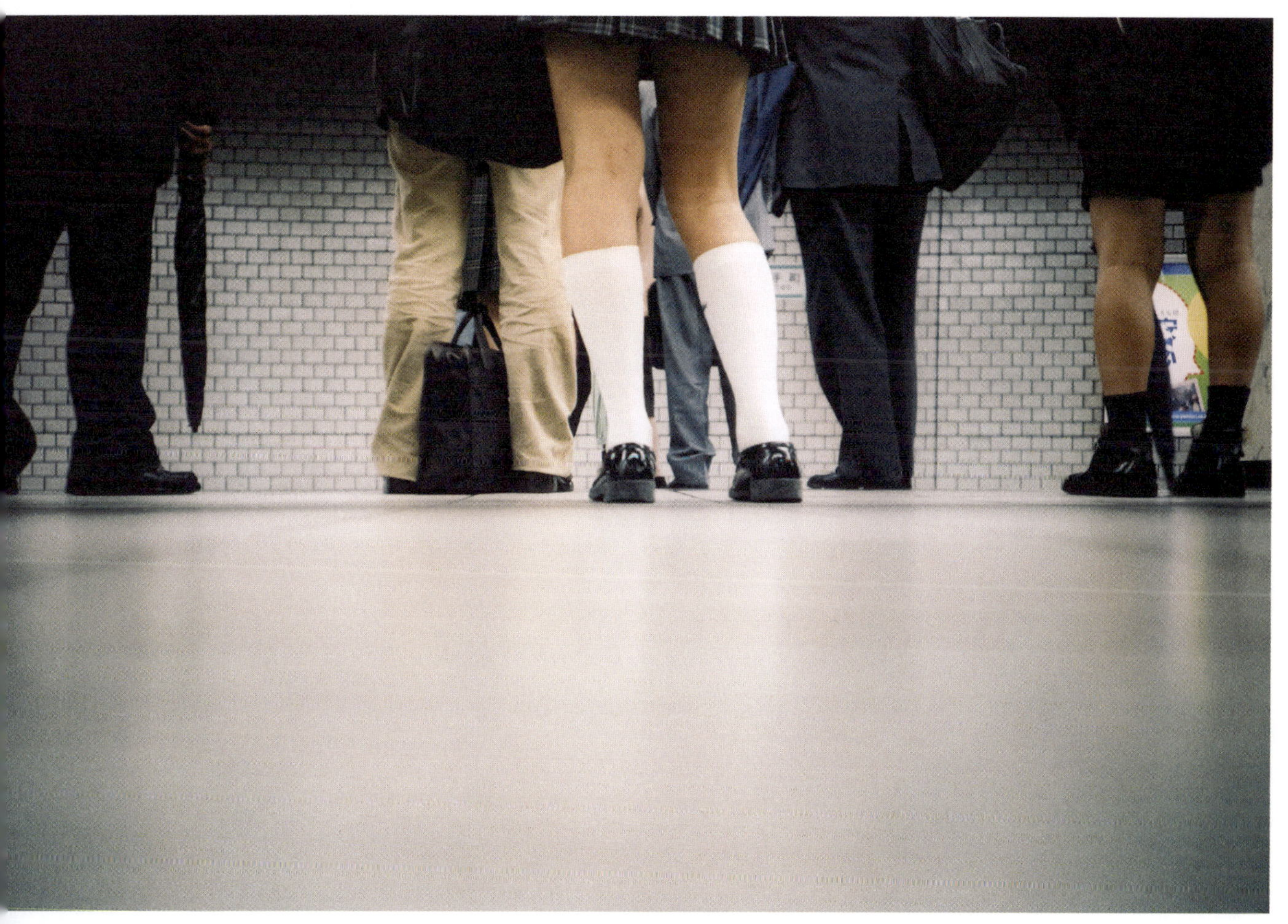

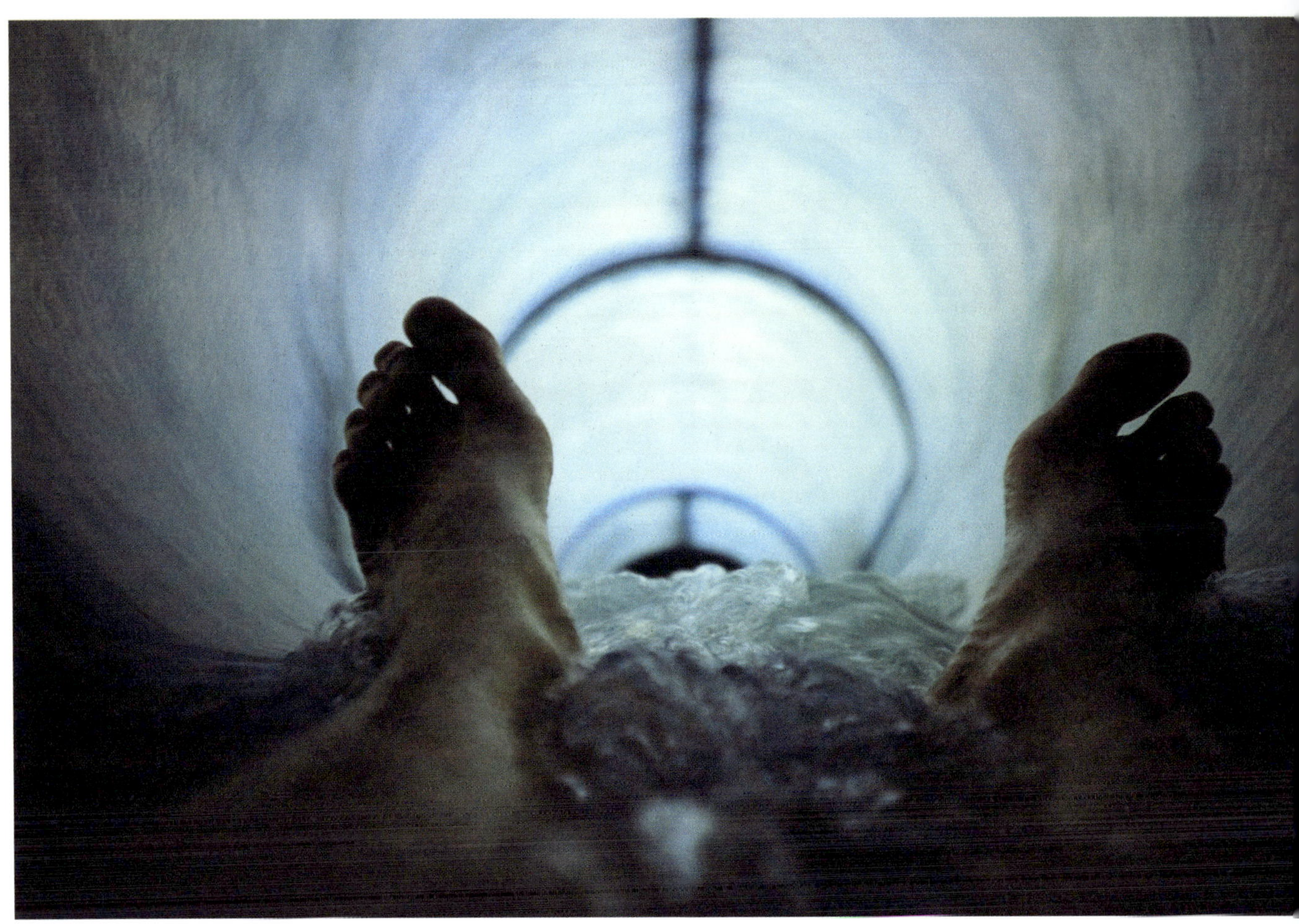

own cultural bubble. Especially with the full English breakfasts, people can't believe that is a breakfast – some people truly believed that I eat that every single morning, and that is completely not the case!

You can easily learn about other people's cultures. Since the age of 16, I wanted to go to Burning Man, in the 90s no one knew of it, but I did as a raver; that was my mecca, I had to go there, but now when you go into a room of people, they all know what it is, because photographs of Burning Man go viral.

On the flipside, is there a standardization of the aesthetic with toy photography?

Especially with an action sampler, you will get very similar images to everyone else using it, and I think to a varying extent, if I give you a camera with the same film type that I have, we will get quite similar pictures. I think that exists with digital photos as well, and especially with Instagram, as that is a very democratized type of photography as everyone is using the same camera. But there is enough variation of cameras and films that you wont get this standard look and feel.

When did you start using social media?

I joined Flickr around November 2004, while Flickr only launched in February 2004. The brilliant thing about that was that I had a backlog of 8 years of the best of my photography so I very quickly became famous on the site, and I probably got recognized as a better photographer than I was. I was also uploading mostly film photographs. Most of the time, digital photographs out of the camera look flat and boring, so I use plug-ins and Light Room, but back then those tools were inaccessible so most people would upload raw untouched digital photographs. So a film shot with really saturated colors would stand out more. So when Twitter and Tumblr came a long, I used those. The early days of Flickr were amazing as there was a real sense of community. At that point, you had be a member of an educational association to be a part of Facebook, so back then Flickr was like Facebook, and all my non-photographer friends were on Flickr and the conversations you would have were amazing.

Why do your students want to use a LOMO LC-A?

For the most part, they are hobbyist photographers who want to take it further. I find that a digital camera can be quite overwhelming. I have an Olympus OMD 5 and the amount of buttons on it is ridiculous: there are about 15 buttons on it and when you are shooting digitally, you are thinking about white balance, shutter, exposure compensation, focal length and blah blah... So on day one of my photography course, everyone is lent a LOMO L-CA because it is so basic, all you have to do is set the focus. All you are doing is thinking about the content of your photographs, so it is like taking it back. It is unfair, if you have someone using a EOS Canon Rebel compared to 5D Mark II. If everyone has the same camera, it is a more level playing field –

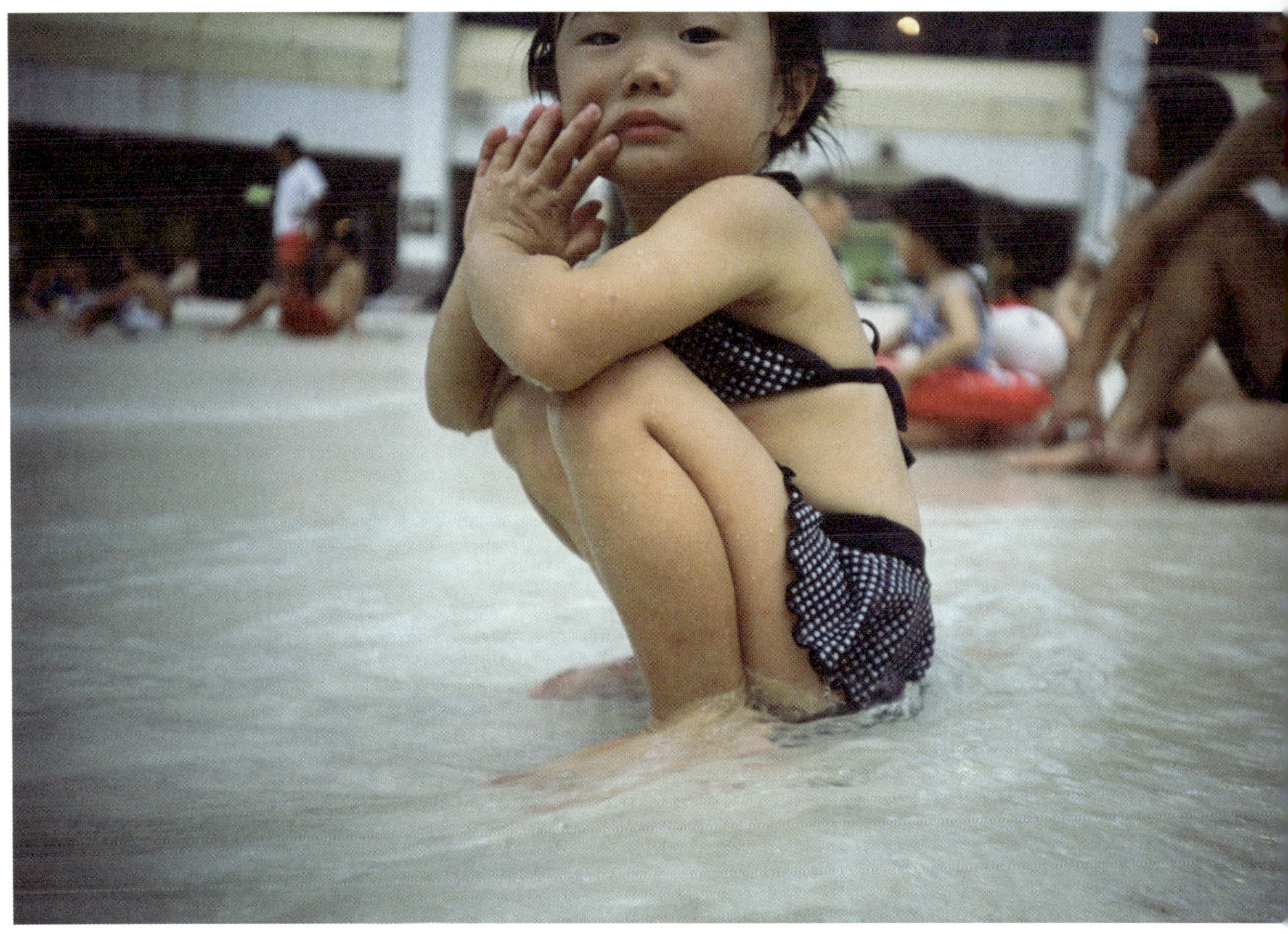

also with digital photography they get stuck in this loop of looking at the back, trying to improve a photo by taking it from a different angle, and I think you get better pictures if you take a picture and move on, rather than take 20 pictures of the same thing.

Can you tell us about your time in Japan?

The reason I was in Japan was for the LOMO Olympics. It is a worldwide photography competition and we had a freestyle day where we could focus on anything, so we started at 3 am at the Tokyo fish market and then I went to a swimming pool.

That was in the year 2000 or 2001 so it was quite early on in my developmental path. It was weird that you couldn't communicate with the people I was taking photos of–it was quite strange–and when I would go into train stations, I was clearly the tallest person there, as I am 6ft2. Up until that point, I had only traveled in Europe and America so I felt it was quite stressful being by myself the last few days, and when I was on the tube, I was like, 'I have to get off at this stop, you are not looking for "ABCD", you are looking for different shapes and strokes.' So that is quite overwhelming, but it was an incredible experience. Japan is nuts; if you are not used to it, it is just a sensory overload. As a photographer it is like, 'Where do I point the camera?'

What were some of the challenges photographically?

I wouldn't say there were many challenges, but I think at the time, I had this chip on my shoulder where I didn't want to take photographs of things everyone else was taking, so I was concentrating on people and stuff. So when we went Shinjuku, I didn't take photos of that, but I wish I did. If I went back, I think I would do a series on grumpy commuters - the people falling asleep everywhere. There was this girl asleep on the counter, and I took a photograph of her; her head raised and she kind of looked at me, and there was a tissue stuck to her face. There were people sleeping in McDonalds. If you did that in London, you would be asked to move on!

Do you use the LOMO LC-A much still?

I use it when I shoot my montage portraits, because obviously I want them to look the same as the first one I did five years ago. I used to have a LOMO LC-A loaded with normal film, and then I used to have one with film to be cross-processed. My favorite film to cross-process was AGFA Precisa - you can get it now, but it is not the same as five years ago and that was the best for cross-processing. Then the Kodak Elite chrome 100 and 200 stopped being made, so even the third best film, you can't get, so if you want to cross-process, your pictures go really green and yellow. I don't cross-process anymore so I only carry one LOMO LC-A and my general camera is a Samsung Galaxy NX, which is like an SLR-style camera. It is small and runs Android so I can Instagram right off it.

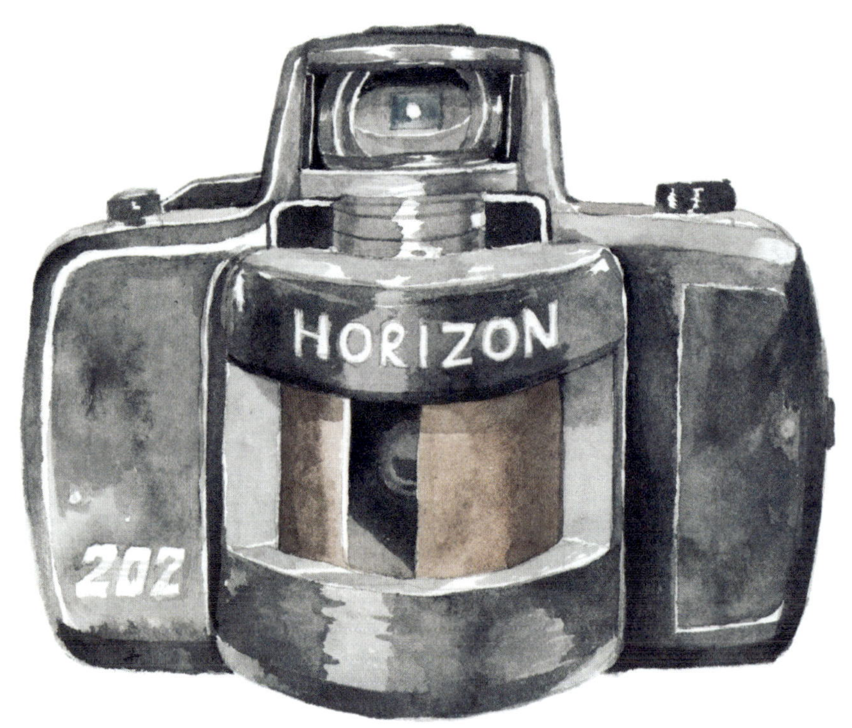
HORIZON
202

HORIZON

The Russian Horizon is based on the Horizont, a Soviet era mechanical swing lens metal camera that was first introduced to the market at Photokina in 1966. The Horizon is manufactured by Krasnogorkiy Zavod in Russia and used to be produced in two formats, the 205pc the 202, with the current model being the S3 pro. The film plane is curved with a 28 mm f2.8 rotating lens, and the images are very crisp; the quality of this camera is excellent.

The Lomography Kompakt also allows for multiple exposure shots. The Perfekt also takes panoramas, but offers more control with full aperture and shutter settings. It is easy to use, gives crisp quality across the entire frame field and there are two shutter modes, day and night.

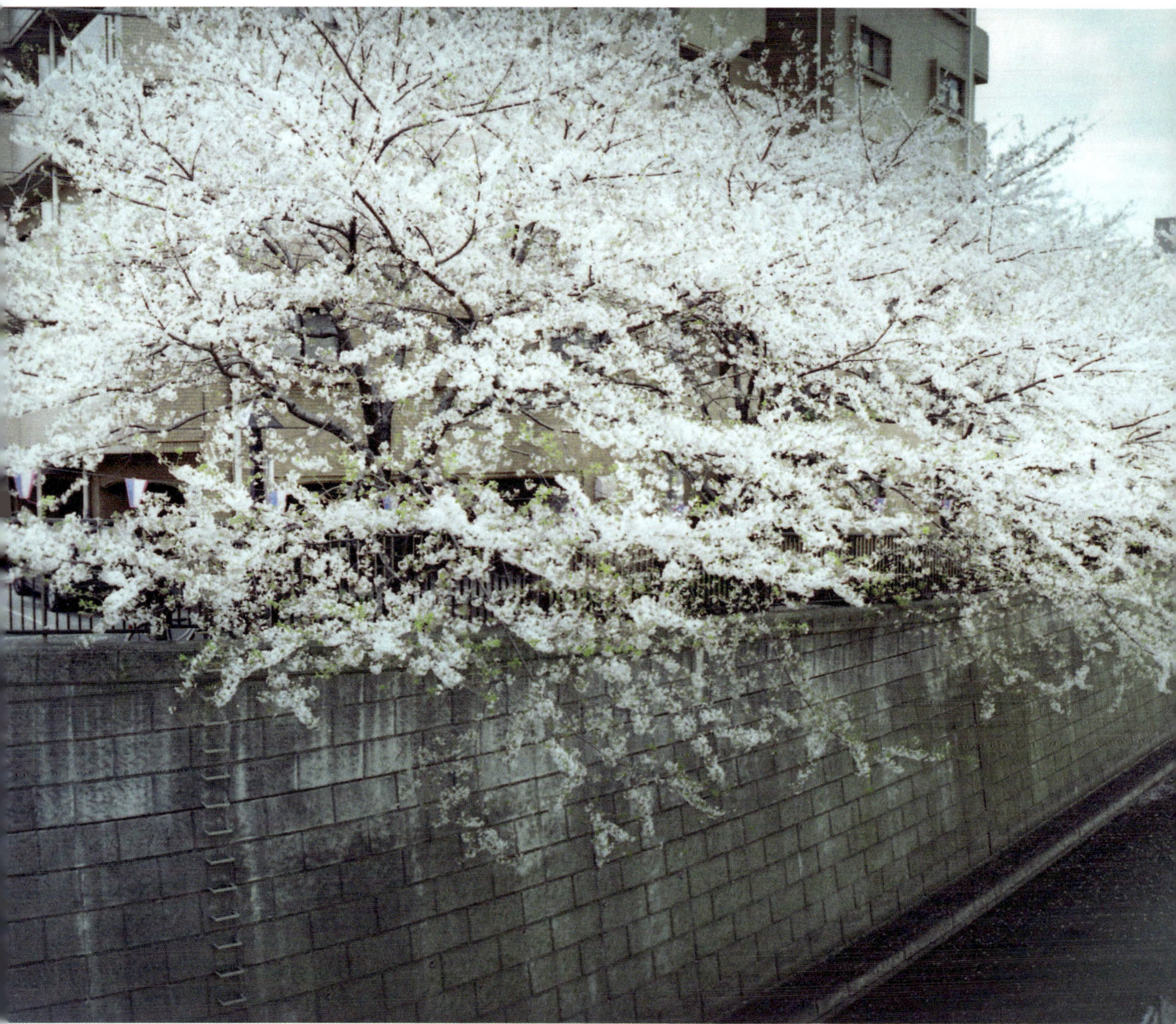

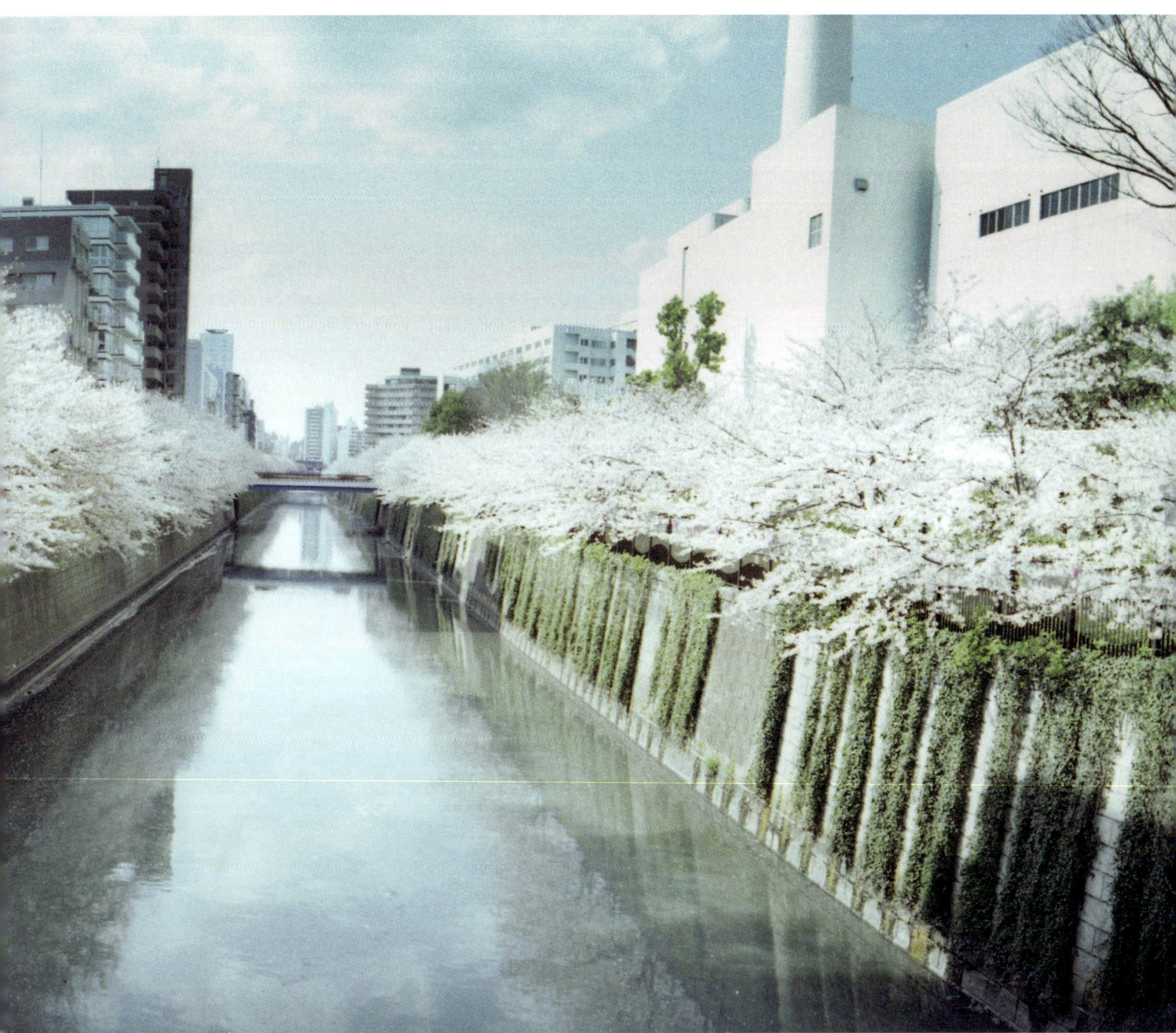

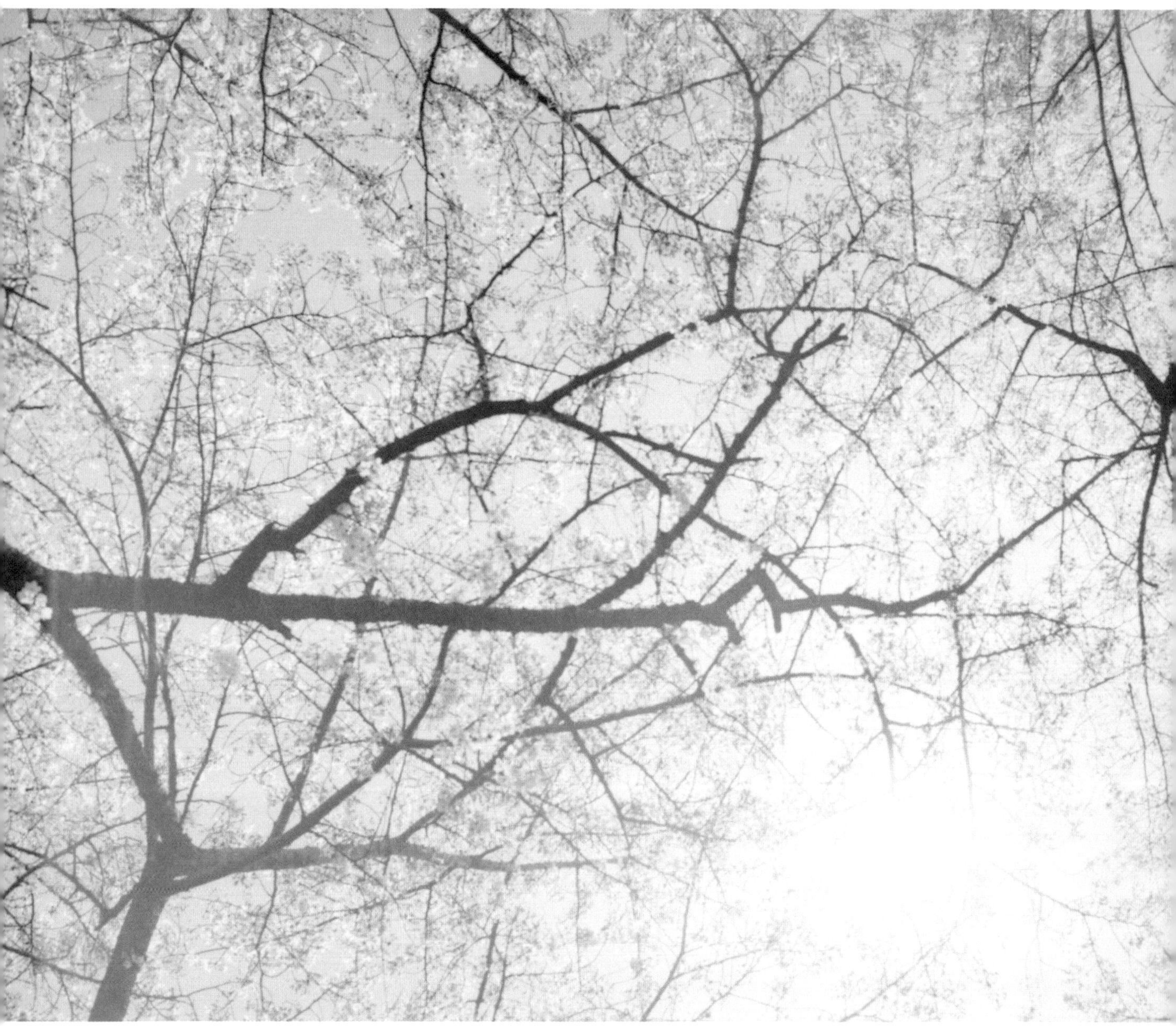

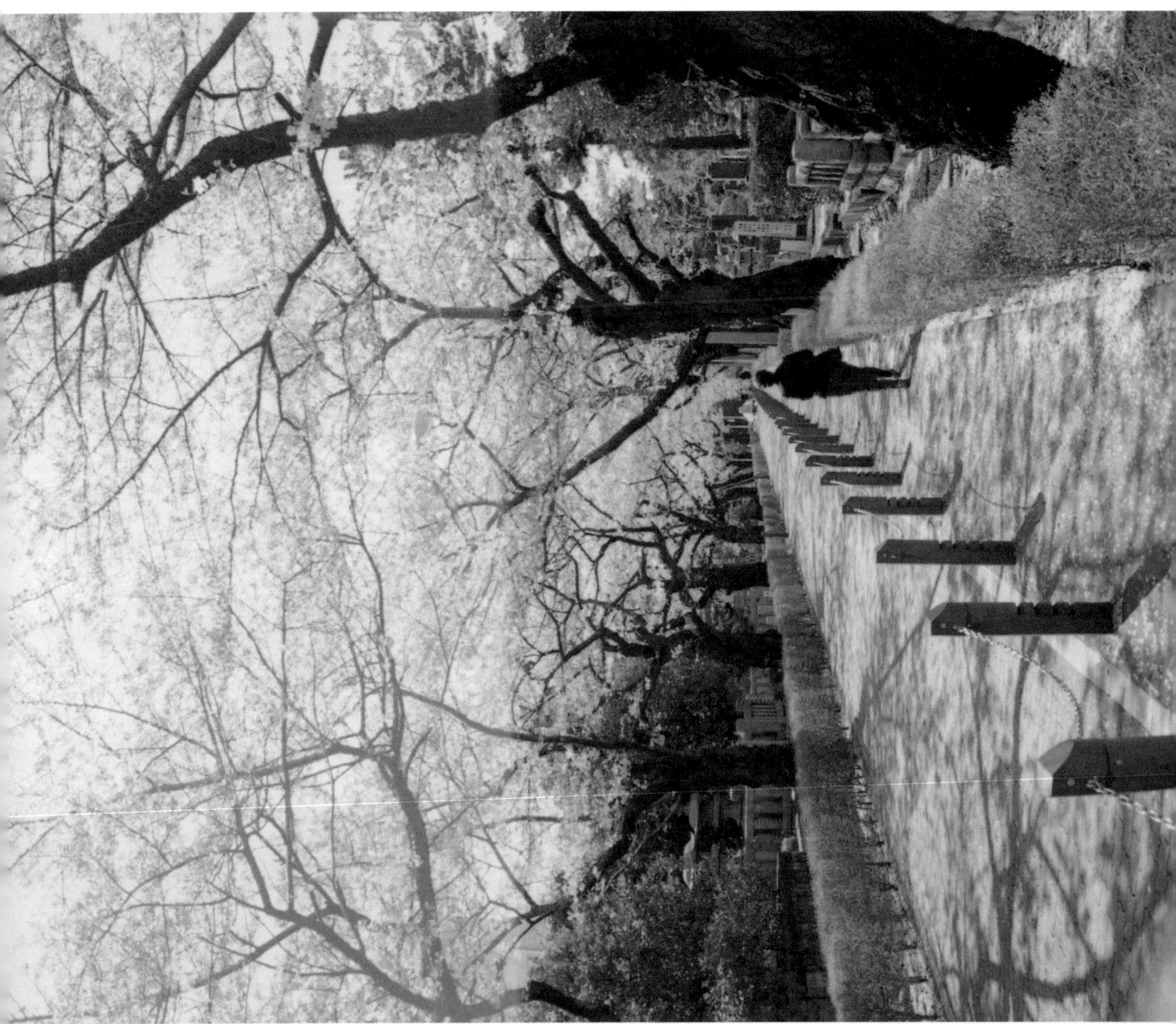

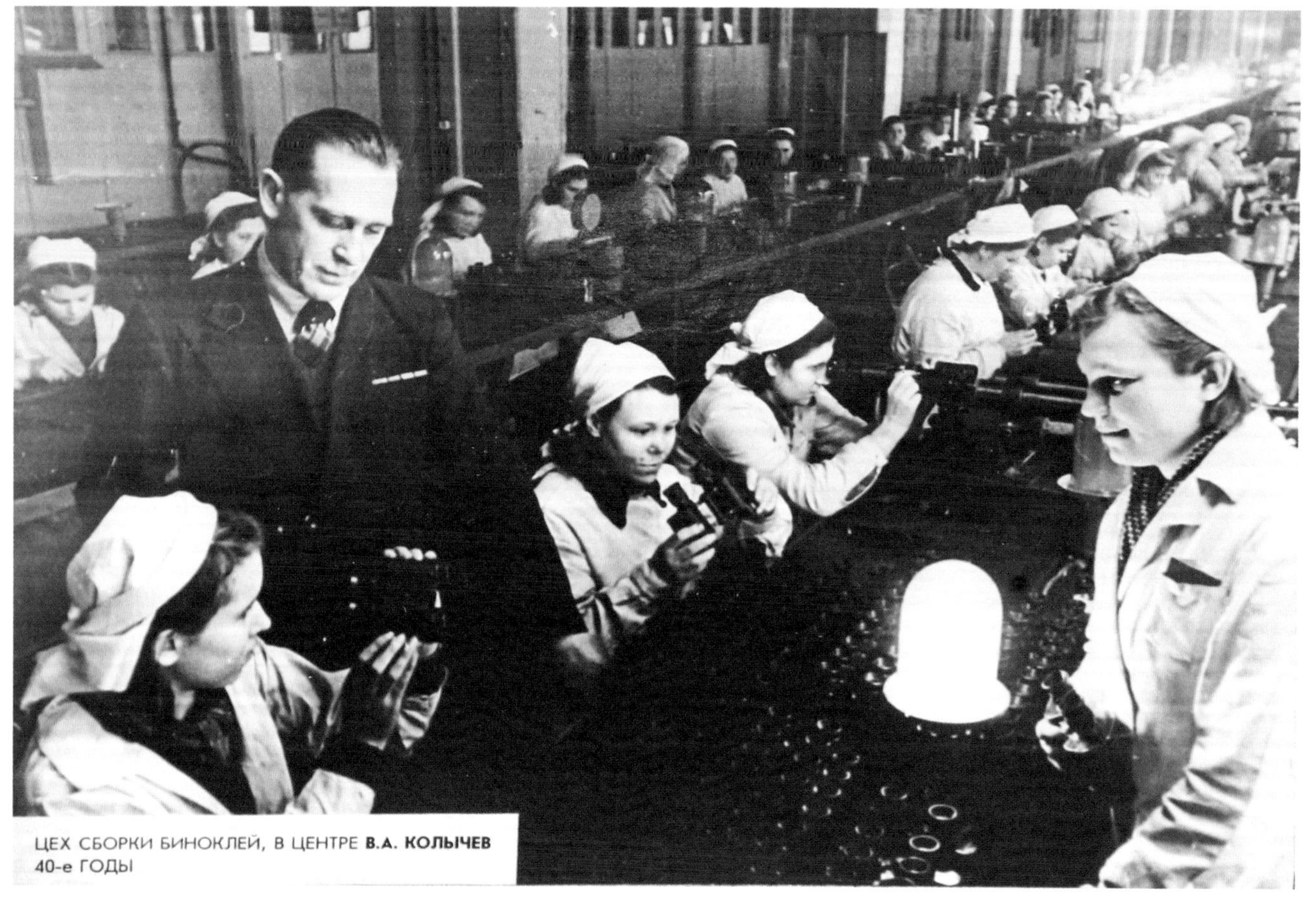
ЦЕХ СБОРКИ БИНОКЛЕЙ, В ЦЕНТРЕ **В.А. КОЛЫЧЕВ**
40-е ГОДЫ

interview 16

KRASNOGORSKIY ZAVOD

DANILOVA OLGA, PR-DIRECTOR OF S. A. ZVEREV KRASNOGORSK FACTORY.

Could you briefly give us the historical context of Krasnogorsk mechanical factory? Who founded it?

The history of the factory dates back to 1905 when the Russian Empire made a contract with Carl Zeiss Stiftung and Herz to establish branch offices in Riga (In 1905 Riga was a part of the Russian Empire). After the beginning of the First World War, Germany stopped the supply of optical glass, which impaired the productivity of the Russian optical factories. After the revolution, Carl Zeiss and Herz factories were expropriated and the production facilities were relocated from Riga to Petrograd. Both factories were reopened as a joint venture, which became the first State Optical Factory.

In 1918, the factory was evacuated to Podolsk. In 1926, the factory was moved to Pavshino (today Pashino is known as Krasnogorsk). In August 1927, the completely fitted plant was named the "Factory of Precision Mechanics." The first manufacturing facilities included assembly lines for glass lens, small medical kits, and magnifiers for textile fabrics testing. In 1928, the industrial township sprang up around the factory.

The "All-Soviet Union Optical and Mechanical Association" was founded in December 1930 and it incorporated the Factory of Precision Mechanics in Ban'ki.

Since 1934, the Factory of precision mechanics became one of the leading factory to manufacture optical and mechanical equipment in the country. In April 1939 it was named V.I. Lenin Factory with 66 workers being awarded military medals. On February 1, 1942 the Factory changed its name into the "State Optical Factory," and later "Krasnogorsk Mechanical Factory." Its area of expertise was special-purpose engineering equipment, including aerial photographic equipment and sighting units as well as civil production; photo cameras, film cameras and scientific equipment.

What were you initially making?

In the beginning, the factory's area of expertise was maintenance and production of optical and mechanical technology. In 1942, the factory produced optical and mechanical equipment for army field forces: large stereoscopic telescope, tank commander's panoramic telescope, periscope aiming circle, mechanical mortar sight. Also, the factory started manufacturing the first moving film aerial camera, the АЩАФА-2. In the period between 1942 and 1945 the factory supplied over 400.000 equipment units for the Red Army and the Navy. The factory began production of: tank commander's panoramic telescopes, mounted surveillance vision blocks, wide-angle hinged stereo-telescopes, periscope aiming circles, periscope cameras for long-distance photos, tank corrective periscopes, optical rifle telescopes, hand magnifiers for topographical maps, and small-diameter tubes for rifle testing.

In 1944, to boost new equipment engineering, the Factory opened construction design centers for the development of aerial cameras and artillery optics equipment. At the same time, the facilities produced prototypes and experimental series on site. These branches formed the basis of the Central Design Bureau (CDB) for the engineering and sample production of aerial cameras, artillery and tank direct fire sights, and infrared equipment. Over the years, the Central Design Bureau became the largest center for optics engineering. For decades the Krasnogorsk factory; based on the Scientific and Technical Center facilities has been manufacturing high-tech optical and electro-optical products for different applications.

How close were the first Krasnogorsk lens to Carl Zeiss lenses? Is it true that they were based on Zeiss optics?

All optical products manufactured in the first postwar decades had German roots. In 1945, by the order of the People's Commissioner, a large group of employees were sent to Carl Zeiss factories in Germany, including the Schott optical glass manufacturer. All German technical documentation was registered, and later shown to the factory commission. German engineers worked at the factory till the beginning of 50s. They assisted in testing the properties of German optical glass and equipment, under the Reparations Agreement between Germany and USSR.

When did the factory start producing civil equipment for the mass consumer? Were they affordable only for the middle class and consumers abroad?

After the end of war, the factory, like other industrial plants began civil production. Civil equipment includes motion-picture projectors, theatrical binoculars (the first run was bought by the Bolshoi theatre), photographic enlargers, and photo cameras.

The first factory camera (the 6x9 "Moscow -1" with the Industar-23 lens) was manufactured in 1946. In 1947, they produced the first model of Moscow-2 camera equipped with focus control and a shutter speed of 1/250 sec. This model became the one to be mass-produced for a long time. The first 25 cameras were made to commemorate the 800th anniversary of Moscow. In 1947, they started engineering the miniature picture camera "Tsorky". 1st May 1948 the factory manufactured the first run, consisting of 50 cameras, and by the end of the year the factory produced 1500 cameras. "Tsorky" and its many descendants (14 models were released over the past 30 years) were destined to become symbols of the factory and Moscow. The first assembly line set up in March 1949 produced Tsorky, and by the end of December they collected 31312 cameras. In 1951, they started manufacturing a new camera - Zenit which started the development of a new generation single-lens reflex cameras which made the factory widely famous.

It is worth mentioning that cameras manufactured in the first postwar year were fitted with lenses produced locally. The first lenses that were mass-produced were Jupiter-8 and Industar-22. In the beginning, the factory produced not more than 300 lens monthly. Within 3 years, the production capacity grew up to 4 thousand lens produced monthly.

Cameras and lenses were affordable for the mass consumer; that is why the demand for photo cameras and film cameras kept growing. On April 25, 1963, the assembly line manufactured the 4 million-th Zenit-ZM camera, which was initially produced in 1962. In 1946, when the factory just started manufacturing picture cameras, they assembled 25 cameras monthly. However, by 1963, the Tsorky-4 was produced every minute, and the Tsorky-5 was manufactured every 1.5 minutes.

Krasnogorsk picture cameras and cinema equipment were exported to 80 countries - not only to third-world countries; but to countries with high level of optics technology.

There was an increased demand for lenses produced by the factories abroad. The most popular lenses were Gelios-40, Tair-

11A, Telemar -22. Since 1948 to 1973, the factory produced 150 models of high quality film, and photo lenses. Most parts of the lenses were produced for export into different countries.

Is it true that the beamer for V.I. Lenin library and theatrical binocular were the first civil production of the factory?

Yes, it is true. It was the first civil production. In December 1945, the factory began manufacturing small-scale series of D-1 beamers for V.I. Lenin library, and opened the assembly line of U-2 enlargers. The next year in April, the Bolshoy theatre bought 20 TB-2 model theatrical binoculars (the first run of this model). Within a year, the factory produced 5 thousand binoculars monthly.

Can you tell us about the Horizon cameras, we love the quality of these cameras.

In 1965, the factory stopped producing FT-2 panoramic cameras, which was followed by the serial production of a new panoramic camera, the Horizon. It was equipped with OF-28 lens with good resolution ability and depth.

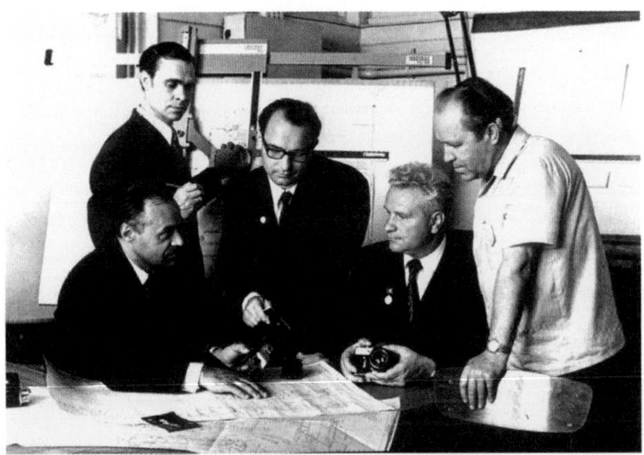

It was awarded with numerous prizes including a prize of Leipzig fair (1967), gold, silver and three bronze medals at VDNKH (All-Soviet exhibition center).

Compared to the FT model, the Horizon had a different photo frame - 24x58 mm. The camera was produced within the period of 1967 - 1973. The Horizon 202, 203 were for 35 mm film, and the Horizon 205 was made for 120 mm film. It took only a year to design the first model - the Horizon 202. The camera was initially marketed internationally, and supplies to the USSR market were not planned. It was a 4-year co-production with a well-known Italian factory Manfrotto.

Horizon-203 designed in 2001-2002 was the next stage in development of panoramic Horizons. The model was presented at the exhibition Photokina-2002 in Cologne, and at PhotoForum-2003 for the Russian audience. The production of the camera began in 2003. The new model differed from Horizon-202 due to its upgraded mechanics, which ensured noiseless performance of the camera and a wider range of exposures. The model also suggested a structural solution of the problem of blanket exposures, which was often the case in Horizon-202. The Horizon-205 is a panoramic camera for 120 and 220 type wide films. Its production began in 2000. The High quality lens of this camera - Zenitar 3,5/50 ps allows for making a vertical image shift.

When did Krasnogorsk invent the motion-picture camera and which directors use this camera? Could you name several movies?

Before the Krasnogorsk factory started manufacturing picture cameras, it already produced motion-picture cameras. In June 1945 Krasnogorsk factory produced «КС-50Б» camera (35 mm motion-picture camera) which was a copy of Eyemo model designed by the American company Bell&Howell. The first manufactured cameras were sent to a Moscow film studio for testing, where they were well-received. However, the production volume was not impressive.

The factory manufactured other motion-picture cameras including the «АКС-1» (a copy of another Eyemo modification), the «АКС-2» (a copy of a aerial motion-picture Bell&Howell), and other cameras. During the period between 1956 - 1961, the company designed and developed complicated film equipment for specific uses.

In the same period, the factory designed speed cameras that allowed shooting up to 200 frames/sec.

In 1959-1960 the factory designed the 'Quartz,' the first amateur motion-picture camera (it was mass-produced for many years). In total, the factory manufactured 224394 cameras.

In 1965 Krasnogorsk factory invented 'Krasnogorsk," the first Russian 16mm amateur motion-picture camera. In 1979, it was used during the Soviet-Canadian expedition over the North Pole. Soviet cameraman Vladimir Pavlovich Ledenyov shot around 2000 meters of film rolls. The Canadians could not shoot much with Sony camera, the camera got frozen but the "Krasnogorsk" camera kept working at any temperature.

The factory also manufactured 16mm cameras for reportage shoots - the "16SP "and the "16SP -M ."

Motion-picture cameras were fitted with an electric motor drive, a large set of shooting frequencies, and a 3 lens turret. These cameras were used for shooting documentaries and TV broadcasts. Initially, the Konvas camera, which we produced, (KSR-2M) was used for shooting inside piloted vehicles. The Soviet cosmonaut Gherman Titov used Konvas for shoots onboard of "Vostok-2" spaceship. However, other cameras of a different type were required for space shoots - they should be lighter, less bulky, and equipped with electric drive.

The Krasnogorsk factory manufactured the 8mm camera «Quartz-8XL, » the only amateur 8mm motion picture camera in Russia. This camera was taken for mass-market production in 1981, the last camera of this model was produced in 1984. This model was the last 8mm motion-picture camera produced by Krasnogorsk factory.

Can you tell us about the pictures of the Moon taken with the Zenit camera?

In the early 1950s, scientists began studying natural phenomena in the Earth's atmosphere, and the Krasnogorsk factory actively participated in this interesting research. In 1957, we launched a rocket equipped with an aerial camera AFA -39. The camera took the first pictures of the Earth from a spatial perspective using 35mm film.

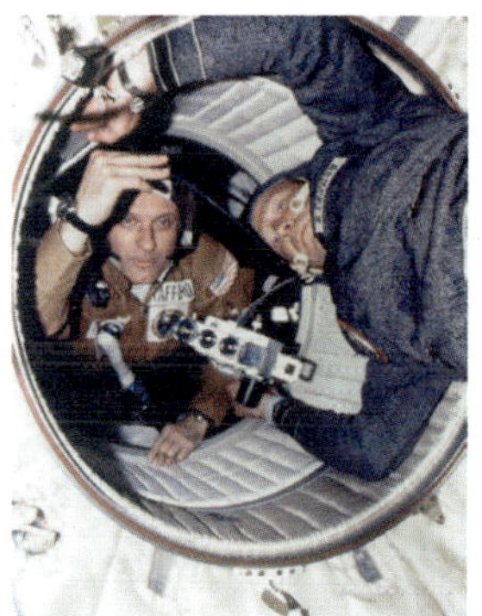

The same year, in October, the world's first artificial satellite, the Sputnik-1, was launched by the Soviet Union. Within a year, the Soviet Union also launched the world's fist space station, and in September 1959, the second space station reached the lunar surface. On October 4, 1959 the Soviet Union launched the rocket

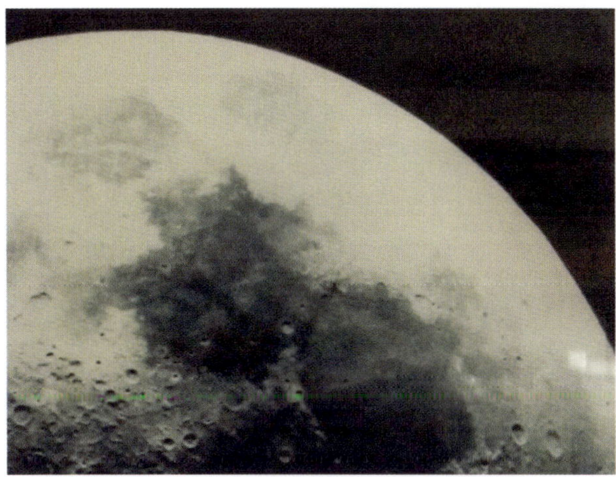

'Luna-3, ' automatic station for exploring the Moon and outer space.

In these studies, the Krasnogorsk factory was assigned a key role: under the scientific guidance of S.P. Korolev and employees of the S.P. Construction bureau; Krasnogorsk optical engineers, using aerial technology, had to develop unique equipment for surveillance from a spatial perspective. A picture camera, the AFA-E1 for use on the space station was developed, and later, Enisey-1 equipment was installed at the Luna-3 space station on Oct. 4, 1959.

On the dawn of Oct. 7, moving along the predetermined track, the camera approached the moon from a distance of 66800 kms and the lens was able to capture 70% of the surface of the backside of the Moon.
The shooting session took forty minutes: using two lenses with focal lengths of 200 and 500 mm, and for the first time, a 35 mm camera captured the previously unexplored lunar surface. Scanned photographs of the lunar surface were encrypted via radio signals and transmitted to the Earth. The ground-based equipment converted them into images. Based on these 17 images, lunar landscape researchers made a map of the Moon.

How did the company change after the collapse of the Soviet Union?
In the time of Perestroika, the volume of orders declined sharply. The management decided to stay within the high and medium technology sectors, and continued to produce civil engineering products, such as night vision devices, medical equipment, laser micro-analyzers, and binocular loupes.
In 1993, the factory became a private limited company, and established the "JSC Zverev Krasnogorsk factory" (JSC Krasnogorsk Mechanical Factory). Since 1998, the factory started developing new high-tech equipment and civil engineering products including the 'Geoton-L1,' optoelectronics device for natural resources exploration and the prevention of natural disasters, and "Gamma," an optoelectronics device for video spectrometers used in small space crafts.

For many years JSC Krasnogorsk was one of the world's largest manufacturers of reflex cameras for amateur photographers. Today, the factory produces panorama film and digital cameras. Lenses have relevant optical efficiency, good color rendering and resolution capability. Today the company is developing a new digital panoramic camera, the Horizon D L3, intended for digital panoramic shooting of landscapes, interiors, architecture, sports and reportage photography. We are also developing SLR cameras equipped with a video recording function.

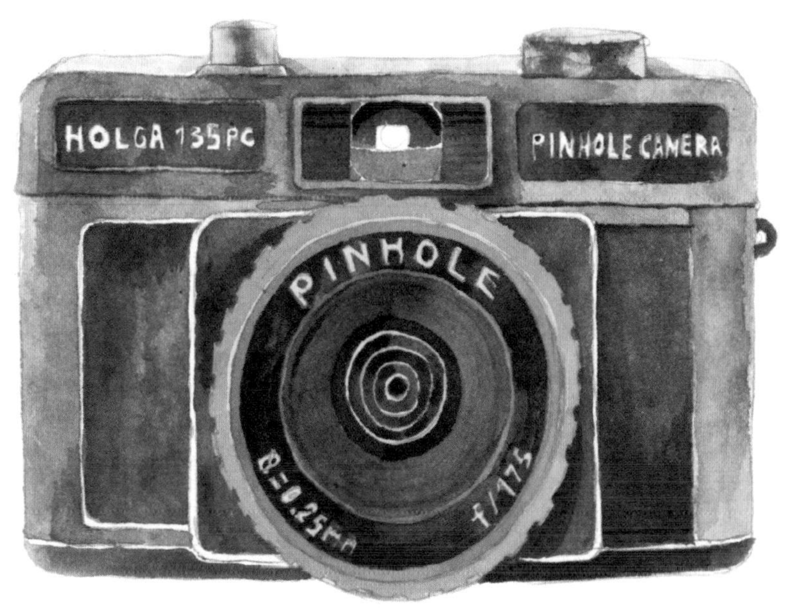
HOLGA 135PC
PINHOLE CAMERA
PINHOLE
Ø=0.25mm
f/175

PINHOLE

A pinhole is a rudimentary camera, consisting of a container, whether it be a box, can, tin, and even as photographer Martin Cheung has used often, a roasted duck, and instead of a lens, it has a small hole on one side. Light goes through this hole, and projects an inverted image. Quite often pinholes need long exposure times. These are extremely simple systems but have a fan base of photographers, and there is even a World Pinhole Day on the last Sunday of April each year.

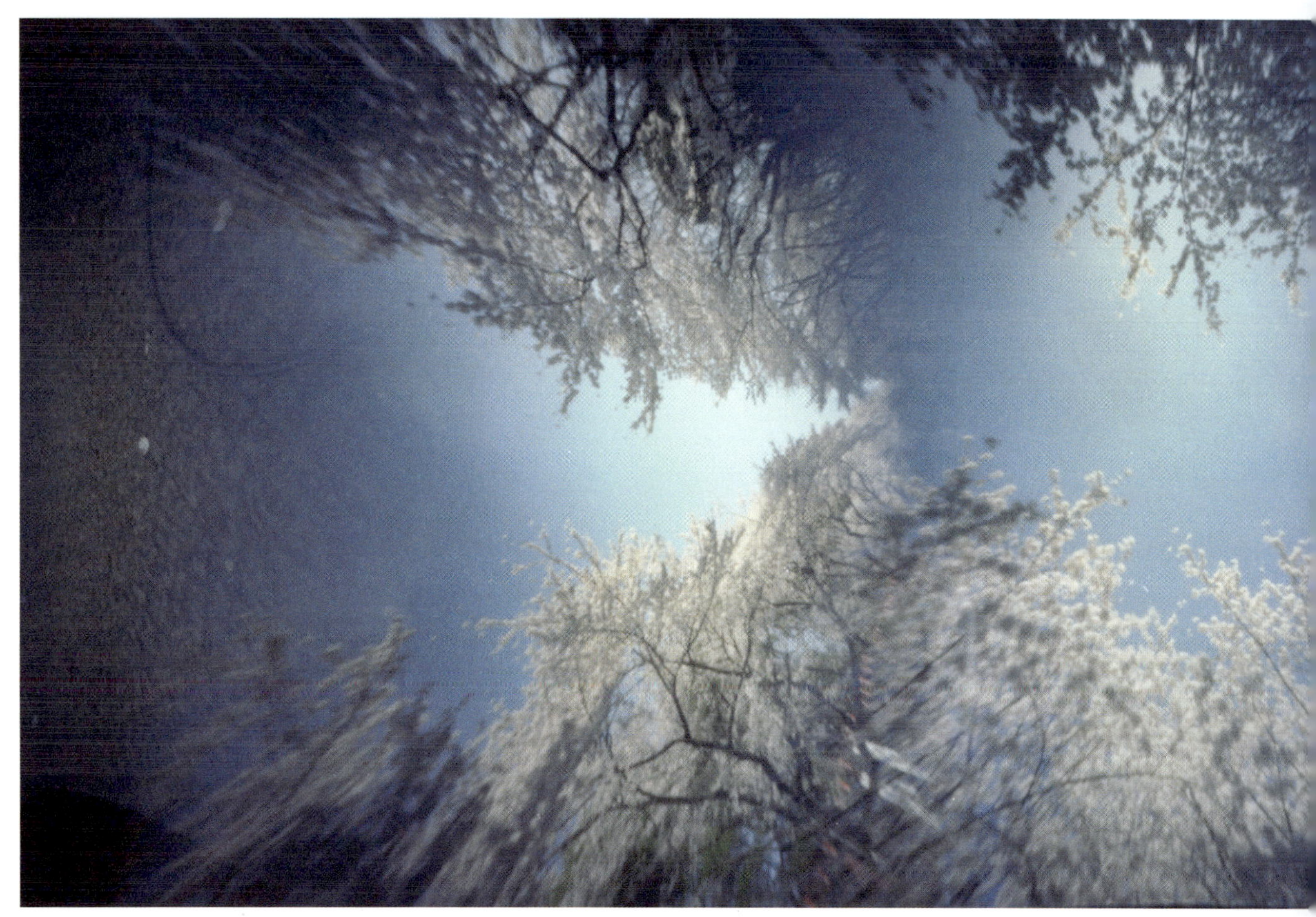

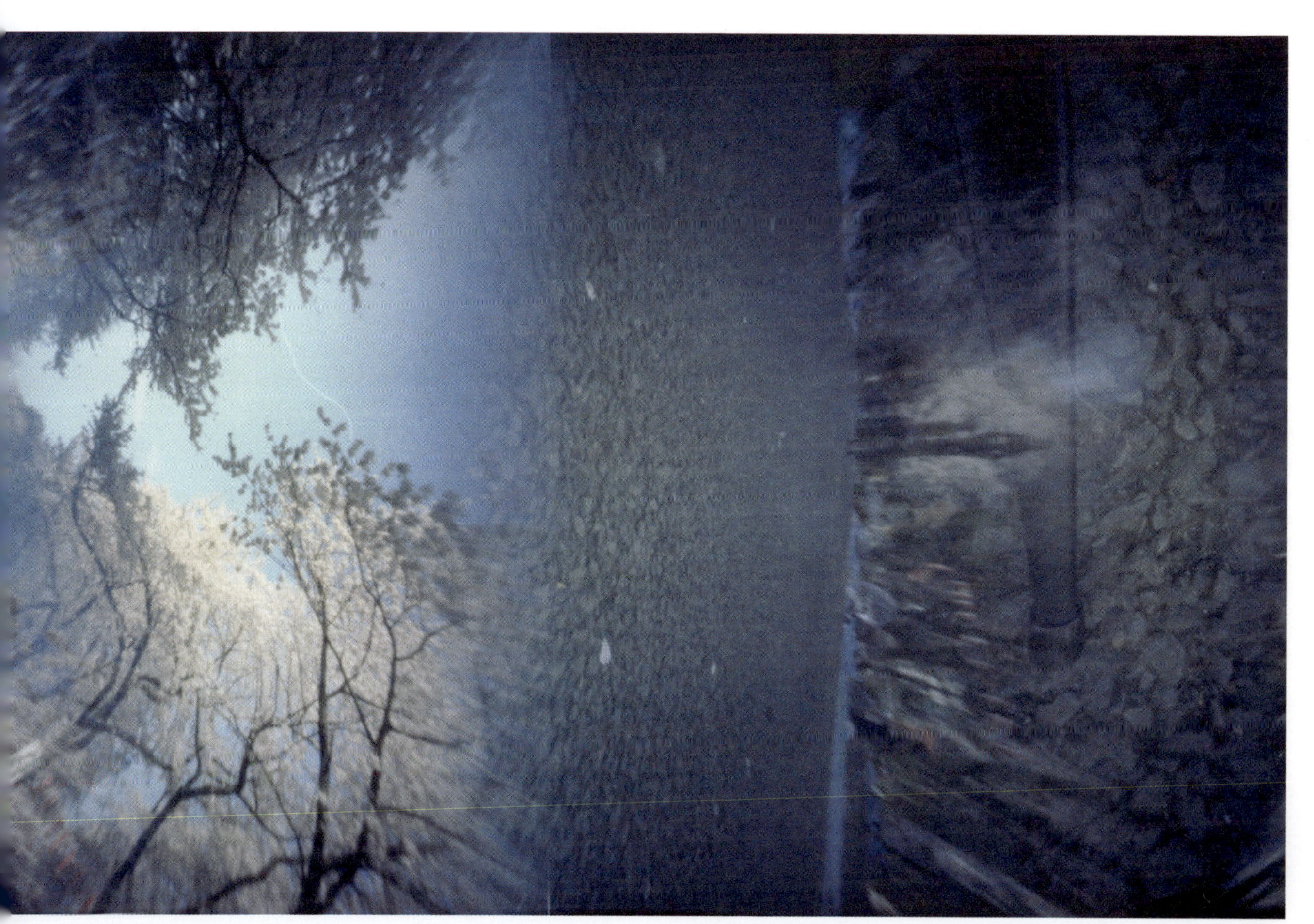

CHERRYBLOSSOMS TAKEN WITH A 6 PINHOLE HEXOMNISCOPE CAMERA.

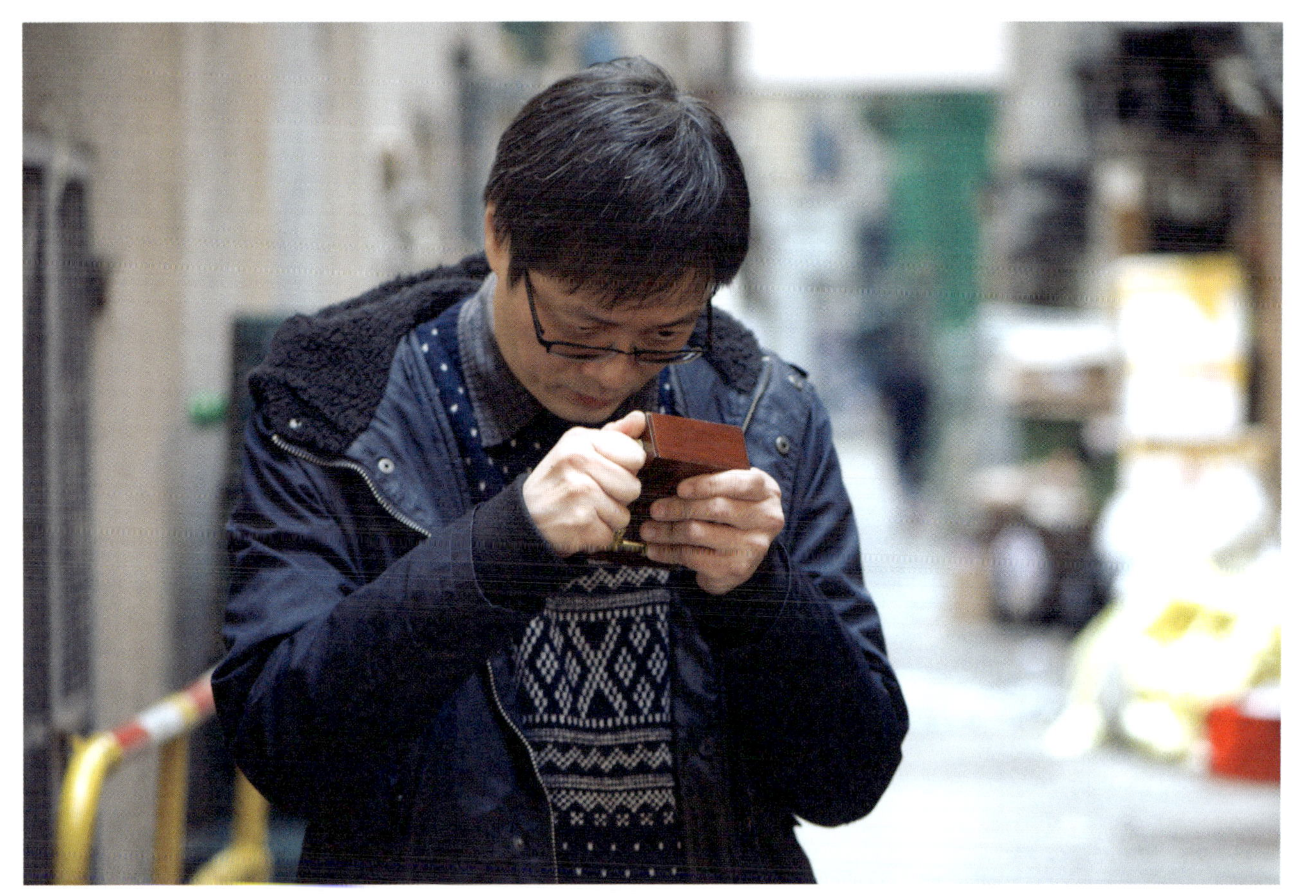

— *interview 17* —

ZERNIKE AU,

FOUNDER AND MAKER OF ZERO PINHOLE CAMERAS

Can you introduce the Zero pinhole camera briefly?

The first camera I made was the Zero 2000, about 13 years ago. The craftsmanship for the 6x6 is a bit complicated because we use an antique method for the painting of the wood. First, we apply the color and then the coating. After each coating, we sand it a bit and then we dry and apply a coat again and let it dry. We have to buy the wood, cut it in pieces, and then store it in a place to let it dry naturally for one year - for some models more than 5 years. We choose teak wood from Thailand as it is very stable with very small distortion in the material itself.

Who was buying them at the time?

Around then, the Internet was beginning, and there was a forum called the "pinhole discussion list" and I posted there and told them I have a new camera. The moderator allowed me to show my camera and after that, it was mostly Americans. My local (Hong Kong) clients were few, however a lot of schools, especially people in photography courses like at Hong Kong Polytech bought them.

Do you work with a craftsman?

I made my first camera, and designed it myself. I studied industrial design in Polytech and I know what product design is, and how to make the parts, because we had to make mock ups, so I have turning and wielding machines. I bought a CNC, and I would design parts in 3D CAD software to see if it works. I can't make that many, so I employed some employees and taught them how to cut the wood and paint it, and when the basic assembly is ready, I make the final parts.

Some people say the price is expensive, but if you compare prices, others' are 200 HKD cheaper than ours, but they are mass-produced. They make a mold and press a button and the item comes out. With us, the whole production period might be a year from cutting the wood to the finished product, because I will not sand the camera if it has freshly applied lacquer, I need to make it dry completely first.

When you first made the first prototype, were the photos OK, or did it take a few goes to make a good photo-making machine?

I first made a very basic camera, and drilled a pinhole and tested it. Before I launched this product, there wasn't a camera that could accept 120 film.

Our film is directly rollover loading, and this is a new installation in the film winding process. It is the opposite of a Hasselblad.

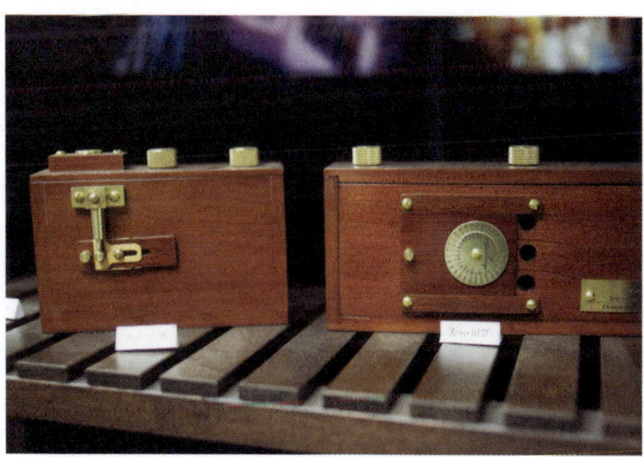

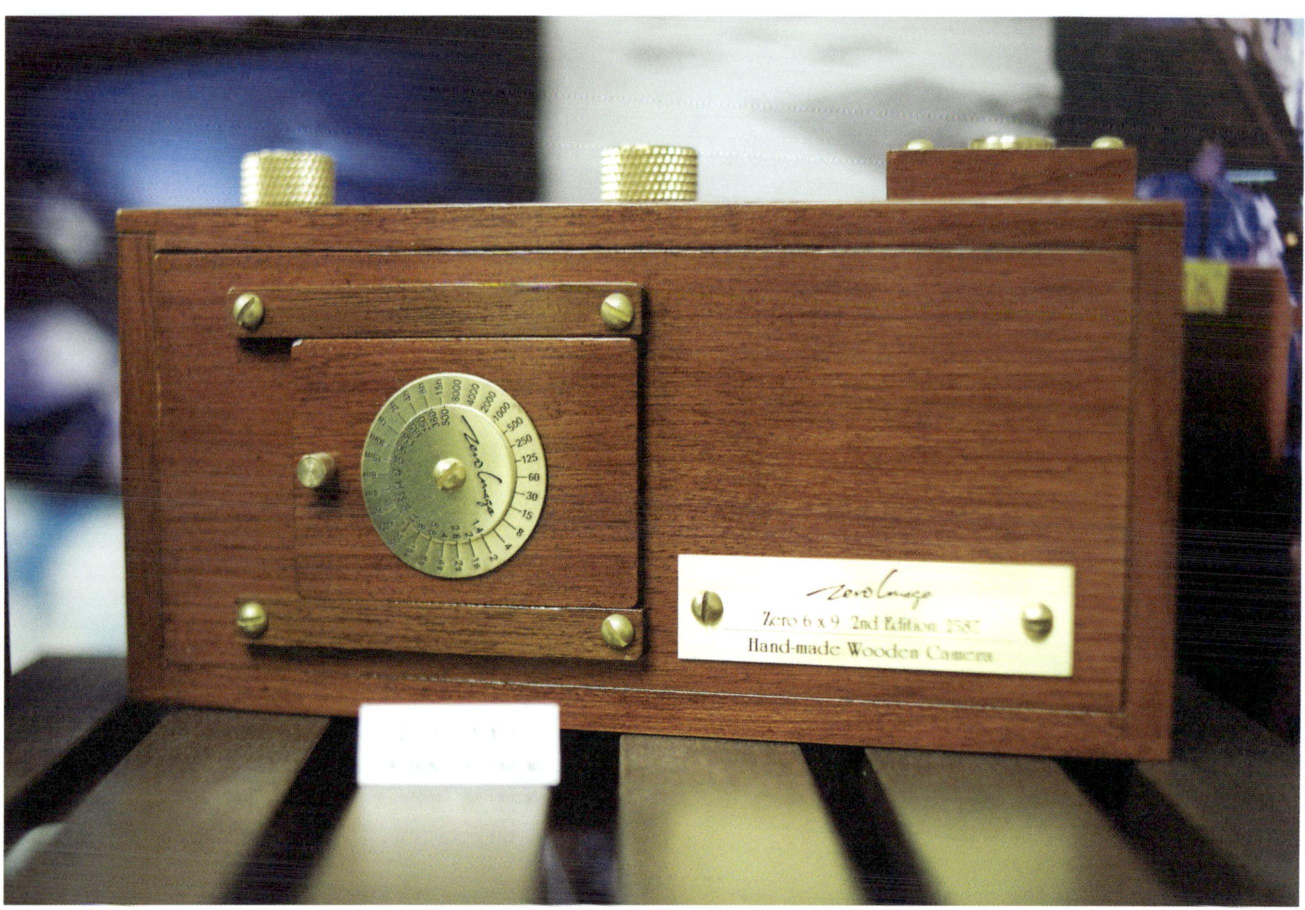
Zero 6 x 9 2nd Edition
Hand-made Wooden Camera

For Hasselblad's film loading, they have a traditional way of making their camera, so they have their own lodge - different cameras have a different lodge, and we have our special notch too. It is one of our unique characteristics, and we used this to fight someone copying our camera in China. They said that anyone can make a box, it is simple, a pinhole in a box, but when the film comes out, we told our lawyer they copied our construction, (because the lodge was the same), so we won.

Because you make them by hand, there is a certain craftsmanship in what you do, so even if someone copies the idea, it is still not the same product.
Sure, we can still exist because people like the wood and the quality.

You can make a pinhole with a tin can; why did you want to make such a luxurious product?
Personally, I love wood so much and at the time, I was working as a product designer mainly in souvenirs, which were in the style of antiques. Personally, I like wood cameras so much, and prior to making one, I bought a few cameras, disassembled them and modified them and tried to make one that would suit my needs. I find a lot of them have standardized everything: the lens, the focal length. I like wide angle so much, and a strong perspective. My first camera was impressive because it was so thin, and the focal length was soft.

Can you explain very simply how it works?
It has a hole, and the light comes through and projects an image onto the film print - and that is it! The pinhole must be very smooth and a perfect circle is better and there are several formulas for the size of the hole.

What are the characteristics of the Zero images?
Many different photographers have different points of view. Our film has no spring at the back, so the film may be curved at the edge, and some people like that, and some like the strong perspective, and the dark corners.
It is a very lateral perspective. The film distance from the pinhole to the print is far; some people make a curved back to compensate for it.

In a word, what do you like about your pinhole cameras?
I can determine everything; I can make my own choice.

So it is the sense of control?
Yes, and also the procedure of taking the photo, it is quite different to a typical camera, with a pinhole it takes a few hours. I don't frame it, and I train my mind to make the image. After a period of time, you know how it will come out. But a lot of people still want to frame the image before they take it, so we made a viewfinder for them, but personally, I try to encourage people to try and train themselves to point and shoot. And the final result is not what we expect sometimes.

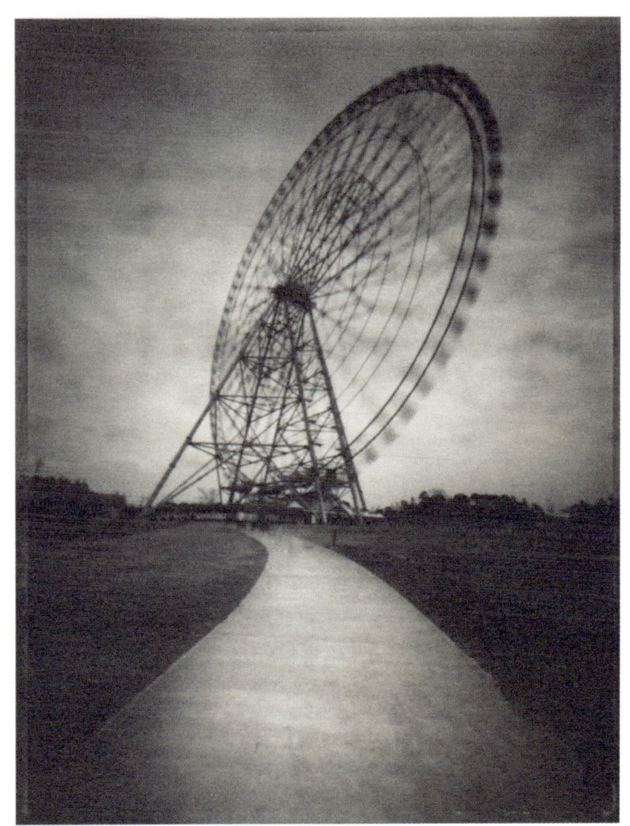

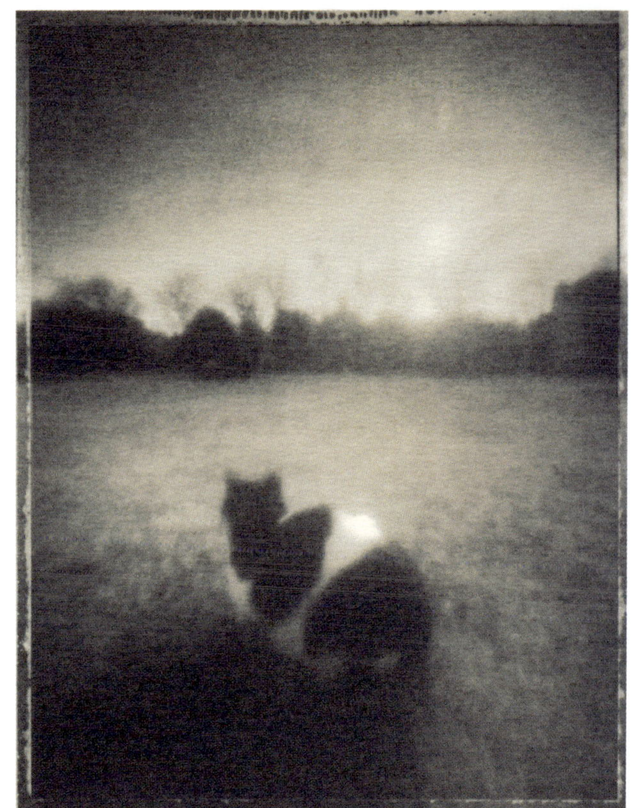

—— interview 18 ——

YUSUKE ABICO

When did you first come across a Zero?

I bought it after it was just released off the Hong Kong website. I bought two of these and I also got the 6x6 type.

I like that the edges of the photographs drop because it is the Zero 50 mm and because of the wide-angle lens, which is different to other photos and not too sharp. I think this is interesting, occasionally. The Zero camera has a zone plate and it makes the photos softer and brighter than a regular pinhole.

The camera itself is aesthetic too. If you compare it to other pinholes, it is quite cute and has a nice wooden design. When there was a pinhole boom, there were ones made out of gold as well as wood but if you compared them, (I liked) the body, the brass parts and the shutter mechanism. It is also light.

So you like the Zero as an object as well?

Yes. I also make a lot of cameras, and I will make them according to a theme, for example, I made one with a wooden photo frame. It is made of extremely light wood. I am not calculating the specs, so some parts are quite bent, as I am making it by hand - I am not that bothered by things like that - but the photos are quite normal actually. In other words, the photos are quite boring.

Was the Zero the first pinhole that you used?

Basically yes, I was making them for fun too before, but to make actual artworks, I think it was probably with the Zero. The Polaroid company had a pinhole contest, and I took a photo and won the prize.

How long did it take for you to get used to it?

Actually it is quite easy to use, as I was using a camera that was quite similar before that.

Can you tell us tips for taking a good pinhole photo?

It isn't that different to a regular photo; to simplify your shot is important. To have a single subject, and don't try and complicate it too much as it isn't that sharp, so at the most, two subjects is probably plenty.

It is a camera you can control and isn't that difficult, especially with the Zero, as it has the zone plate. It is a camera where you can envision the results. For example, when I shot this cat, the cat is clearly not sitting there still for a minute, but if you use the zone plate, the exposure time is short, and that makes it easy to shoot. I can shoot a lot at night. Usually with a pinhole, you can't shoot at night, even though the pinhole function on a digital camera makes it easier to shoot at night. But when it is with film, I always thought night shots with a pinhole camera are impossible, but I was able to use it. This Ferris wheel was around winter, 4pm it was dark already.

I used a Holga in the beginning, around the year 2000. When I won the Japan polaroid company pinhole competition I won some money and also some goods; I received 3 6x6 Holgas and I gave some to my students. The Holga has a plastic lens so we burnt the lens with a flame and I gave them to my students and we did an exhibition.

You shoot overseas, as well as things extremely close to you, such as people sitting next to you in the office, how is the

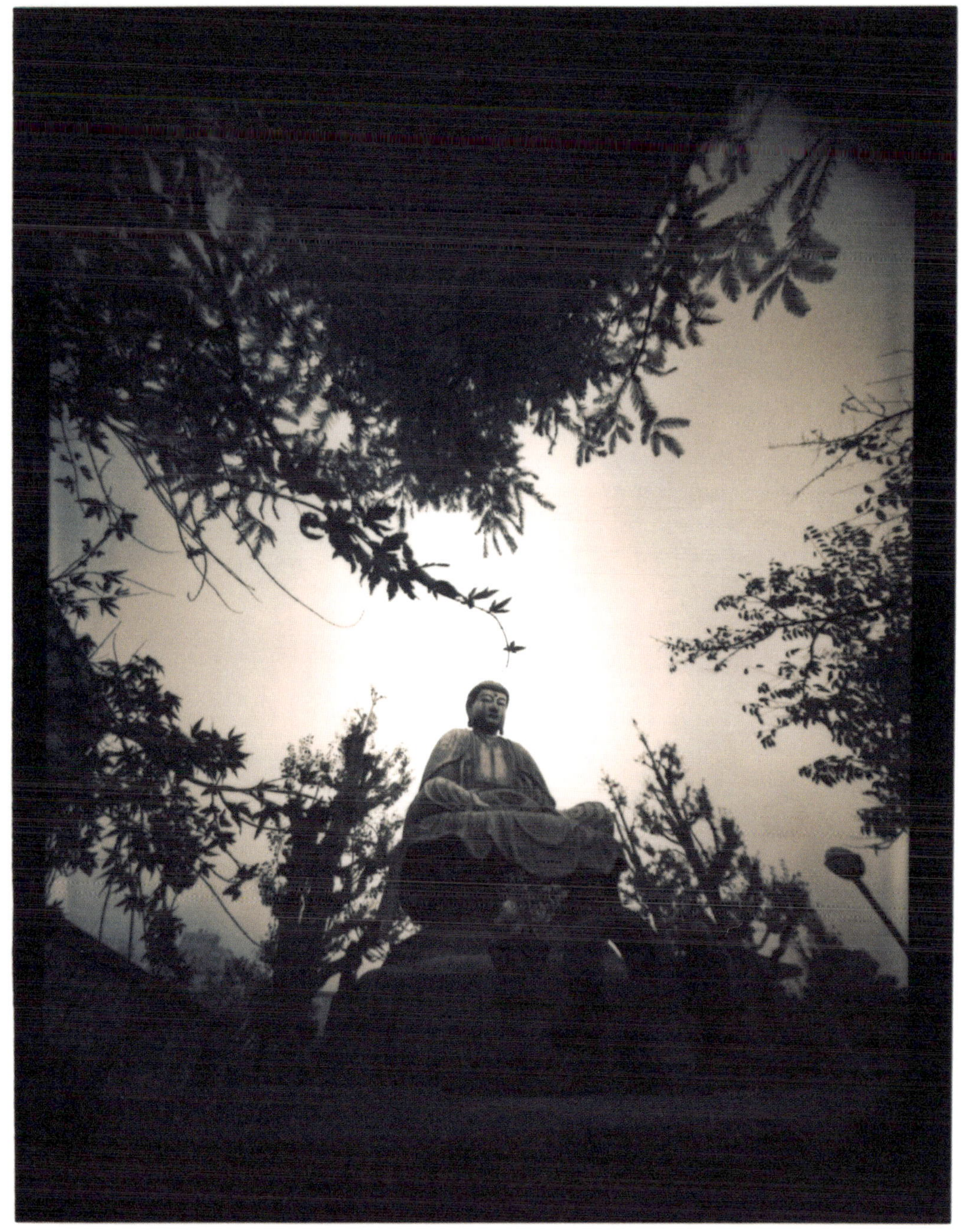

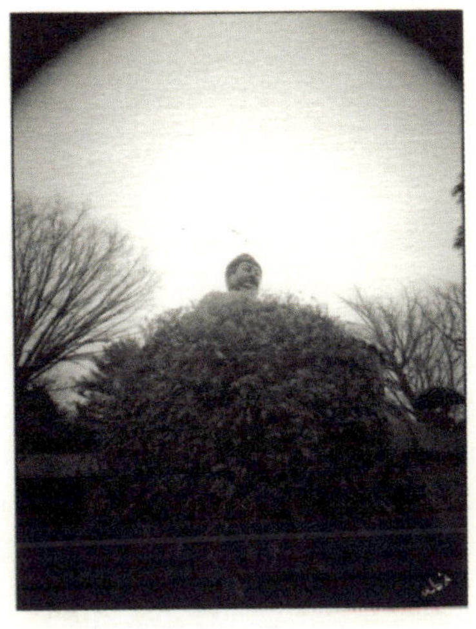

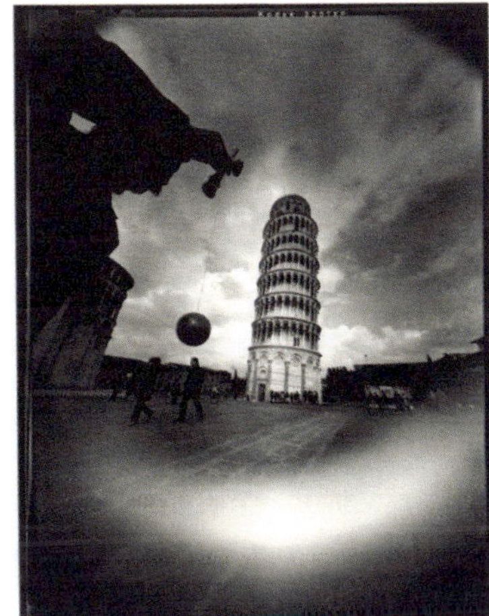

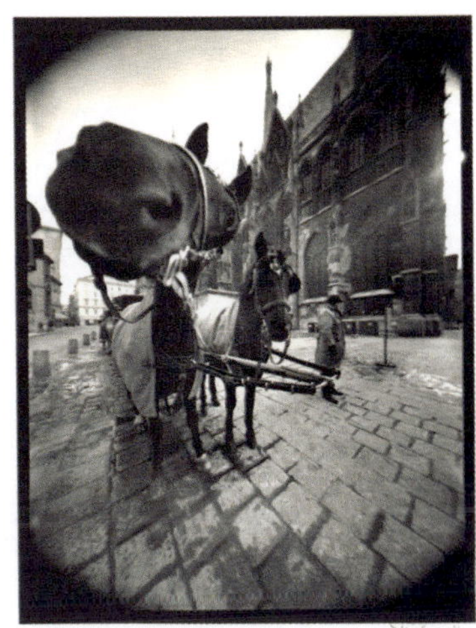

shooting process different?

I went to Europe with the school I teach at (Nihon University College of Art) and used a wide-angle that I made. It was basically taking distorted tourist photos, and shooting things that were somewhat extraordinary. I was just snapping photos with none of the sense of irony that I have in my local photos. They are just tourist shots.

When you talk about things that are close by, I think there are a lot of things I am inevitably overlooking. It is about the choice one makes when selecting a subject, these kinds of dangling carrots. For example, I have a photo of a guy slumped over a counter asleep and for me that was a dangling carrot.

Before, I was taking a lot of fluorescent lights and it was quite interesting. If you buy a new camera and you are sitting here in my office, there isn't that much to shoot, so what I took was the fluoro lights. I was taking them while standing up straight as soon as I got a camera.

What are some other projects you have worked on?

I would shoot some Polaroids with double exposure, and printing the back of the Polaroid. I also made a camera that doesn't focus at all. My eyes are bad, and when I take off my glasses it looks close to the images this camera produces.

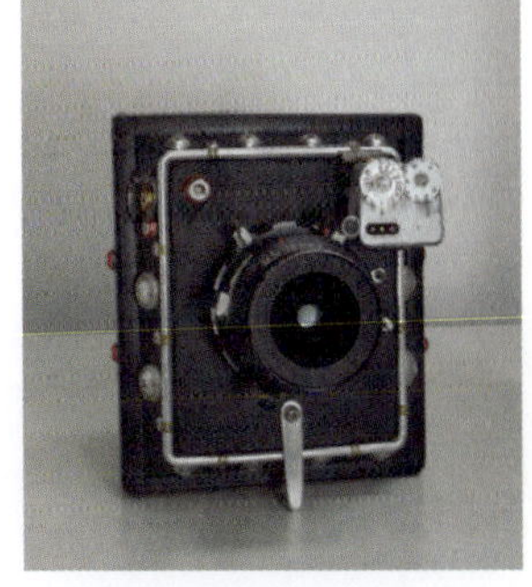

PHOTOS TAKEN WITH ONE OF ABICO'S MANY HOME MADE CAMERAS.

What makes a good photo?

Composition. It is very basic, but it is important. It is instinct but you can practice and improve that as well.

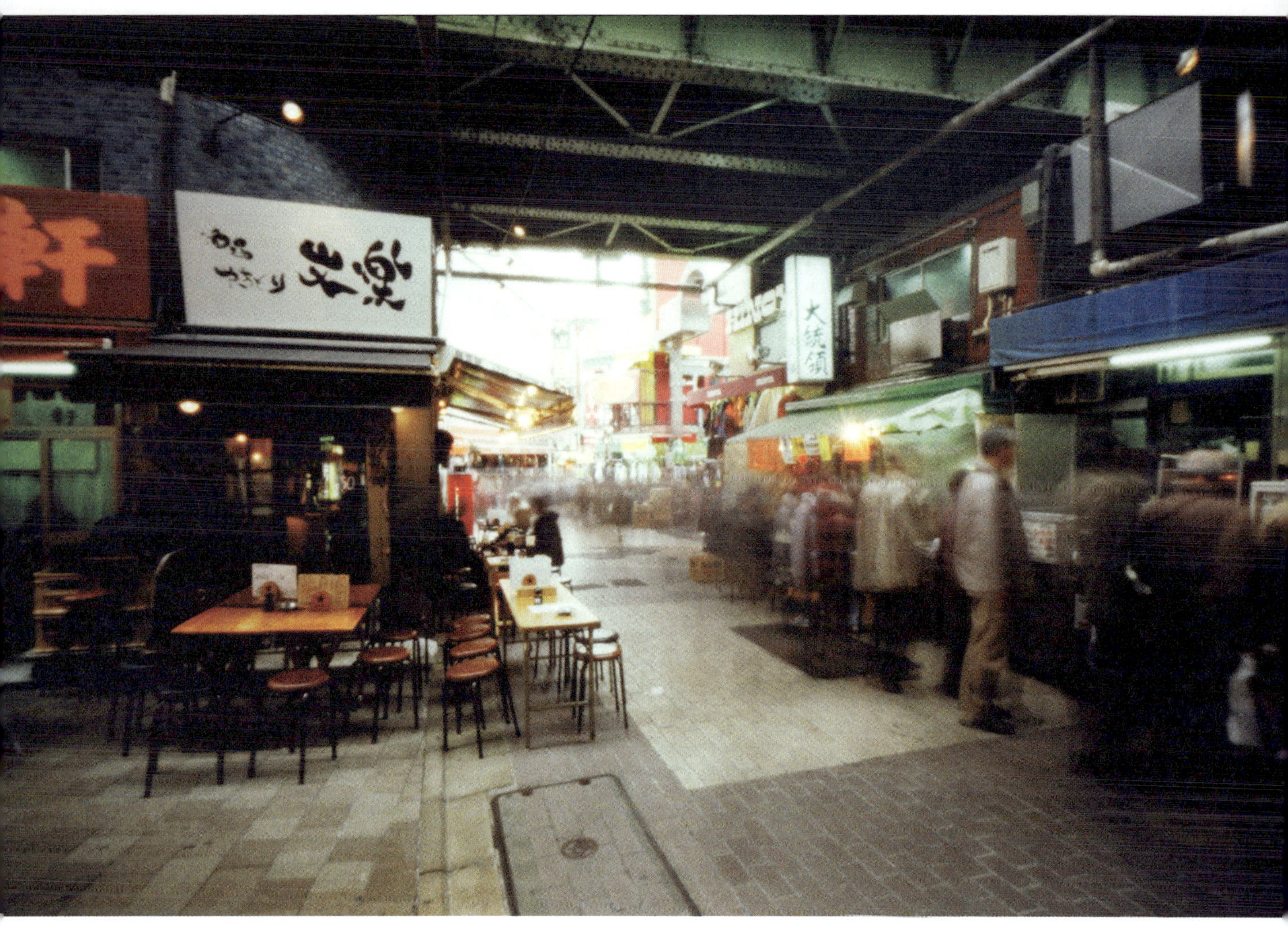

— *interview 19* —

MICHAEL FEATHER

It's quite ironic because I found your work at an exhibition at the Hasselblad gallery, but yet you are shooting with a Zero camera!

Yes, I had an exhibition at Chinsanzo, and Elizabeth Addyman (the Hasselblad creative coordinator) happened to come along with some of the Hasselblad people to a talk that I did. I had various works up, I had black & whites and cyanotypes and a small series of pinholes, but because of the space I could only put small ones up. I was saying that normally I would do the pinhole prints 2m x 1m and Elizabeth said to bring them to Hasselblad. They just want to promote photography, whether you are doing cyanotypes, Holga or pinhole.

I found that when I would interview people who are doing commercial photography as well, no matter how jaded they are, they would suddenly get an interest in the topic when you start talking about these kinds of cameras.

I think the thing is, I imagine a lot of people are a little like me, when you work in commercial photography, you always have deadlines, clients and designers you work with, and it is commercial photography.

I am not a fashion photographer - fashion is a different area where there is a more creativity for the photographer to have freer reign, but with advertising and commercial photography, there is always a client and it is design agency-led.

When you break out of that to do personal work, you do get excited about it, because the only client is yourself. People see it on the wall, some people love it and some hate it, but it is what you wanted to do so, that is most important thing - you can make all the choices.

The reason I went with the pinhole is partly because commercial work is mostly digital, so to get away from that aspect, and with digital now, and iPhone and smart phones, we can shoot anything any time and stick a filter on it. You are playing around. You don't start out with an actual vision, you just snap away. Whereas, when you start using something like a pinhole, with film, you start to think about what you are doing. You have made a conscious decision at the start. For me that was to use the Zero, and I shot with film with the 6x9 format.

What appeals to you about that format?

It is quite cinematic and I actually kept away from the pinhole wide-angle effect of putting it close to subjects and making them look huge, with exaggerated perspectives. I went for a more cinematic look - I like landscapes anyway.

A lot of pinholes are done in black and white because it is not sharp, so they rely on the contrast of black and white to give it shape, form and depth. And because of the inherent lack of sharpness they tend to print them small. With the type of the film and the speed I used, the texture held together and it was all very conscious decisions. Otherwise, I don't think you can do it that big otherwise it will be too blurry, but by choosing the film and getting the grain that I wanted, I was able to hold the texture to the page. And I think it worked quite well.

The pinhole is quite interesting because you have no viewfinder. Also when you do a long exposure and the light is changing, you

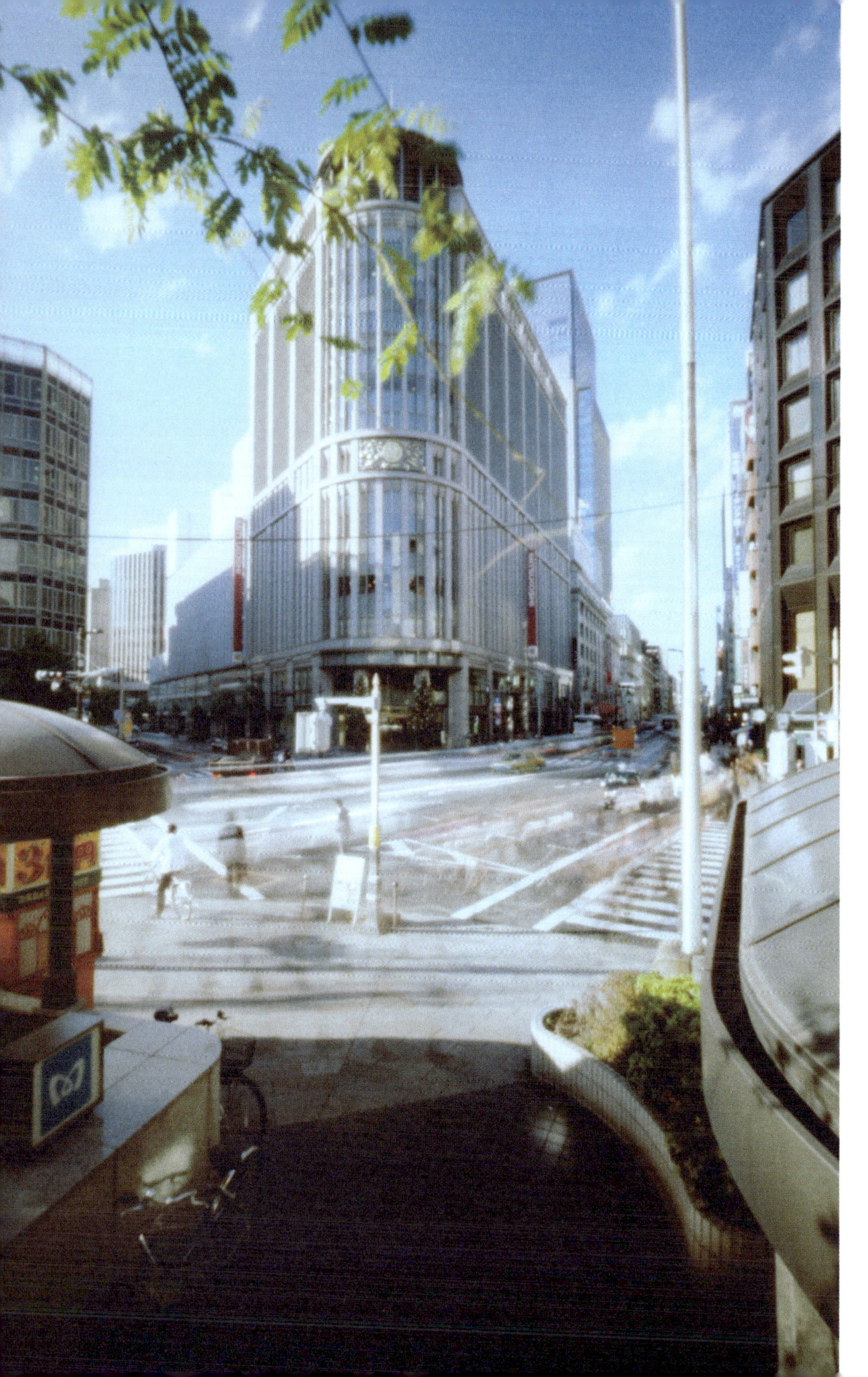

get a lot of interesting things happening – some of the shots in bright sunshine would have been 4-8 seconds, while on an overcast day, 20-30 minutes. I did a shoot at Asakusa when they had a Chinese lantern festival, and obviously it was full of people – it was just rivers of people – but that is why I went there.

When I set the camera up, you have the temples and the stillness of the temple and you have people that have merged into the shape of a river. Many stopped looking and talking for 10 minutes and then walked on, so you get these shapes of people. It is nice when you get things like that. It is things you hope will happen but, without a viewfinder you really have to pre-visualize and think about what it is you want to do.

How long did it take to get used to the Zero and not having a viewfinder?

To be honest, I am quite a technical person and I like technical things, so I worked out that it is the equivalent of an 18mm lens and I know roughly where the back of the film sits, if I look through he side of the camera and imagine a line going through the pinhole. I can roughly guess where and what I am getting in the shot.

Obviously, you get a lot of things that don't work, but the picture that set me off was the picture of the tree at the emperor's moat at the imperial residence. Everyone goes there to see if they can see the emperor and I went around the corner and it was shot on an overcast day. Because of the wideness of the lens and because I got close to the tree, you get from the roots to the sky and the water on the moat is moving with the breeze so it is very smooth. The exposure was about 30 minutes and there is a bit of movement in the leaves from the breeze. When I got that back and looked at the negative, I scanned it and looked at the print, I was like, I like this, it is not reality. But actually it is the reality that I felt on the day.

Do you find with the pinhole, that you can express what you were feeling easier than a clear image because we don't remember things like that?

It is funny you should say that because I had a shot that I took with a Holga of two donkeys on a beach in Blackpool in England. I shot it with cross-processed film and I put it in for a competition in England. And it got picked to be in the competition, and a book. When people look at it, they ask if it is in North Africa, and I say it is in a British seaside town, and they say, 'But it is like a dream!'

Well actually they were right – when I was a boy, we would go to Blackpool and it is raining, cold, and grey; and if you swam in the water you would probably die, but when you are looking back to that time, it is like a dream and you remember the sun was shining and the sea was warm. But it wasn't like that at all. I took that picture with the Holga with the feeling of a dream, because that is how I remembered Blackpool – not as the reality.

What are some specific things about shooting in Tokyo that differs to other places?

I was playing with the Holga and the long exposures – while I was moving, as well as the people in the shot, it made me think that Tokyo for me, couldn't be still – still images of Tokyo aren't

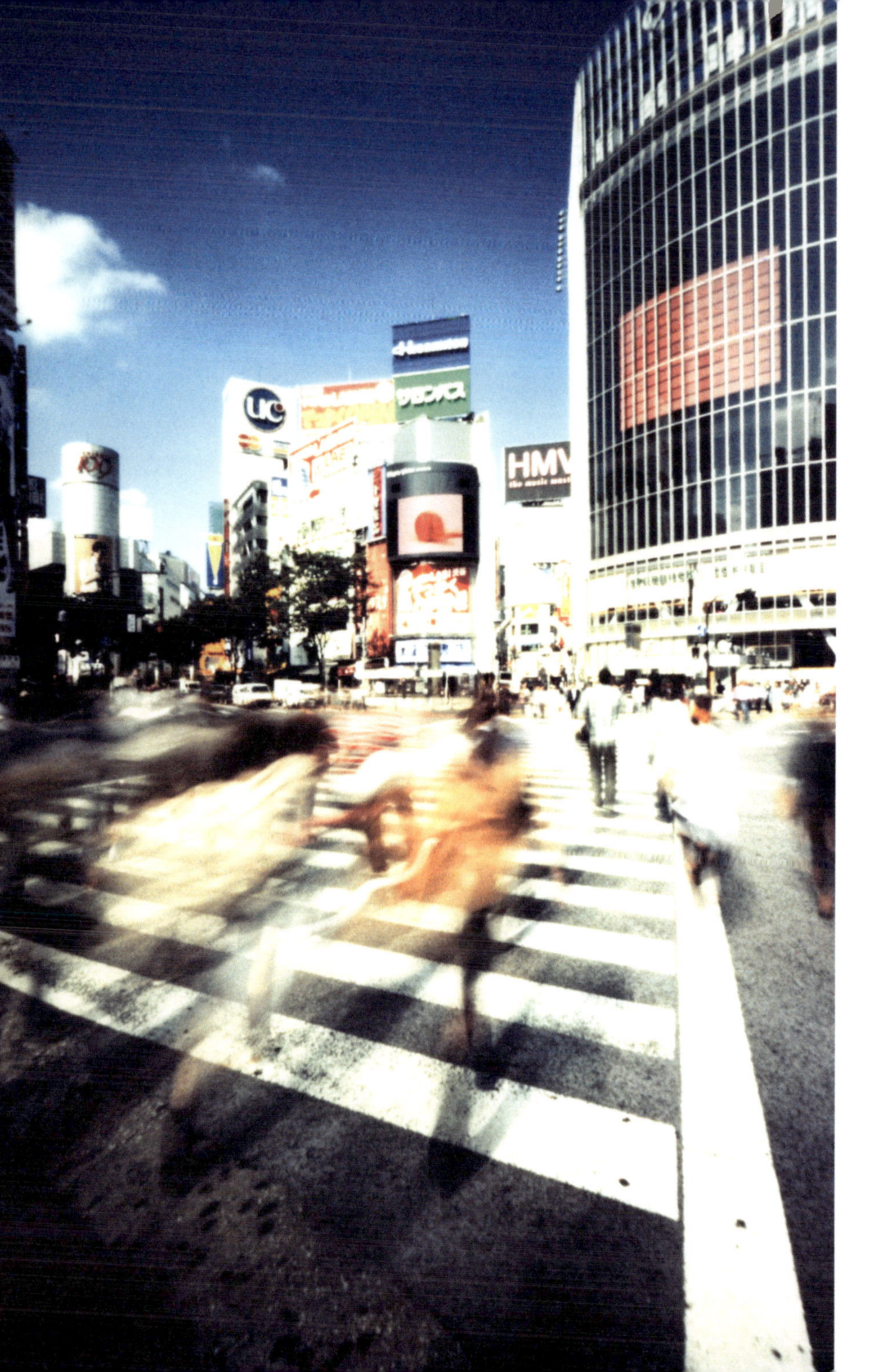
UC
HMV

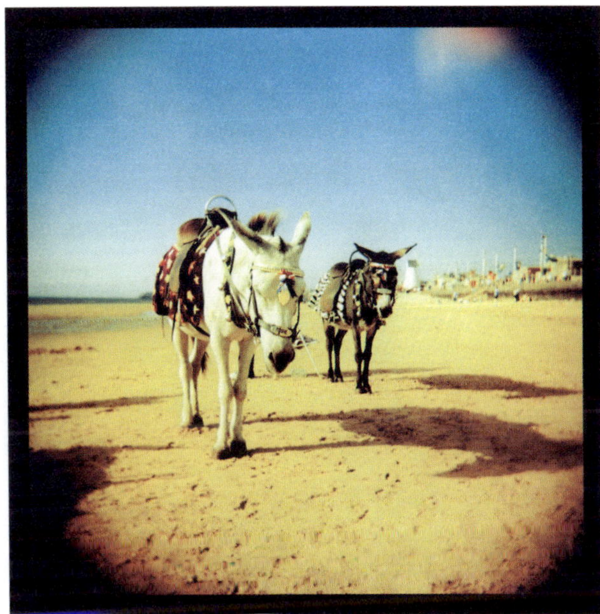

right! It is always moving. When you are in the underground you don't see people's faces in reality, because they are moving all the time - to work, to the izakaya (bar), they are all going somewhere. There is no stopping to pass the day, it is always flowing. So after working with the Holga, I thought that maybe I can transfer this notion to the pinhole camera and do long exposure images with that. That is why I chose the pinhole, because a frozen moment in time wasn't right for what I wanted to do.

What made you want to explore the pinhole camera after using the Holga?

It was the wideness that you could get with the pinhole and the dynamic. I was always attracted to landscapes, and the 6x9 matches more of a cinematic, 35 mm format. What I like about the Holga is the simplicity, you are limited by what you can do, but that limitation makes you work at it a bit more. I like how the plastic lens causes a little bit of vignetting and distortion and that sort of the dream-like quality.

The pinhole is just a very simple thing, it is just a box with a hole in it, but the thing that I like about it, is that it imposes restrictions on you. You have just one lens, you have to work out the exposure by the daylight, I have to work out the angle that I want and think about the image and how it will look after an 8 second or 20 second exposure.

With pinhole, you get lots of people who stick them on the floor or on the table next to their lunch so you get a spoon the size of the Eiffel tower, and an egg bigger than Godzilla, and that is cool and nice, but there are other ways to use it to get a beautiful image.

Why did you want to do the workshops? What did you want people to reflect on in the digital age?

The digital age is amazing, don't get me wrong: the learning curve is fantastic. If you think about it, years ago a family would have one camera in the house and when they process the roll there were probably three years of summer holidays on the one roll of film. And then they get the film back and the pictures they took on the first holiday are all out of focus, and the pictures from the second holiday, everyone's head is chopped off and on the third holiday, they drop the camera by accident and they didn't learn anything.

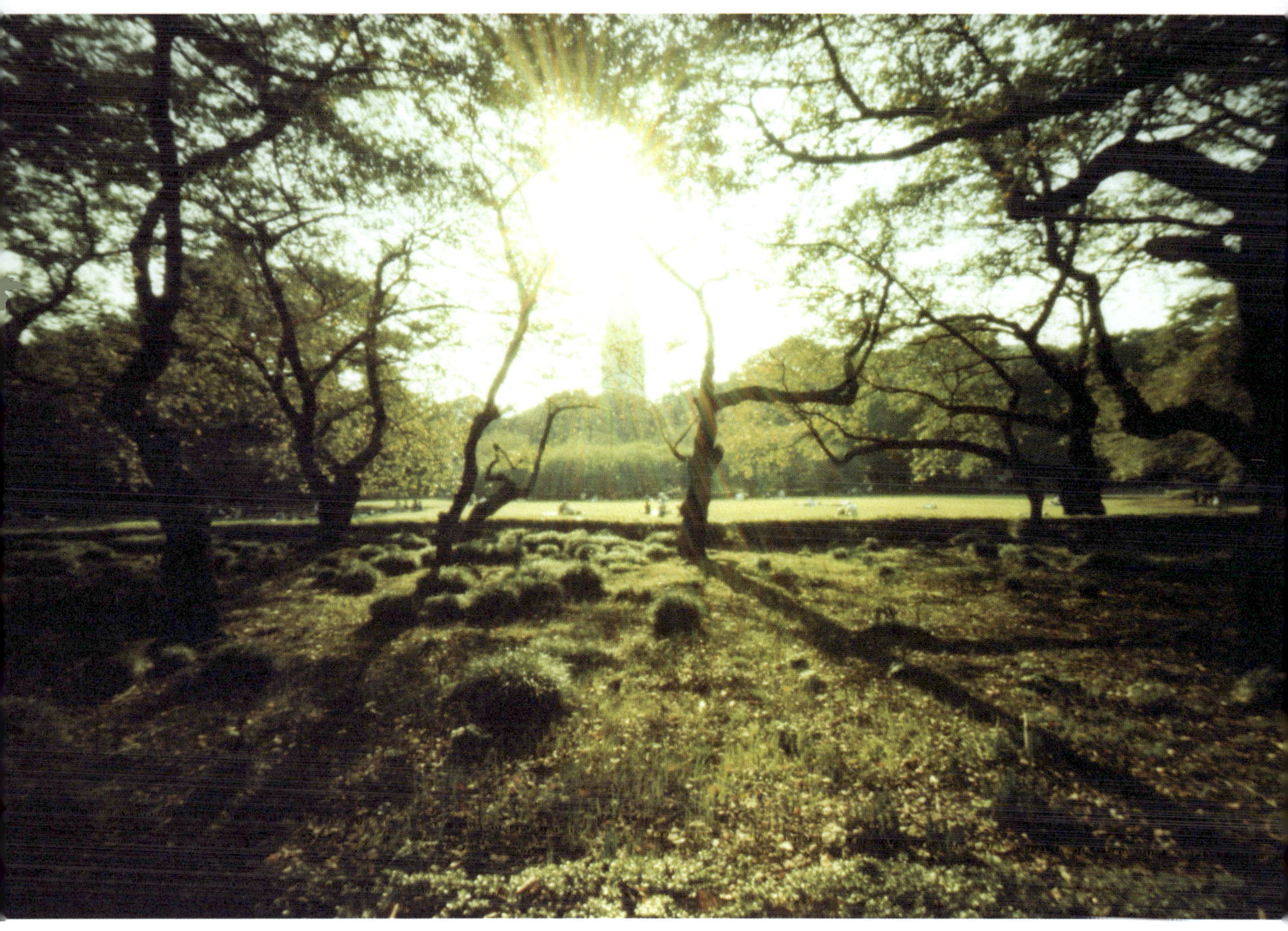

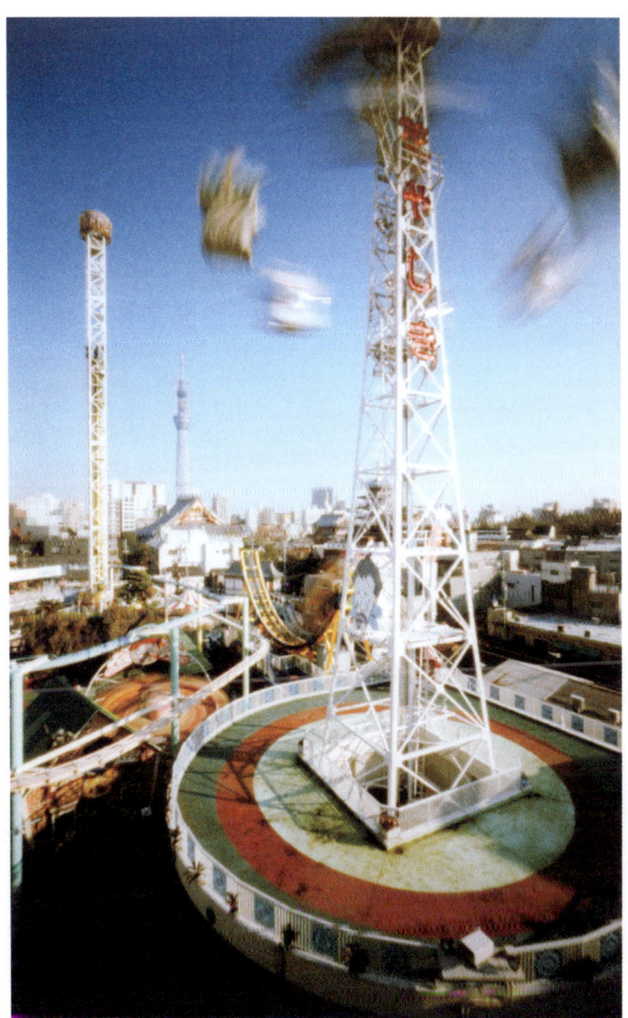

Now you get feedback straight away if it is out of focus or not sharp, so there is a steeper learning curve and it is making people much better photographers. But it is also producing so much rubbish as well, and people are shooting because they can, not because they should. It is not for me to say what is rubbish, but we can all see it.

With film and toy cameras in general, going back away from digital is not so much a rebellion against it, it is more like I want to do something where I just focus on the image and not worry about technique and having x amount of lens. I think sometimes photographers, especially amateur photographers, get weighed down with lenses. You see some guys with three bags, a film jacket and a zoom lens that even a top sports photographer would never buy, and of course in Japan, there are a lot of otakus (geeks) as well. Sometimes I see these people and I think they have more gear than me, and I am doing it for a living.

Today, we have so many options that it is difficult to know what to do, so if you restrict yourself, by creating boundaries, then you hopefully create some more interesting images.

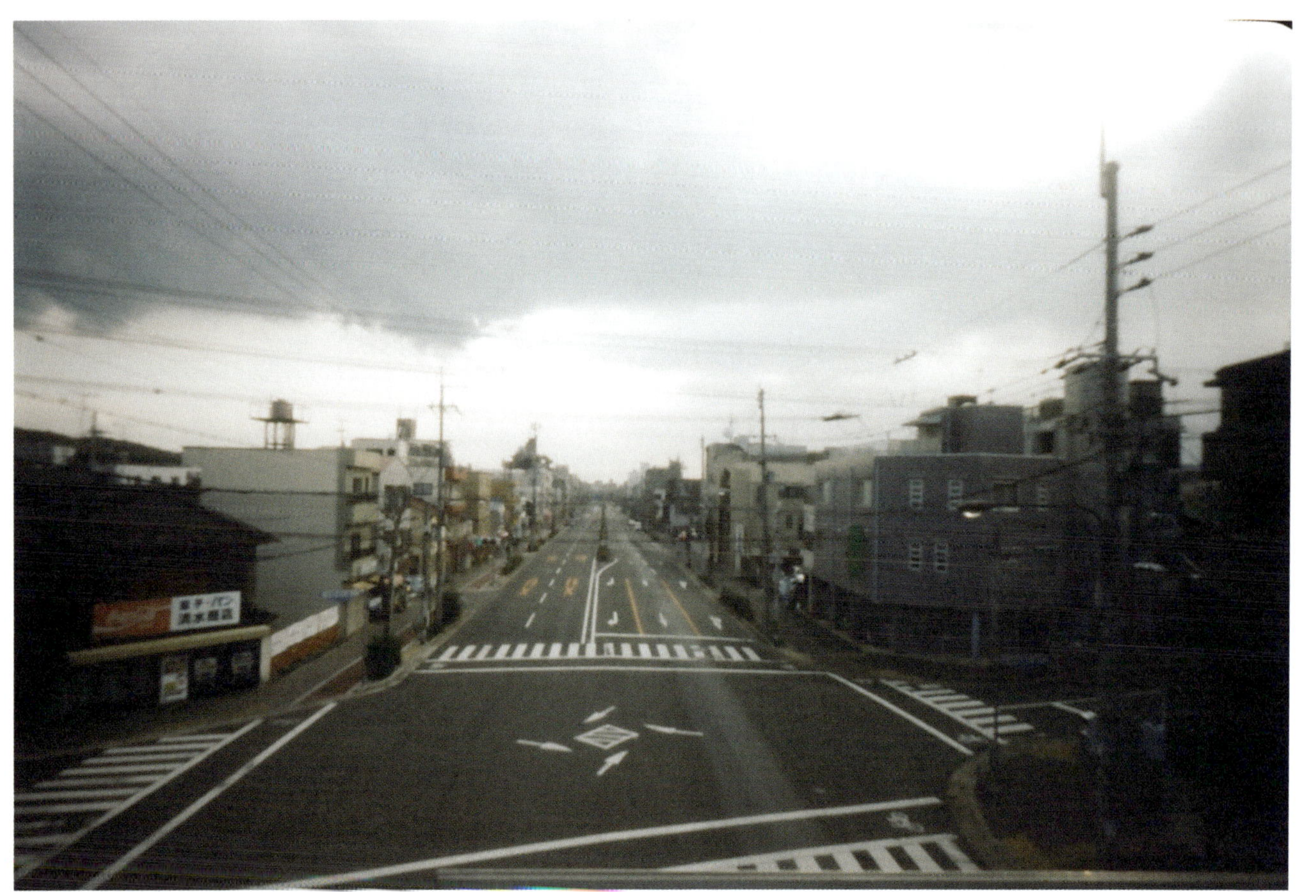

—— *interview 20* ——

MICHAEL LYONS

Can you tell us about your background as a photographer?

I became interested in photography as a teen (in the late 1970s) and took up developing my own 35mm b&w pictures as well as dark room printing. I also experimented with self-made pinhole cameras, infrared photography, b&w slides, and holography. After much effort I succeeded to make a transmission hologram of a dice, which involved setting up a beam splitter and HeNe laser on a table resting on balloons to reduce vibrations.

In those days I considered studying photography professionally, but I became interested in science and followed a career as a research scientist. However, I've kept taking pictures over the years.

How did you end up in Japan, and what keeps you there?

I was invited to speak at a conference on face and object recognition in Kyoto in 1996, and came back later that year to spend some time at a communication science research lab in Kyoto (Advanced Telecommunications Research). My stay has extended until now! Initially, I was fascinated by learning about a different culture. I've published some research works on visual perception of Japanese dry landscape gardens and Noh masks. I've continued to stay because I enjoy the comfortable lifestyle in Kyoto and especially that I can get around nearly completely by bicycle. Kyoto offers a rich cultural life, including a fairly active experimental arts scene. Before living in Kyoto I lived in L.A. for nearly five years. Interesting place, but car culture is not for me.

Why use a P-sharan, and what are the characteristics of the images that appeal to you?

I bought P-Sharan pinhole camera kits in 2009 as presents for my niece and nephew (in Canada) then decided I'd better build a kit myself so I could help them properly. The first roll of pictures revived my teenage interest in pinhole photography and another outcome was that I started to use film again - I had been fully digital since 2002.

Another reason is that since 2007 I have been a professor of Image Arts and Science at Ritsumeikan University. Since some of my courses touch on various image technologies, I wanted to re-examine film as a technology and expressive medium. Some of my seminar students were interested in projects involving film. In fact, one of my students started a toy camera circle in the university a few years ago.

As an exercise in my seminar, one year I gave everyone a P-Sharan kit with a roll of film. We had an very interesting session comparing pictures a couple of weeks later!

Film offers a creative process different from what is possible with digital technology, so naturally the outcome also differs.

Do you use other types of pinhole cameras?

Yes I have a Zero 6x9 multi-format pinhole camera made by a company in Hong Kong. It is made from wood and brass parts and it is a pleasure to use. I had a Holga pinhole camera and took some interesting pictures with it, but I didn't enjoy the plastic material so much, so I gave it to a student. On the other

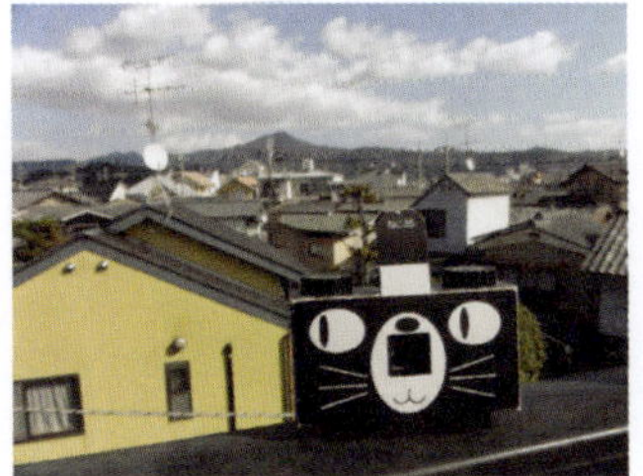

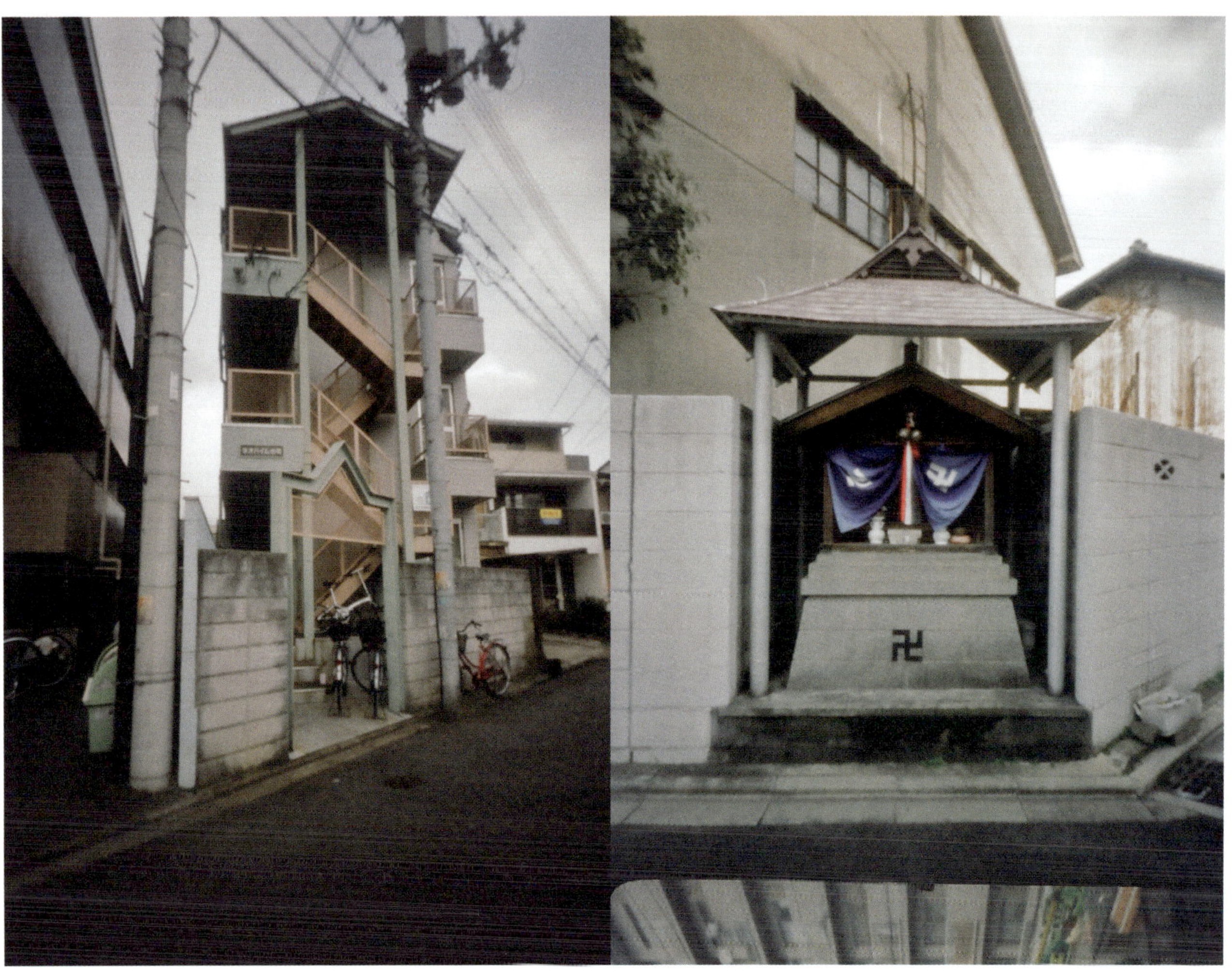

hand, the simplicity of the P-Sharan, its small size and efficient design really appeal to me.

What kind of atmosphere or mood can you achieve with these kinds of low tech cameras, that you can not with a high precision camera?

I agree that there's a special quality to the pictures and I'm very much interested in the element of indeterminacy involved in the process of using such cameras. It forces me to relinquish conscious attempts to overly compose or achieve a certain kind of image. Paradoxically, the 'accidents' of LoFi photography can make an image a more faithful record of the contingencies of time, place, and atmosphere present when the image was made.

Are there subjects or themes that for you suit pin hole photography?

I tend to photograph whatever interests me and don't think about it too much. Other than the technical aspect, which I do think about carefully, photography tends to be an intuitive, perhaps even subconscious process.

Are there parallels between for example, musical expression and photography?

What can one learn from using a camera such as a P sharan?

There is much to be learned from techniques which involve an element of chance, whatever the domain of expression may be. It's a question of learning to "listen" and be receptive towards unplanned and unexpected outcomes. Counter-intuitively, releasing control of the creative process often leads to outcomes more reflective of oneself. This is an area where the viewpoints of art and science have considerable overlap: it's necessary to learn to see value in what we normally ignore in everyday life.

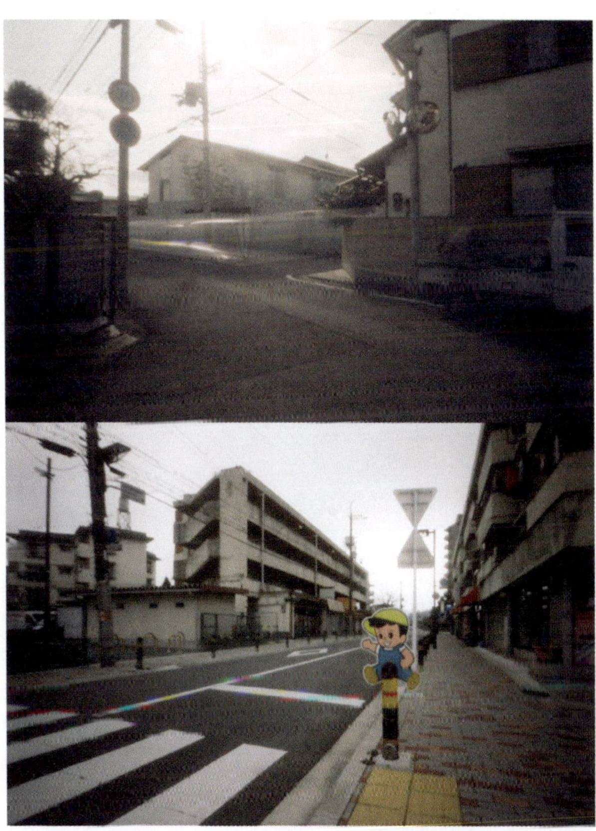

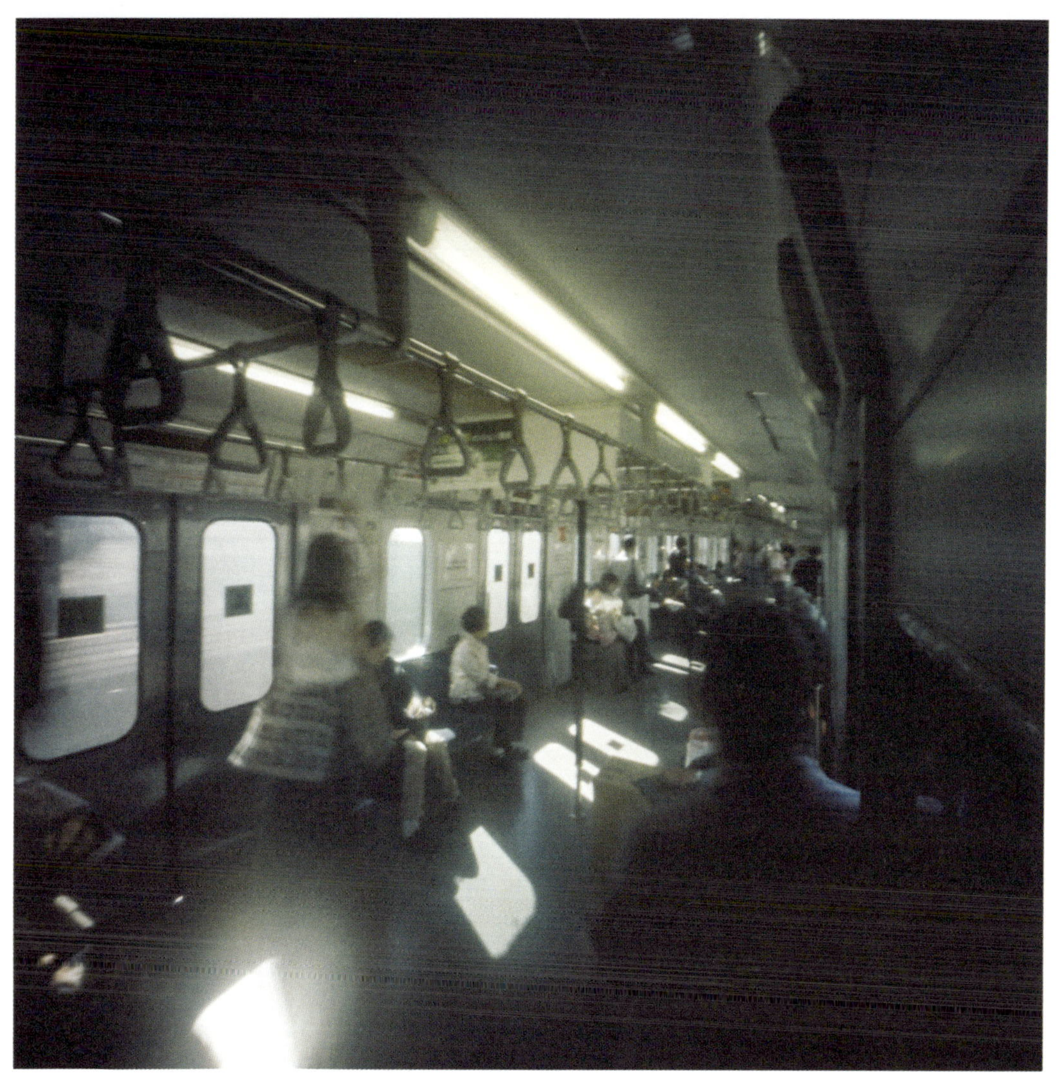

—— interview 21 ——

MARTIN CHEUNG

When did you start making your own cameras?
In 1998. In 1997, I was at a Fine Arts school in Melbourne, and the school organized a workshop for all the first year students to make pinhole cameras. We attended it for one day, and we used a can to make a camera, and I had very good results, very sharp with good exposure. And then I thought it was easy.

At the school we were learning technical photography by using large format cameras to photograph still lifes that were very precise, so I felt that pinholes were too "toy" for me. So after that workshop, I didn't continue until that summer which was Christmas in Australia, and I saw some tin cans on the street. I thought that they could be cameras, and I thought: "Why don't I make a camera out of different boxes or tin cans?" At home, I started to make some cameras, and the result was very bad because I couldn't control the size of the hole. During that time, I didn't have internet – it was still dial-up internet – so I started looking at books. There wasn't that much information at the time, and I was relying on information from second hand bookstores.

What was the motivating drive?
When I was younger I would go to flea markets every week, and I would see a lot of cameras for 2 or 5 bucks and I was so amazed at how simple the construction of the camera was. It was based on a curiosity, and I would disassemble the camera. Like the Kodak brownie, which was old and super mass-produced, I would open them and make some changes. So part of it was because of this, and part of it was being a Hong Kong-grown kid, we used to buy Gundam models to disassemble them, or some mini cars, and you would assemble them. It was like a habit to construct things.

So you liked the camera as an object?
In the beginning, I would be looking at a chocolate box on the street and I would be saying, 'Yeah, that could be a camera!' By buying these cheap cameras and disassembling them I became curious about the mechanism of the camera.

Also, during my study, we were mainly talking about why we do photography. I guess it was more than 20 hours on tutorials and art history, and 3 hours on technical classes; we were always talking about theory, and how people use photographs in the history of humankind.

I gradually found out that photographs are not real, and we talk about the decisive and particular moment in photographs, but the more I do photography, the more I realize that it can be composed, like a self portrait on Facebook. We take many and select, it is based on someone behind the camera and they choose what moment to publish. I don't believe photographs are real, and I don't believe they are the moment. That actually pushes me to use a pinhole camera because I don't have to act like a hunter to grab the best moment, and somehow it is a burden to 'capture the moment.'

So you think understanding the mechanism of the camera changes the way you actually take the photo
Yeah, if I didn't go to flea market every week, I would just use my 35 mm camera and just take pictures, like pressing the shutter. There is nothing wrong with it, but my development of photography would be totally different. I will end up being a photojournalist. But I think the best photographers actually think before they press the shutter.

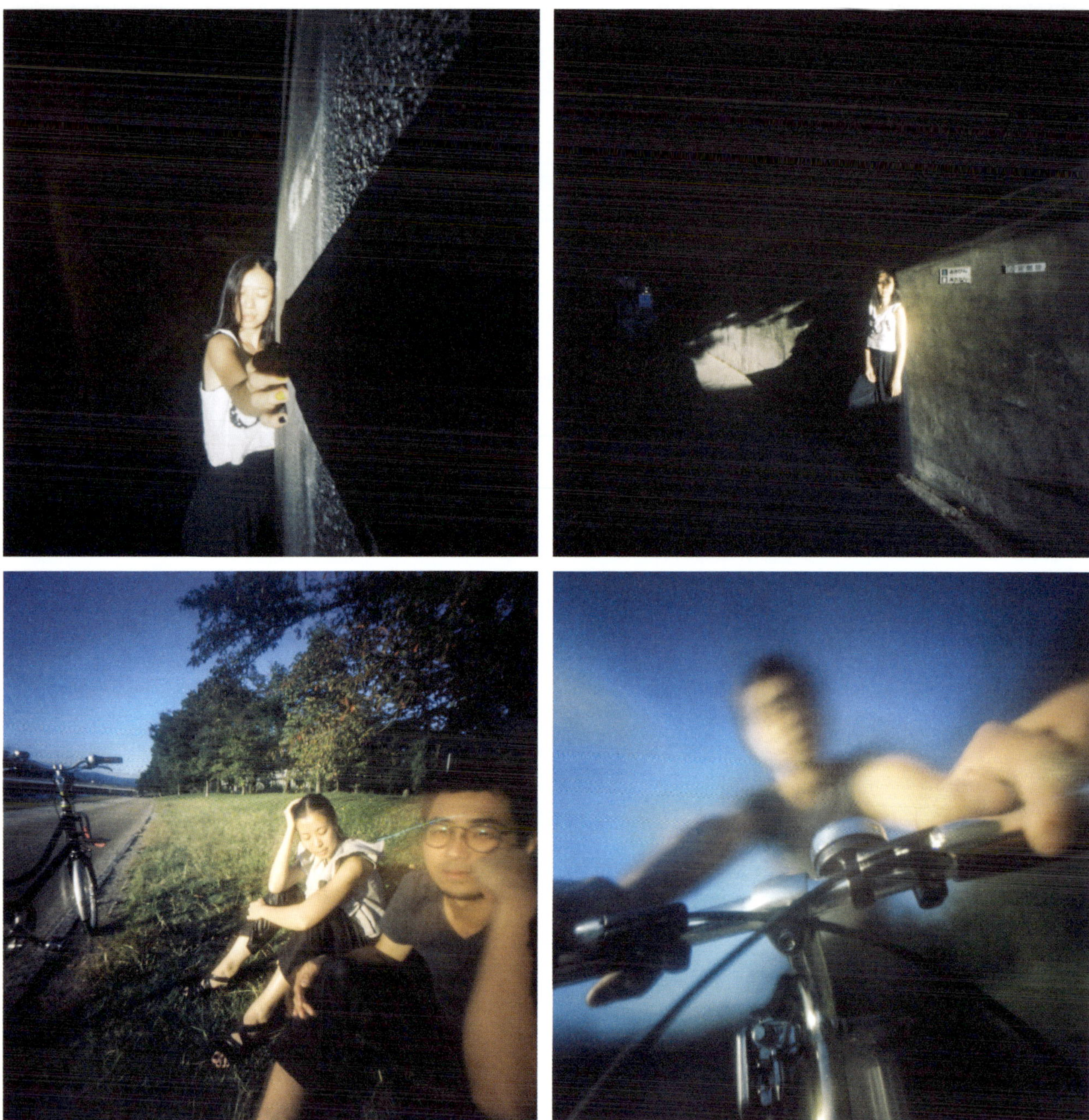

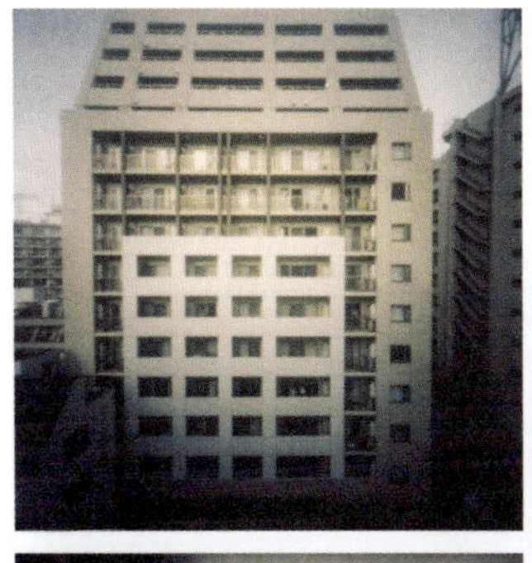
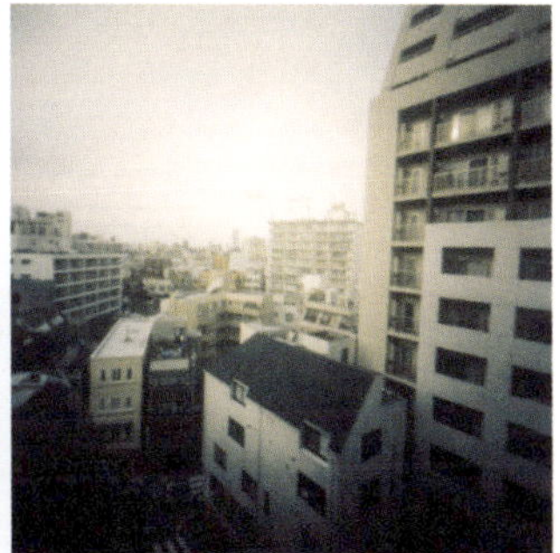
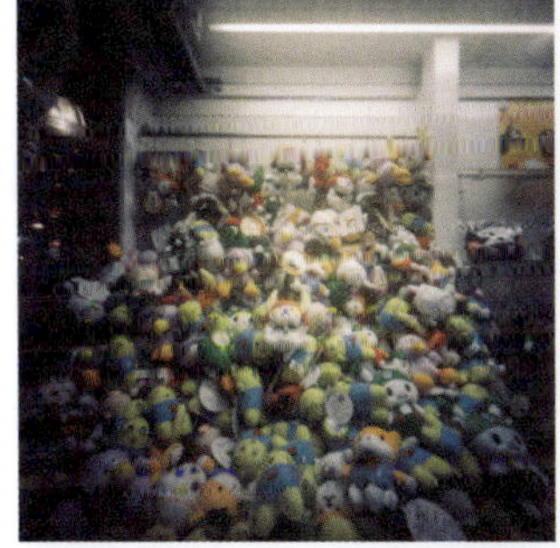
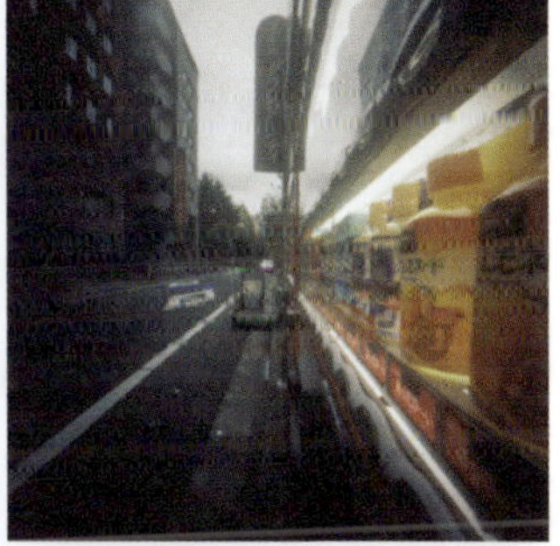

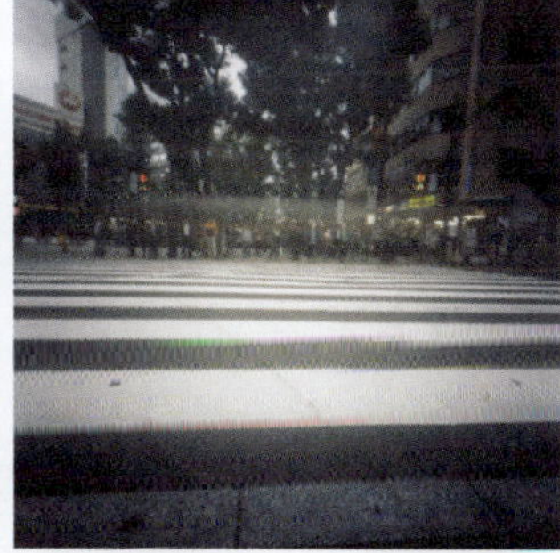
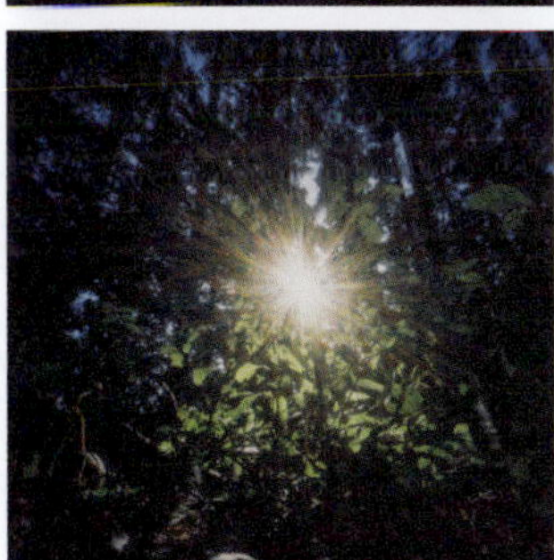
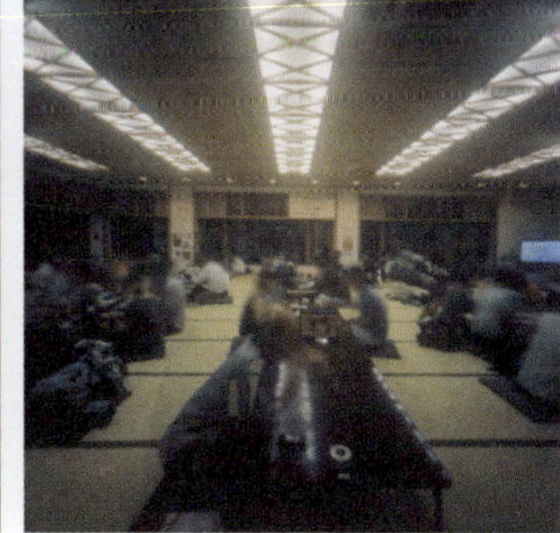

If you are thinking like that, is it hard to use something like a pinhole with unpredictable results, especially as you are known for making them out of things like BBQ roasted ducks.

Yeah, actually it isn't unpredictable. It is a very controlled medium because it requires you to have some technique to master it. Of course there are people who have mastered the technique already, then ignore the technique. It is like using a toy camera. With the so-called actual proper cameras, you can adjust your aperture, your shutter speed, and that is about it. With a toy camera, it doesn't have many adjustments, so you can only take a picture with limitations, so you actually have to figure out what is the best situation for you to take the picture.

So for you, what is the best situation for you to take photos with a pinhole camera?

I like taking photos with a long exposure. I don't have particular reason, but if I really have to name one, it would be that I like to be a passive monk. I don't like to be the hunter. I find it hard to catch the moment. It's not that I don't have the ability. I mean with commercial work, this is what I do, I catch the moment for an event, I have to.

Do you think it just suits your personality?

Yes, it suits me better. I don't like to hunt. It is not me.

When you use a camera that is manufacturer made, and the lens and aperture are controlled and the optics performance is controlled, but why they control all this is based on the market. What kind of people are buying this camera? So the camera is more and more geared towards to the taste of the people using it.

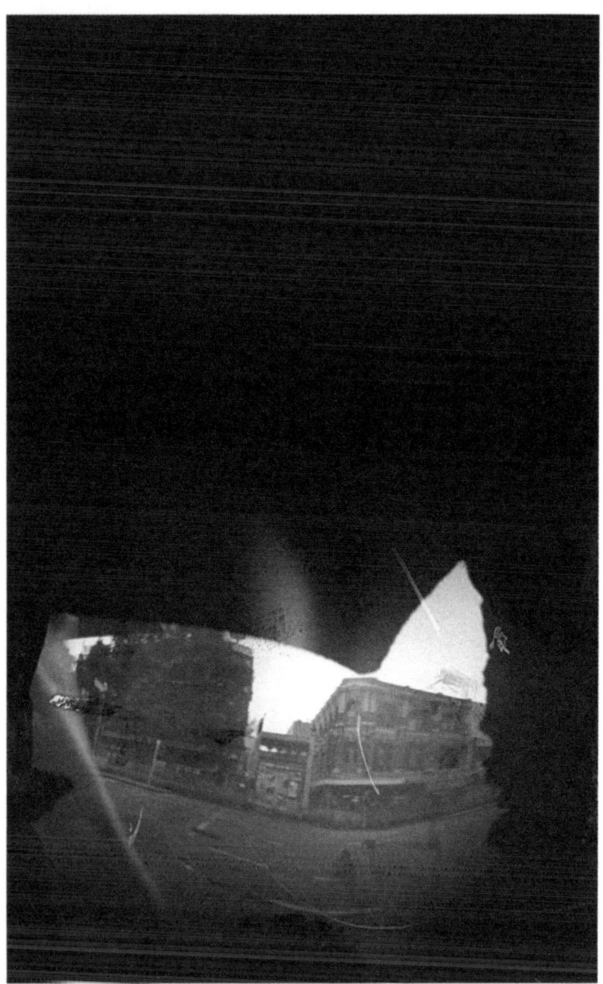

PHOTO TAKEN WITH A BBQ DUCK HOME MADE CAMERA.

And what do you think that is?

Say everyone uses a Canon Mark II or III for pictures and videos, your picture and my picture are maybe not the same, but they have a similar certain visual quality - you cannot deny it. If we use the same pen the color is similar, of course the brush-stroke cannot be imitated or the same, but I think making my own camera is the important part. If you and I make a pinhole camera, we will not have one thing the same, image-wise.

What are the qualities of the pinhole camera photos?

Usually there is a tunnel-looking effect, a vignette but a pinhole is more exaggerated because most people use it as a wide angle, meaning the focal length is short, which means the hole and the film plate are close, so that it produces a wide-angle effect visually.

I am recently at this point, where I am in a circle and I can't get out of it, and it is because of the visual effect that pinhole produces with the black corners. It feels like every time I take a picture it is not quite what I produce, but rather an effect the universe has produced. So when you look at the picture, you say "Wow! Very cool!" but it is hard to look at the content, which is what you photographed. With photography, we are trying to create a one or two second "wow" effect for the audience whether it be Facebook or Instagram, which I don't really like very much, but the characteristic effects of the pinhole photos are impressive.

When you see that everyone can achieve this effect, part of creating this visual impact means there must be something about the content.

Why do you think you take photos then?
I don't know why I am taking photos right now, I am lost right now. I think I am overpowered by the pinhole camera.

Do you feel bound to your technique?
Yeah, really honestly I don't think photography is about making a camera and making a sharp pinhole photo. I don't think photography is about sharpness. Every picture should be more about content, no matter what camera you use.

Do you take photos to capture memories?
Right now it is the only reason I keep taking photos. Or to talk about something.
I enjoy keeping memories but I think photography, as an art medium, can be more than that, so for the past 3 years I haven't produced much of my own work that I think is qualified. I only like having sharp photos as a test, like photos of my cat. The amazing part of photography is the machine and the camera can produce an image sharper than your eyes can see.

The memory part comes from our mind. The moment of the picture doesn't reflect the whole story, but your mind recalls that after you see something. I think the human brain is the most important element to create this notion of art.

Photography is really hard because you can't escape from reality. That thing that you photograph has to be there. Most of the time it has to be there: I was there, and it happened. This is very difficult. There is always a subject. Even Sugimoto, he has to photograph something. At the end, the picture shows some kind of graduation of tone and grades, but it was a subject. Photography is hard because the manufacturer always controls it; we are relying more and more on the machine. With painting there is a lot of variety, you can use a smaller brush, or you can be like Jackson Pollock and pour paint, you can be Mondrian and paint strips of colors, but with photography you can't get away from film manufacturers and camera manufacturers. I don't know which is first and they produce things based on the mass market. This is one part that I like about pinhole.

I think in my father's age, say in the 60s, selling a camera was almost like buying a car, and you are learning a technique and mastering it, to make images. But these days they are selling the camera like a gadget or a fashionable item. I'm not saying it is right or wrong but I'm just saying it is more like buying a lifestyle.

There was a movement to use a Diana, to use uncontrollable cameras because 35 mm SLR interchangeable lenses were so sharp and the new standard of photography, whereas the artistic world was looking at a different medium. Like for painting, you see textures and brushstrokes, whereas with photography in a gallery it is usually framed and mounted so asides from the grain you can't see the medium. I think people started to question what photography was even in the 60s.

After saying the camera is evil and all this, I still love them. As a machine they are so well made.

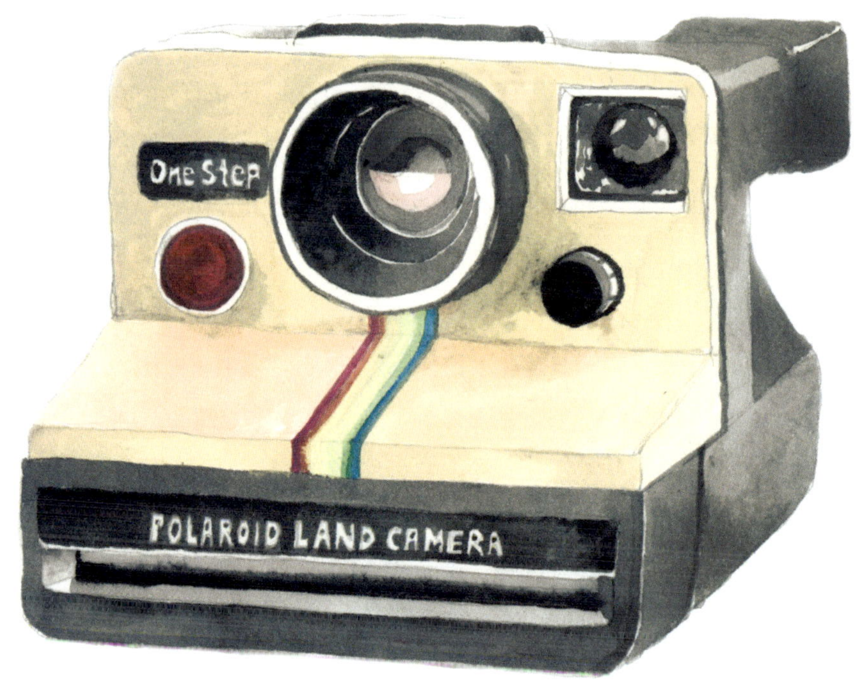
One Step
POLAROID LAND CAMERA

INSTANT FILM CAMERAS

Instant cameras that produce a developed film image are said to have been invented by Edwin Land, an American scientist who developed the Land Camera in 1948. The most well-known self-developing film is the Polaroid, which was made until 2008 by the Polaroid Corporation. After the Polaroid Corporation ceased making film due to a drop in demand, the Impossible Project took over and is now creating instant film, with warm tones similar to the original Polaroids. Fujifilm also makes instant film, and their cheki cameras are hugely popular with Japanese schoolgirls, producing close to real life, instant images.

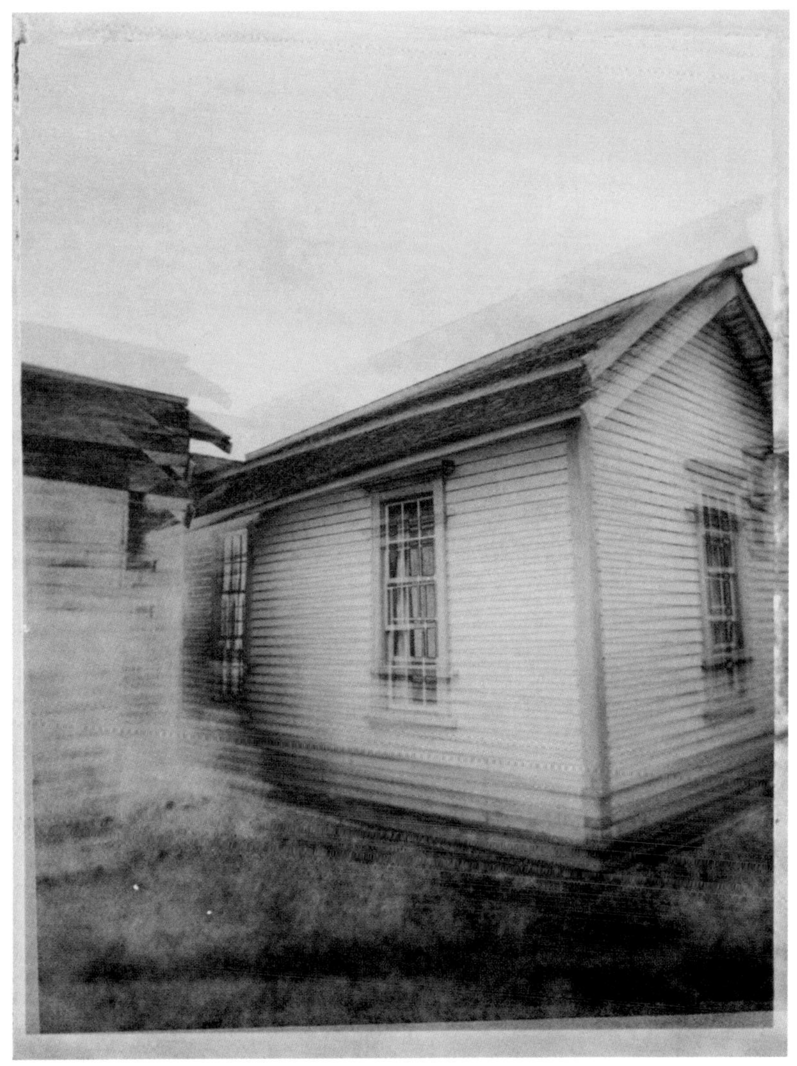

YUSUKE ABICO PHOTO

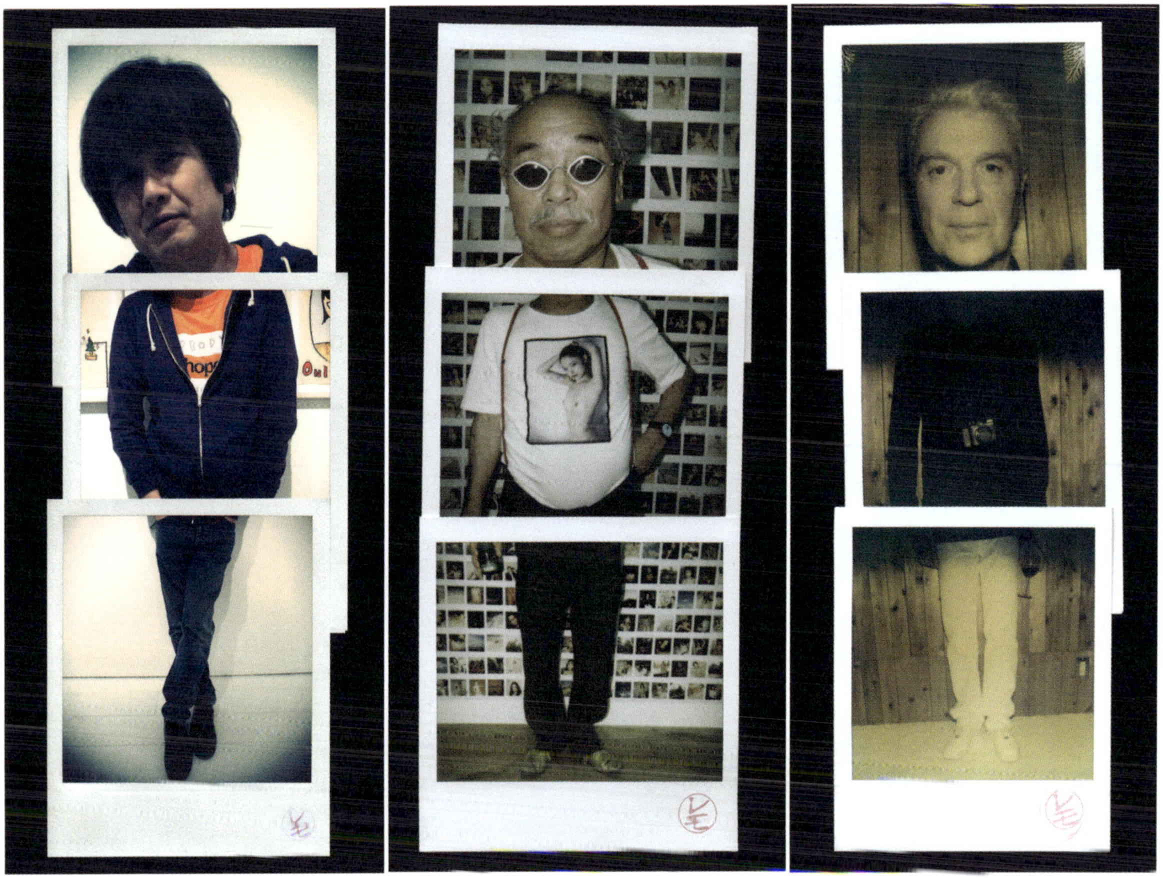

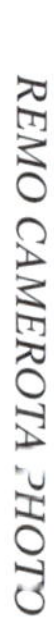

interview 22

OSKAR SMOLOKOWSKI,

IMPOSSIBLE FILM

Where will Impossible succeed where the Polaroid Corporation didn't?

There were a lot of factors that led to their bankruptcy, but what they did in the end was they led themselves to their own demise because they were so big in a way, so they couldn't sustain it. The reason we can't do it the same way that Polaroid does it is because we don't do it at the same scale. I think they were doing something like 30 million films a year, and we are doing under one. There are many factors that went into why Polaroid went bankrupt, such as them investing in Polavision. But if you focus on just instant film, it didn't really make sense for them to make less than those millions of film a year. Any less, and they would have to shut down their factories because they wouldn't be profitable. One hundred components were bought from different factories they were all running, and Polaroid was basically keeping a lot these factories afloat – they were the only customer for many of them, and some of them they owned. They saw that demand was going down, so they said, 'Let's make a 5 year plan, make a bunch of film and shut down all the factories and sell out all the film.'

They did that, but there was still a lot of demand. They were not thinking about making this whole operation small scale, they just said, 'We can't run it at a big scale, so let's forget about it.' I think they could have made a small scale operation that was very profitable, if they chose to do that, which was the perfect opportunity for Florian (Kaps), the founder of Impossible to say, 'You know what? You guys are crazy for shutting this down. Let me buy this last factory that assembles all these components from these other factories that had to be shut down.' So they said, 'Go ahead, it is a ridiculous idea because you won't be able to use that factory because all the components are gone.' But he met with one of the guys who was working at the factory and he said, 'OK we can remake this whole thing and make it run at a smaller scale, and take the risk and do it.' So, that is where Impossible will work, to make it at a small scale – of course it is really expensive because we had to do it that way, but we had completely different targets. But in terms of Impossible succeeding, the market is still sizable, if you sell a million or two a year, that is not nothing. So we saw a good opportunity. People wanted to play with this film and shoot with it, especially in the age when analog is so rare.

How do you maintain the heritage that Polaroid has, and still progress?

Instant photography means something totally different now, so Polaroids used to be about low art, it was not the photographic medium of a photographer. Some photographers of course used it, but most would go for a high quality film, and Polaroid was

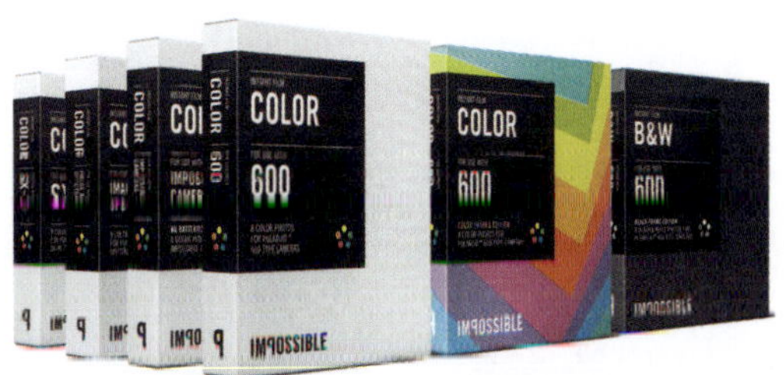

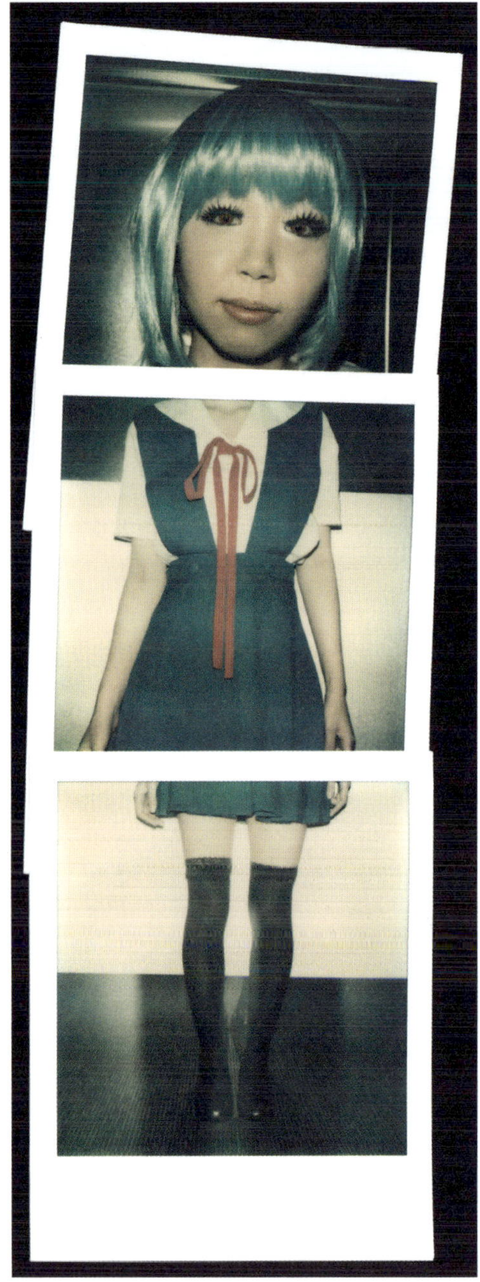

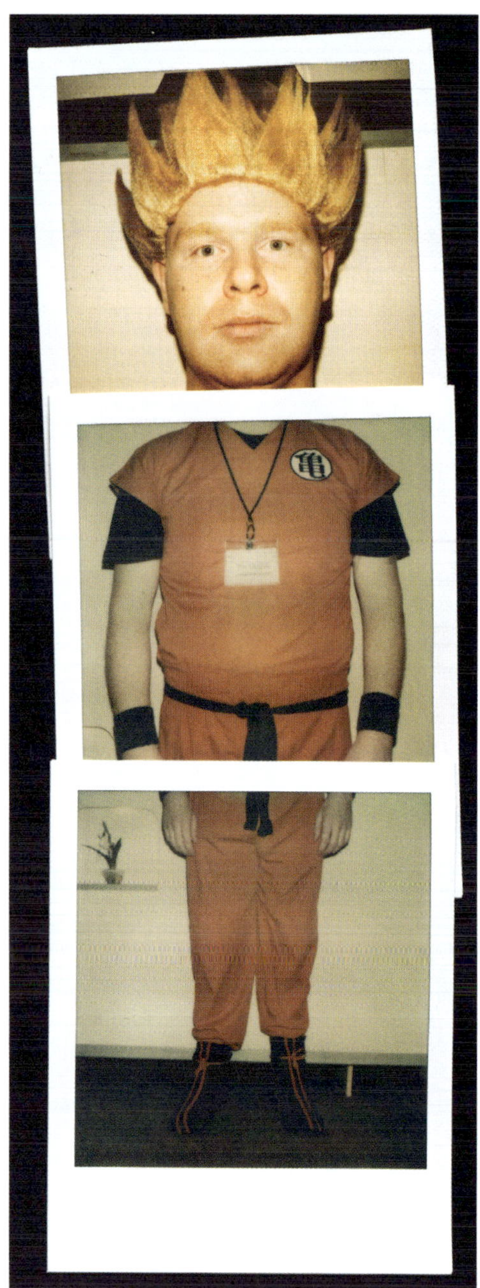

REMO CAMEROTA PHOTO

like, 'Ok, we will take a shot to check the light.' Whereas now, a lot of our customers have no idea about instant photography. So I think it is redefining the heritage, not preserving it. Before, it was the easy, amateur way to do photography, and now you can't get easier than an iPhone. I think iPhone is what Polaroid used to be. There is this great video of Edward Land predicting this; he was walking through a giant factory that he built to sustain the giant numbers of film they were selling. He was like, 'In the future, you will be able to take out this device from your jacket!' It is exactly what is happening right now.

Film takes a completely different role; It is a different product in today's market. It is something quite special, and rather than being the amateur low version, it is something that people can do a bit more rarely. You weigh every shot, it costs you money. You have to think about the light and you have to remember what photography is about and a lot of people don't even know that. A lot of people have no idea that you have to have good lighting to take a good photo; 'If I point my iPhone in the right direction, it is going to make it work, or sometimes it doesn't because, that is cause iPhone screwed up.' It is interesting to see how little people know about photography and how much they have to learn.

Do you think with iPhone filter users it is an either or situation, where they love the apps, or they are fans of analog?

If there is any analog company that will bridge that gap it is us, because you just have to point it and shoot it, whereas with a Lomo camera you go to the place, you give your film and wait for three days. It is not an "either or", any Instagram user would be pretty interested in taking the photos that we have, they just don't want to pay that much money. In my opinion, they all want to do it, and the ones that really want to experiment, do.

I don't think it is an either or, a lot of our users do both and that is the instant lab, if you take a thousand some have to be good, so basically you want to have the best ones as physical objects. So that is something that people have been missing as well, the physicality of photos. In Japan, it is more developed with Fuji and people trade photographs and stuff like that, it is much more physical and in Europe and the States that is something that was lost and people are rediscovering it a bit.

How often do you evolve the product, and how?

So basically, we started with a team of six scientists, maybe it was five in the beginning and they were doing the job that 100 to 150 people were doing at Polaroid. When they were inventing the film, to be perfectly fair, it kind of sucked. What we did was involve the people. And then we did that for a while and the film got to a place where it works, but it is super slow. You take a photo and it takes 30-40 mins for it to develop and that part is really difficult, but I think we will have some pretty good news on that by the end of this year, if not earlier, as we recently hired the person who was the chief technical officer for Polaroid for 20 years. We do it in cycles, and we do it as fast as we can, it just takes time when the team is so small.

What point are you evolving to, as Polaroids were never perfect, and I presume the consumers aren't wanting a super clear image either, they love the warmth and the cloudiness of the

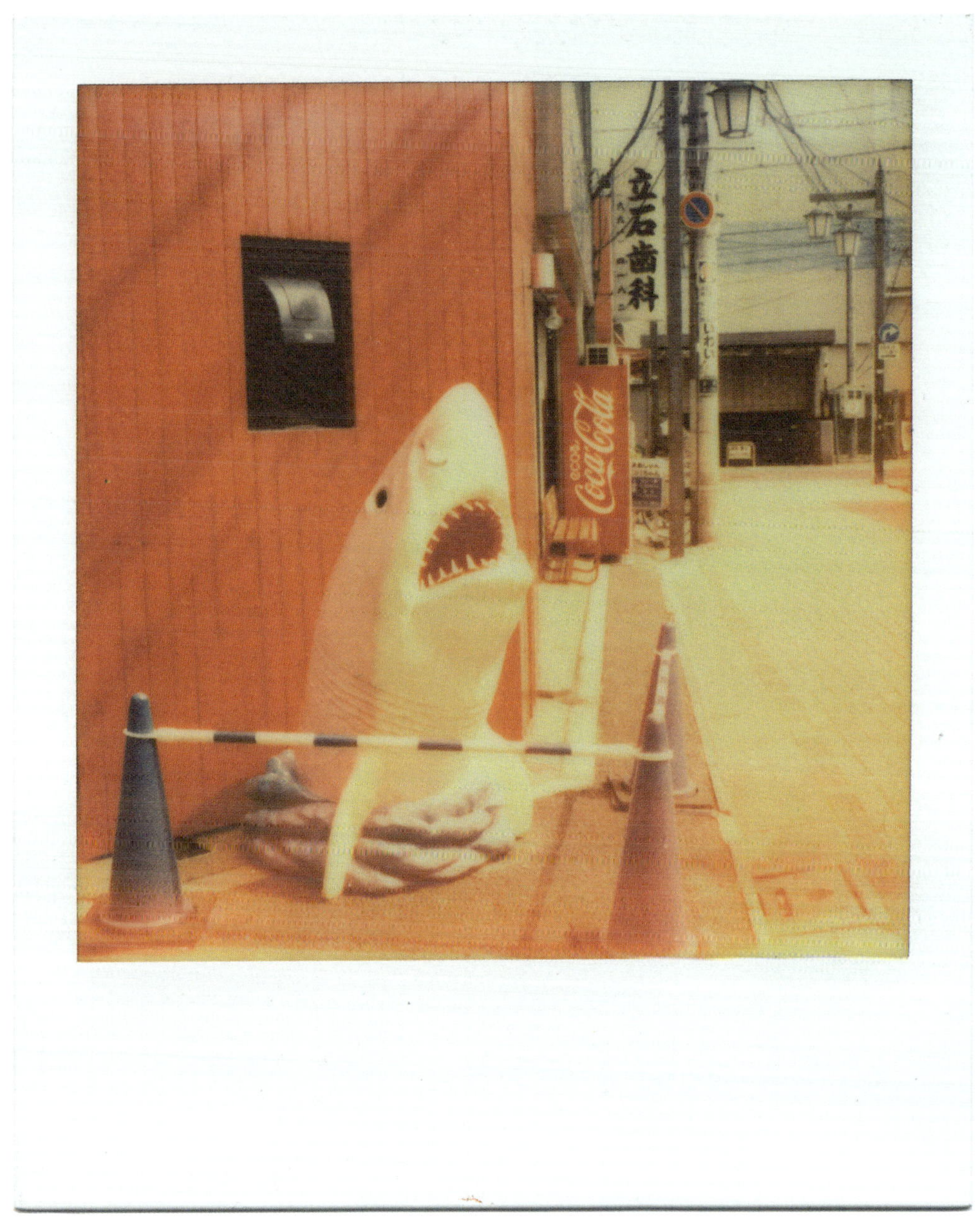

KUMIKO SEKIGUCHI PHOTO

Polaroid images.

Fuji has good color rendition and it is spot on, and close to reality. The answer is that Impossible film has personality, and you take a photo and it looks special and different and we don't want to lose that. The warmth and the tone is something we don't want to lose, of course there are faults with the colors, I wish the red was more red, and we are working on that every day, but the main goal is not to lose the warm special feel it has, that Polaroid used to have.

Polaroid is much warmer than Fuji's film right now. The first target is speed, back to Polaroid timing. The second is more vibrant colors and a sharper image, and the third is to not lose sight that we want to keep this warmth and personality in the film.

Why are you growing?

I just think people want to experiment with things like that, like vinyl is growing, people want to get more in touch with the stuff that they have, they want it to have more meaning because you have everything online and you have everything digitally, but that makes everything physical more valuable.

People are discovering that they can all be photographers. If they buy a digital camera, it is going to be marginally better than their iPhone, but if they buy an analog camera it is going to give them something completely different. People want something different, people are over the fact that you get a digital camera every year because it does the same thing, but unfortunately the iPhone is catching up to it, as well, and not only the iPhone, but other smartphones as well.

Who are the main clientele of Impossible Polaroids?

It's not that it is limited to 18 to 24 year olds, but it is something that came about naturally to have a younger crowd who is really receptive to this stuff because it is so novel. I was walking down the park with my friend the other day and we were talking to people, and showing them the film. They didn't know what a Polaroid was! It is amazing because if you look at every billboard in the city there is a fake Polaroid frame around it to say 'This is a photo, and when we show a photo that is how we present it, and without the frame it isn't a photo, it is a billboard image!'

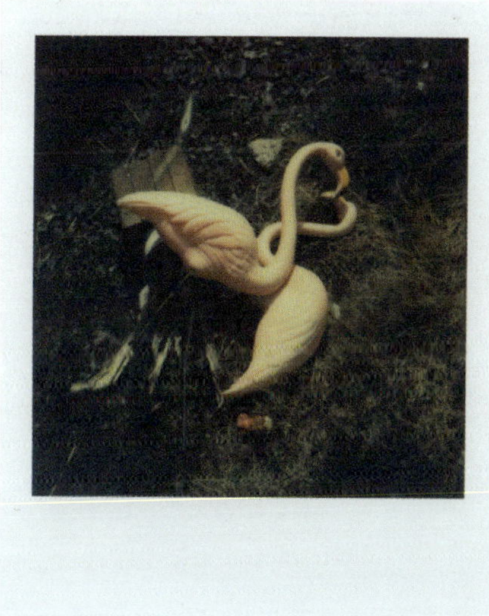

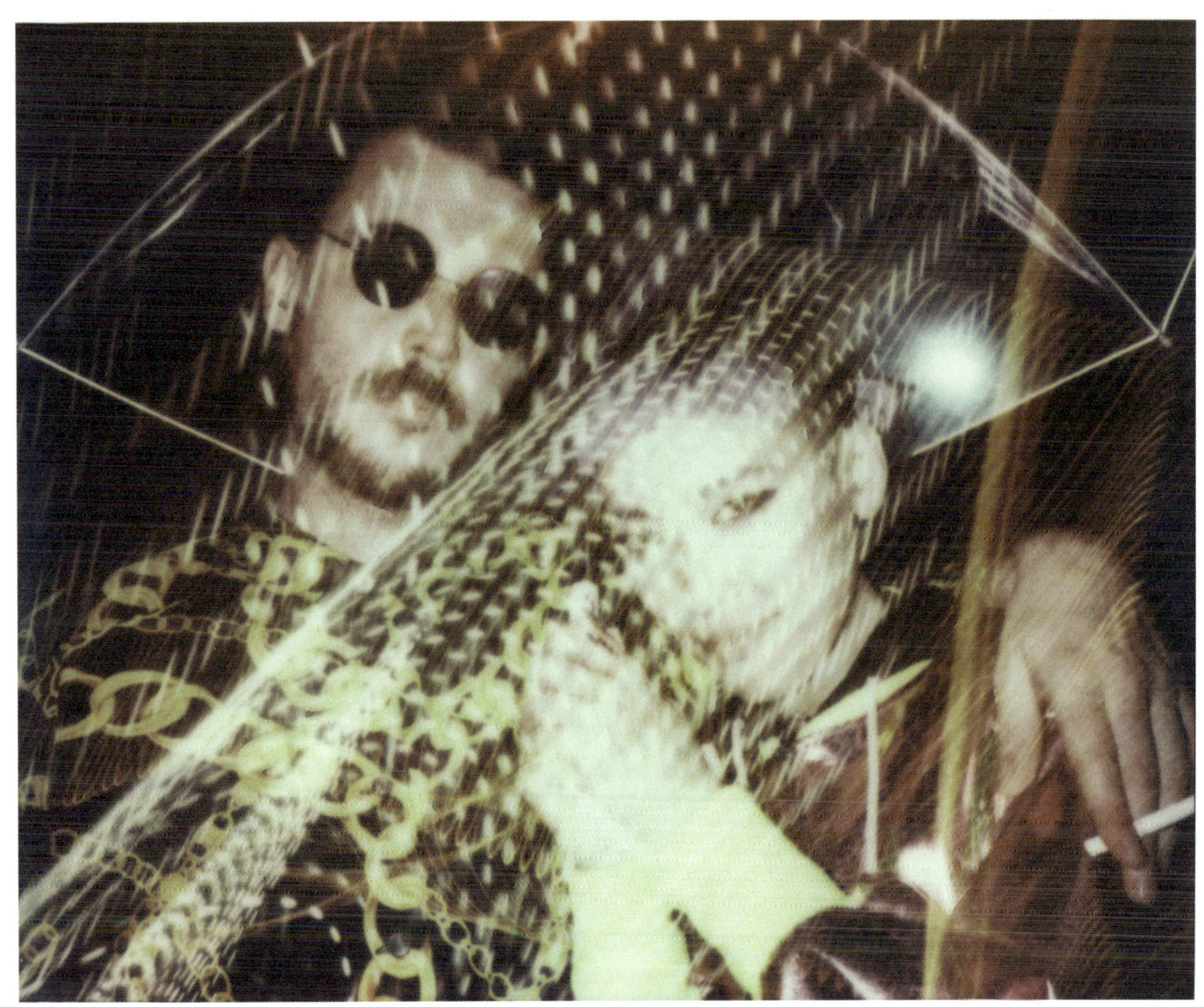

interview 23

LEO BERNE

What are your main reasons for traveling?
It refreshes my mind and my eyes. With the western culture being globalized, I feel the need to meet what's still alive from other cultures.

Can you tell us what you found interesting about Japan, photographically?
In the cities, I love the way the iconography of the market world is integrated to the urbanism. The neons, the big screens, the lanterns, the typographyies... I think all of that lives within the architecture, modern and old. I think the lights in the cities are great for night photography, especially when it's raining.
In Europe, all the new shops just ruin the old architecture, it's not well integrated, especially in the old villages, the phone shops, the Subways' sandwich logo, the banks, all this terrible iconography just doesn't match with the mood of the houses. It's pretty depressing.

I also think the way people dress in Japan is fascinating, there are so many styles, while in Europe it feels that there's only one fashion and if you don't respect the rules you just suck. Besides, unlike what people think, there are not so many people who really pay attention to how to dress in France. Most people are just wearing regular casual stuff, with nothing special to define themselves. They just more or less follow how people dress on TV shows.

I think Rachel Zoe's quote "Style is a way to say who you are, without having to speak" is taken more seriously in Tokyo.
Also my childhood was influenced a lot by Japanese culture, like video games, anime, movies... Even more than American culture, I guess. So when I travel in Japan there's like a Proust Madeleine effect on me, it's even stronger than when I go back to my childhood village, maybe because imaginary fascinations are stronger than reality.

How would you describe the energy of Tokyo after dark? These photos you sent me really capture that frenetic energy of Tokyo youth at night.
I love the energy of Shibuya, with the lights and music everywhere. I think girls are beautiful there and very creative the way they dress. I love karaoke and bowling. Those activities are very rare in Paris, and no one takes you seriously if you ask them to do something like this.
However, I feel that people are sometimes too shy to let themselves go in parties, I must admit that in Taiwan people are crazier. I've never been to Fukuoka though, I hear people are less shy there.

What is the appeal of Impossible film – have you used other brands like Fuji etc... and how does it compare?
I'm really happy they came up with this project and I think their new system gives very interesting images.
I like the soft tones on the skins, and the natural bluish in the darks. I never tried the Fuji film and even if I like what they do camera-wise, I'm not convinced by the polas I've seen, for me it feels too digital in some way and I don't really see a polaroid feeling in the texture of the images.

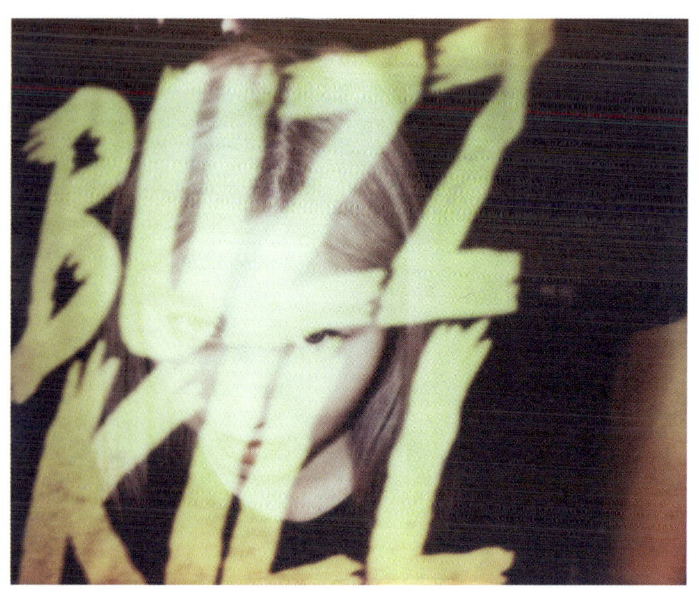
BUZZ
KILL

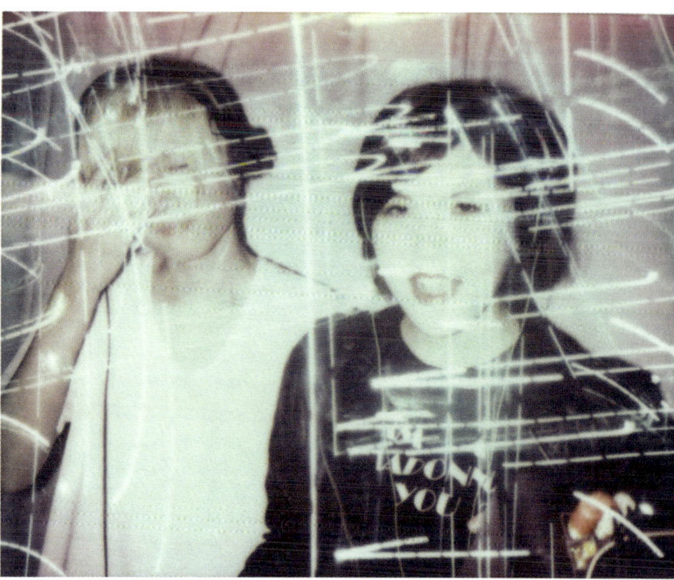

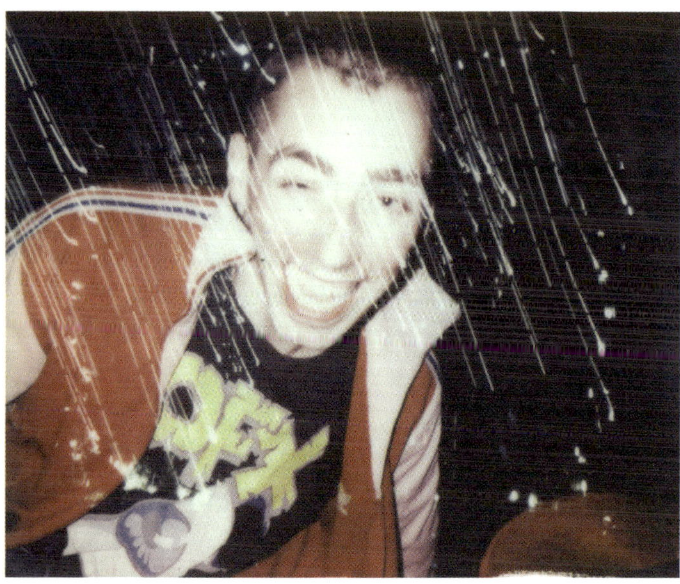

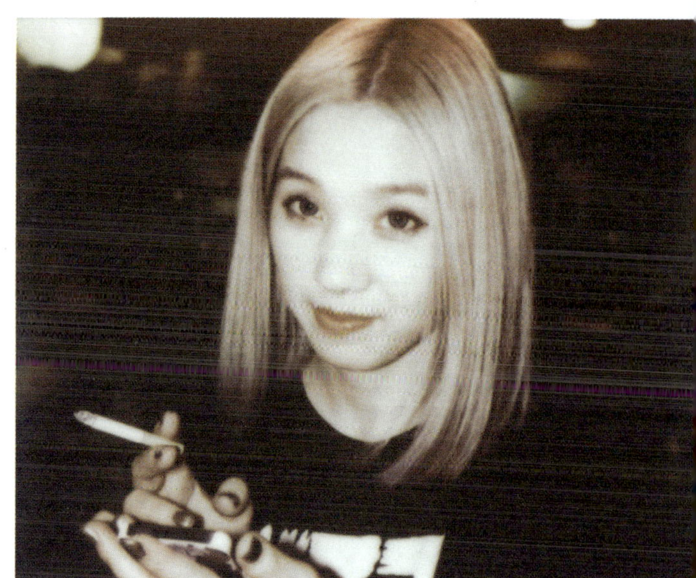

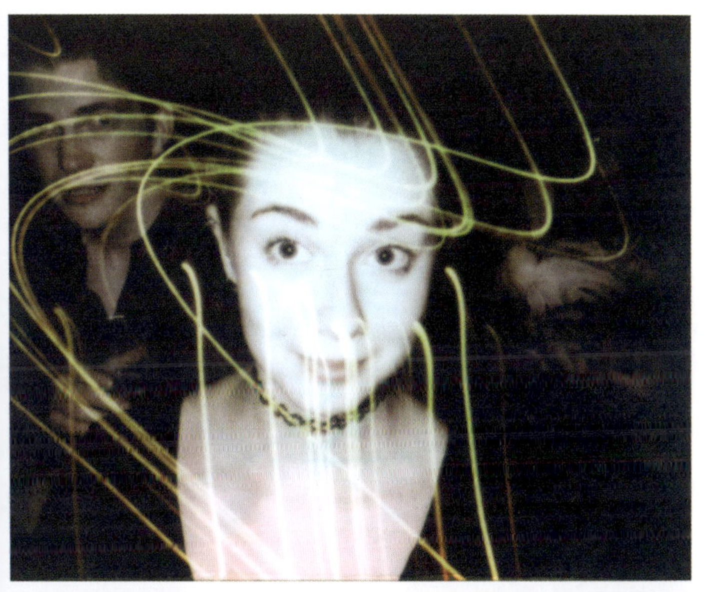
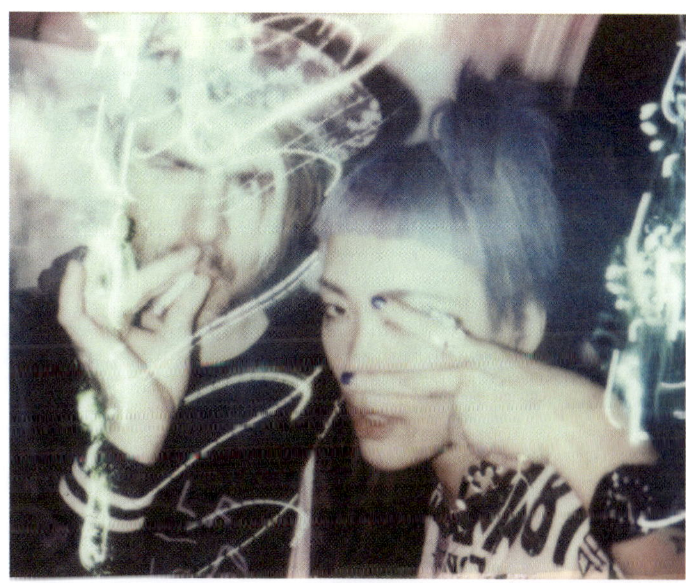
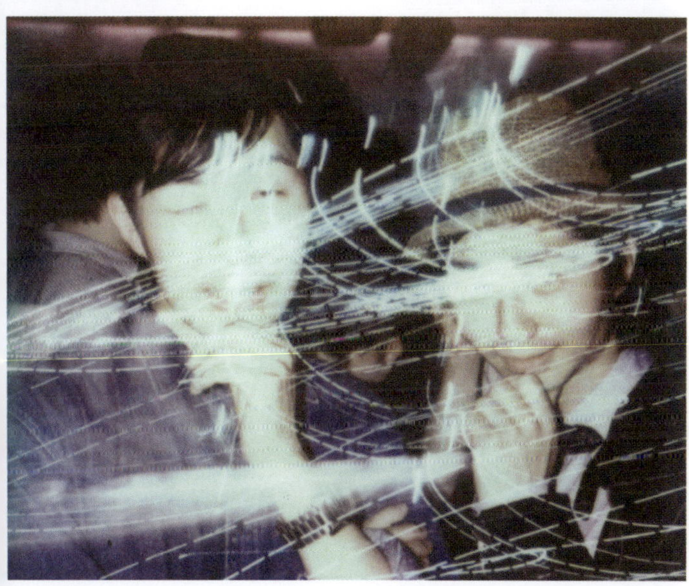
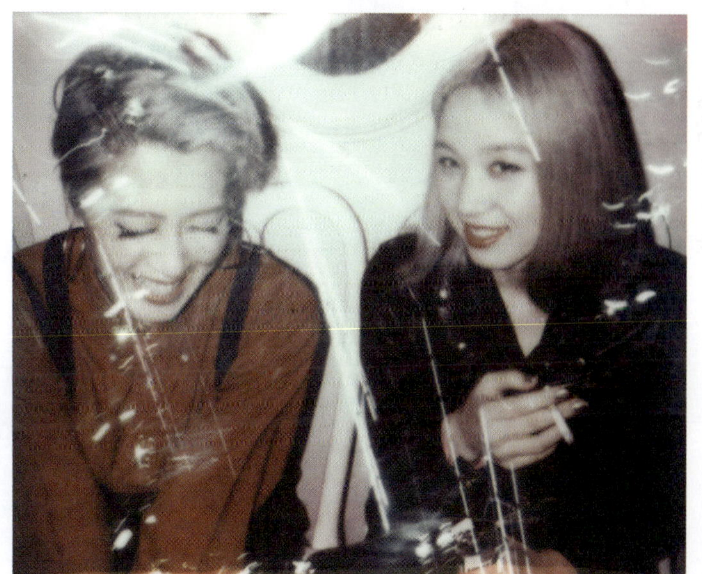

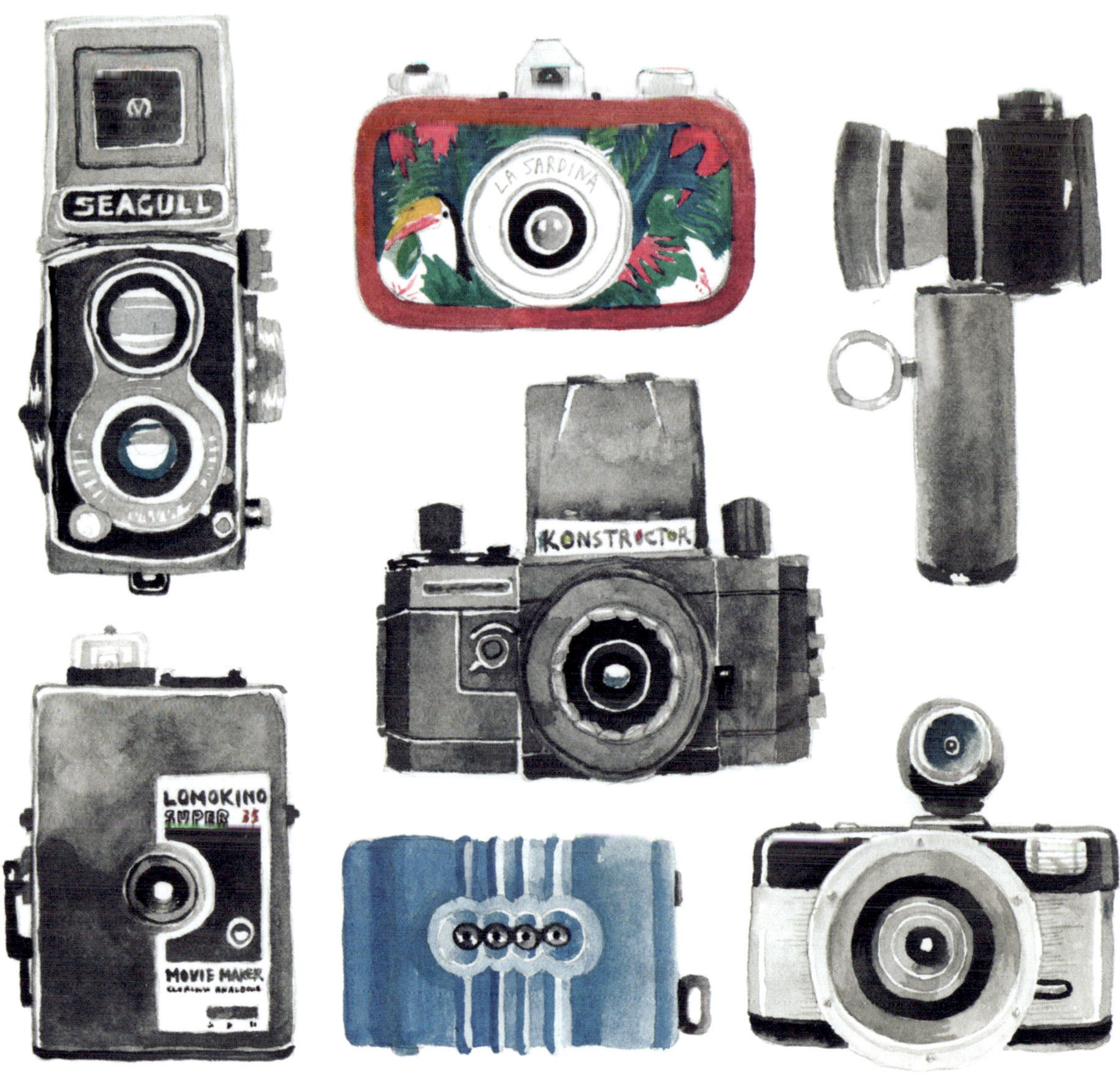
SEAGULL
LA SARDINA
KONSTRUCTOR
LOMOKINO
SUPER 35
MOVIE MAKER

LOMOGRAPHY CAMERAS

— *interview 24* —

LOMOGRAPHY

TOMAS BATES, KIEKO HOSHI

What is the concept behind Lomography?
(TB) The concept behind Lomography is to create beautiful, fun, crazy, unique, special, experimental photos. We live by 10 Golden Rules which encourage people to shoot in a very free way. Lomographic pictures are moment catchers; characterized by vibrant colours, shadowy framing, surprise effects and spontaneity. As Lomographers, we seek to document the incredible planet around us in a never-ending stream of images.
The ten rules of Lomography:

- *Take your camera everywhere you go*
- *Use it any time - day or night*
- *Lomography is not an interference in your life, but part of it*
- *Try the shot from the hip*
- *Approach the objects of your lomographic desire as close as possible*
- *Don't think (by William Firebrace)*
- *Be fast*
- *You don't have to know beforehand what you capture on film*
- *Afterwards either*
- *Don't worry about any rules*

What do you attribute to the success of Lomography?
(TB) The success of Lomography came about for various reasons. It captured a moment in time with the rise of the LC-A and has continued to grow over the years because of people's love for creating unique, exciting, experimental photos.

How important is the image and fashion surrounding the cameras?
(TB) It was incidental - the most important thing is the photos the cameras produce. The fact that the cameras look awesome and are used by celebrities is secondary to the photos they produce. We are a company dedicated to photography firstly, not fashion.

Is there anything particular about toy camera users in Japan?
(KH) We believe Japanese Lomographers are very passionate about learning more about the camera. Once they start using our camera and feel the excitement of using them, they will try to understand it completely. They are very eager to take beautiful pictures using their favorite cameras.
Compared to other countries, I think at least in the cities, Japan

has very good facilities and places to develop or purchase films. Of course, the Japanese are known to be camera lovers. There aren't any other countries that have so many camera brands.

When did toy cam usage first become popular in Japan, and why?

(KH) Since there are many more companies that produce what is called a "toy camera," we cannot specifically state the dates. However, we think easy to use, small size, fun cameras like Lomography cameras became popular maybe about 10 years ago, when we first launched LC-A. Back then, digital cameras were already becoming very popular. However, people were looking for more interesting cameras - which in fact were easy to use film cameras.

Compared to other countries, I think at least in the cities, Japan has very good facilities and places to develop or purchase films. Of course, the Japanese are known to be camera lovers. There aren't any other countries that have so many camera brands.

What are the most popular cameras and why?

(KH) The most popular cameras are the following.

LC-A+ - The radiant colors, knockout contrast and vignettes are unique characteristics of LC-A+ and even after so many years it's still the iconic camera of Lomography. It is a compact and useful 35mm film camera.

Lubitel 166+ - It is a twin lens, medium format camera that shoots square photos. It can also be used with 35mm film.

Konstruktor - This is a new product that launched in 2013: Lomography's first SLR camera that you can build by yourself! This product has been very popular since its launch. Anyone who is interested in understanding more about how film cameras work can build this first and understand the mechanism.

What has been the effect of Instagram and so on the industry?

(TB)Well what we do and Instagram do are very different still. These kinds of apps and photo filters give people some sense of what Lomographic images can be. But lots of people become interested in Lomography after using these kinds of things because they are after a real, authentic analog experience.

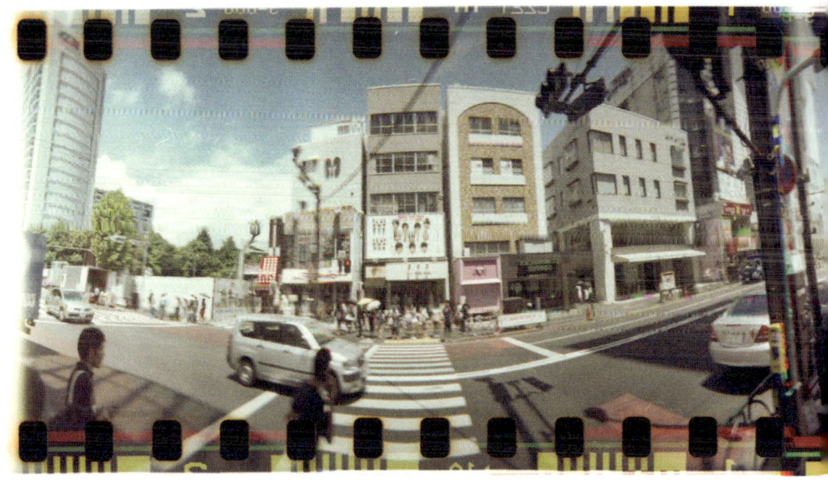

SAMPLERS ——— The ACTION SAMPLER is a light, simple, four-lens camera. It has a fixed aperture, and four 26 mm plastic lenses. It takes under a second for all of them to shoot in sequence. The resulting photo has four separate images inside the one photo, each showing a sequential movement and is great for subjects with action (or if the photographer spins the camera) – otherwise you get four identical images. There is also a flash version of the camera. This camera really has no focus or exposure settings and encourages spontaneous shots. The SUPER SAMPLER is similar to the Action sampler, but the frames are displayed stacked on top of each other. The camera has two shooting speeds, 2 seconds or 0.2 seconds. The camera has a cord to wind the film. The OKTOMAT has 8 individual lenses that shoot over a 2.5 second time frame.

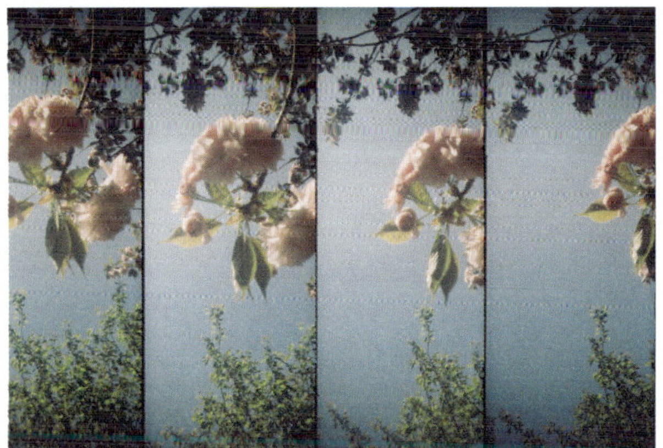

FABIAN REUS PHOTO

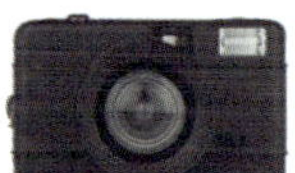

FISH EYE ——— This light, fun 135 mm camera with a fixed fisheye lens and a 170 degree field of view, creates wide, distorted images. Lomography also has an underwater housing for this camera. The FISHEYE 2 is the later version of the fisheye, which has an additional bulb setting (the only two modes are the standard 1/100 shutter speed and bulb). There is also a hot shoe for an external flash. The FISHEYE BABY110 uses 110 film, and is tiny. It has a 13mm plastic fish eye lens and also has a bulb mode.

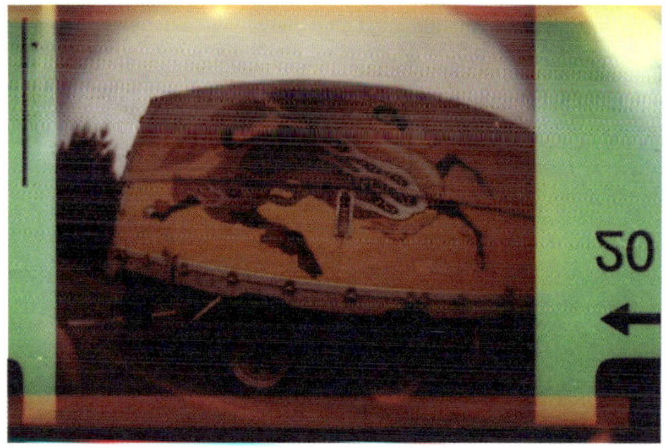

REMO CAMEROTA PHOTO

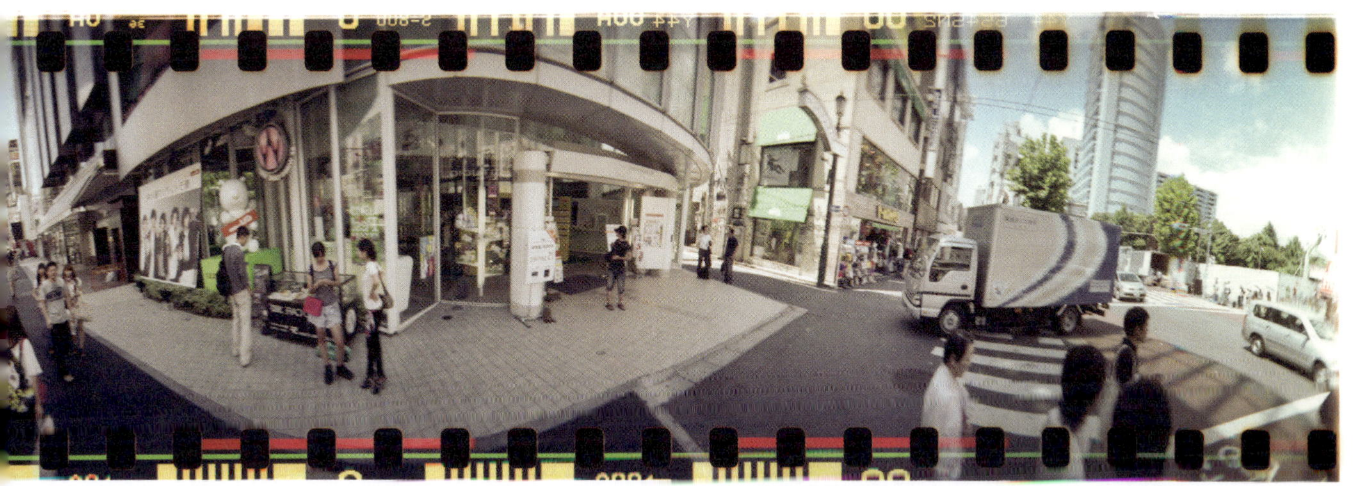

TOM JACKSON PHOTO

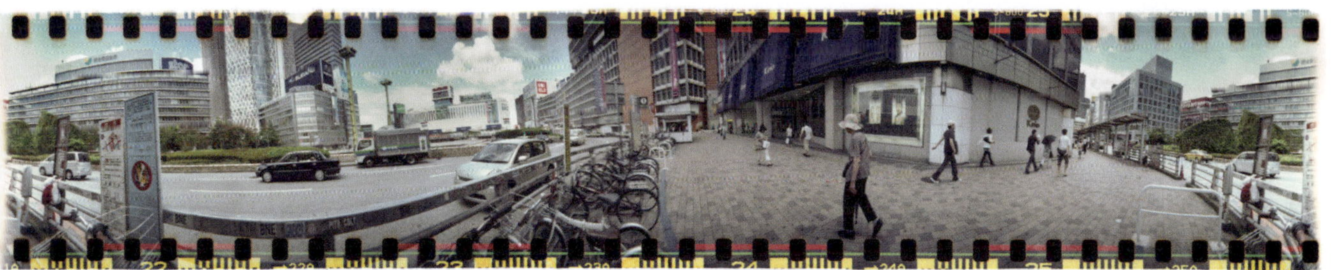

SUMMERSOUND PHOTOGRAPHY (SUMMERSOUND.CO.UK) PHOTO

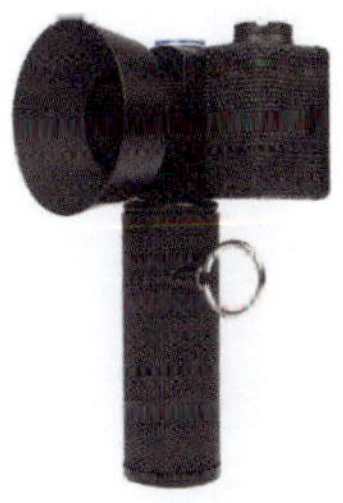

SPINNER 360 ——By pulling a cord the camera rotates on its handle fully, enabling 360-degree photos – including the photographer in the shot(if so desired). It uses conventional 135 film, but it also exposes the sprocket perforations as well. There are only two aperture settings, a sunny f/16 setting, or a cloudy setting at f/8. There is also a "Spinner Motorizer" that allows the photographer to shoot remotely on a single spin, or continuous spin mode, which is like the bulb mode.

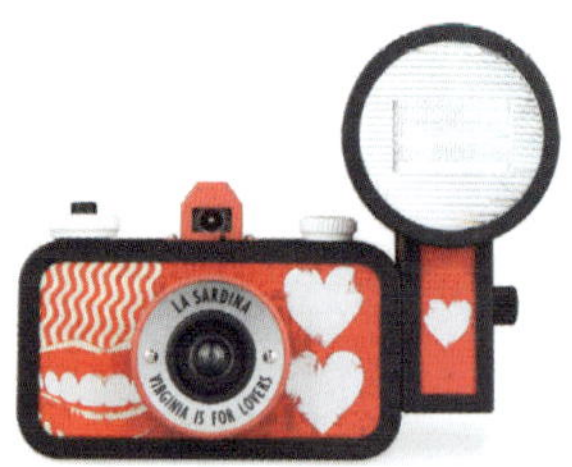

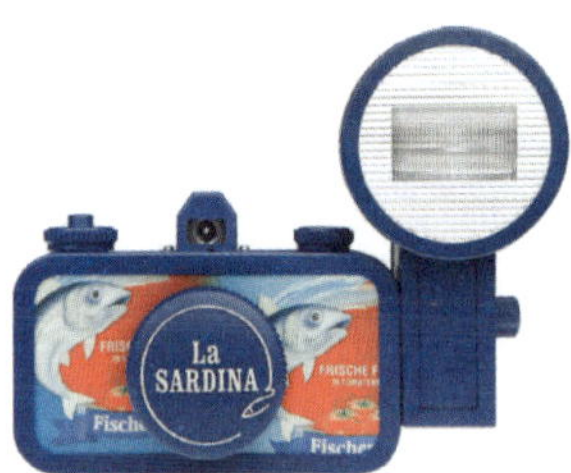

LA SARDINA ——These beautifully designed compact cameras are inspired by the Kandor Candid cameras that resembled sardine cans from the 30s. It takes 135 roll film, and has a 22 mm f/8 wide-angle plastic lens. It also includes a flash. Asides from the regular shooting mode, there is a multiple exposure setting.

YUKO C. SASAKI PHOTO

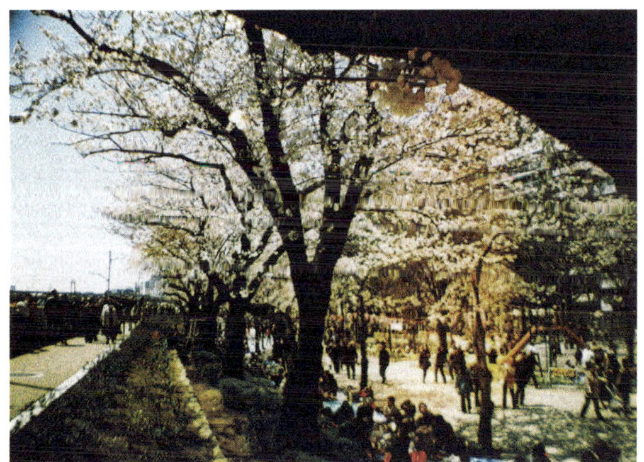

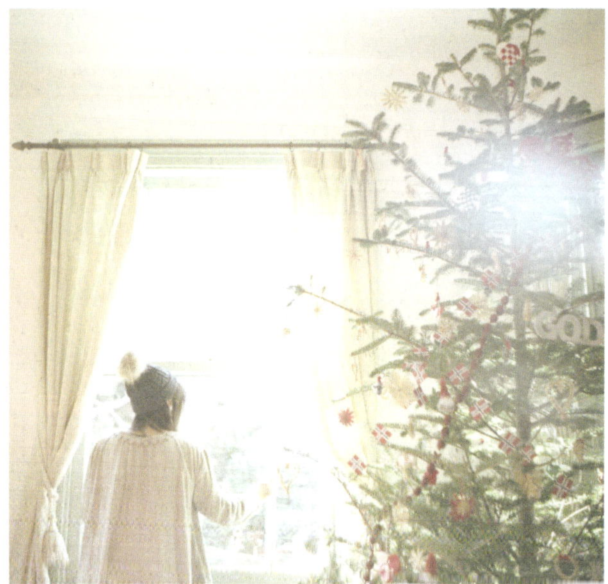

DONA YAMAZAKI PHOTO

SEAGULL TLR ——Twin Lens Reflex camera from the Shanghai General Camera Factory, which first made an appearance in 1959, is based on the Rolleiflex. While often called a toy because it is distributed by lomography, this camera produces high quality medium format photographs.

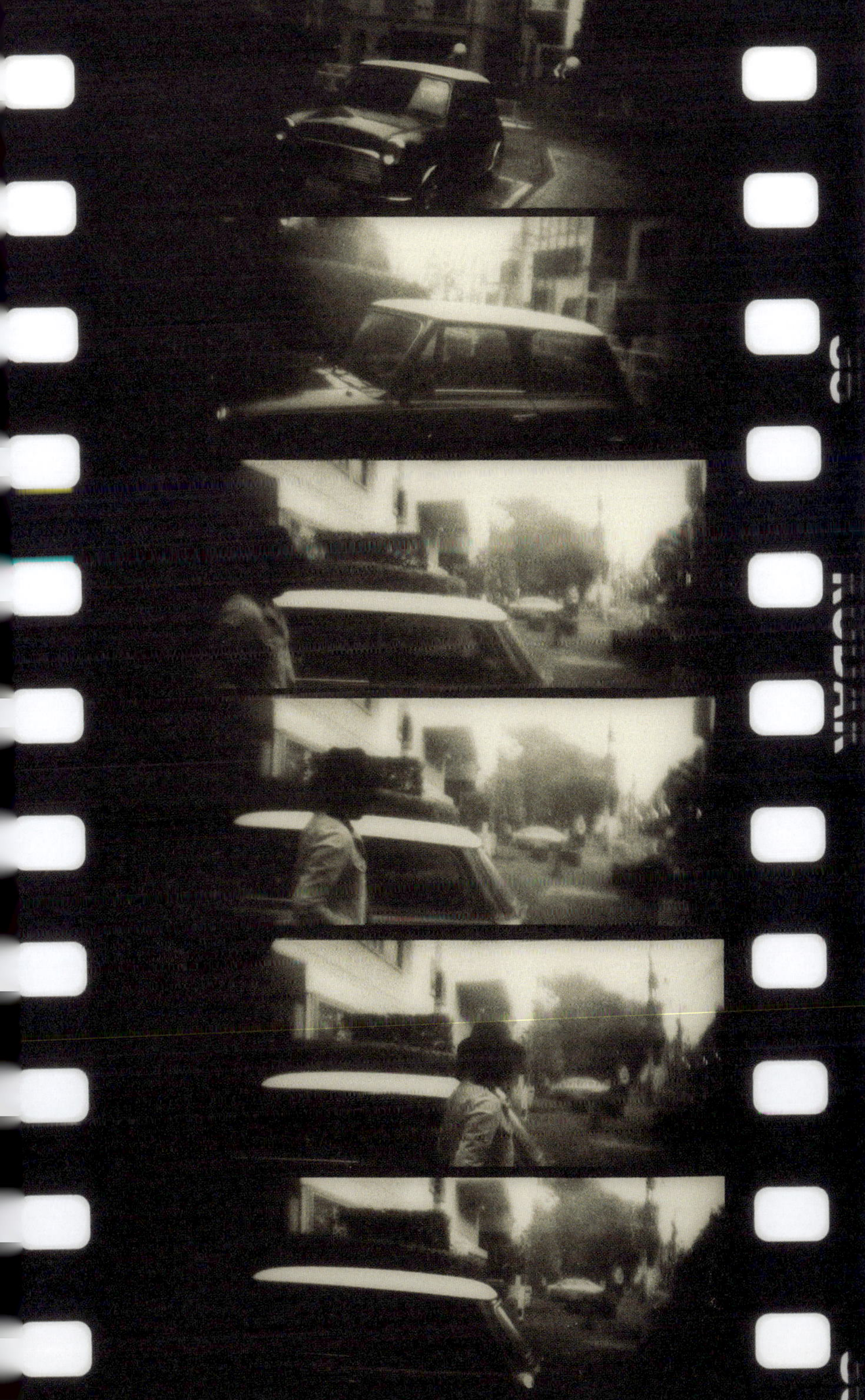

LOMOKINO — A 35mm silent film movie maker with a 25mm lens. The film is wound with a crank, so the frame rate is dependent on how fast you wind it. The aperture settings are f/5.6, f/8, and f/11. Movie imaging software is needed to stitch the images together

TOMMY OSHIMA PHOTO

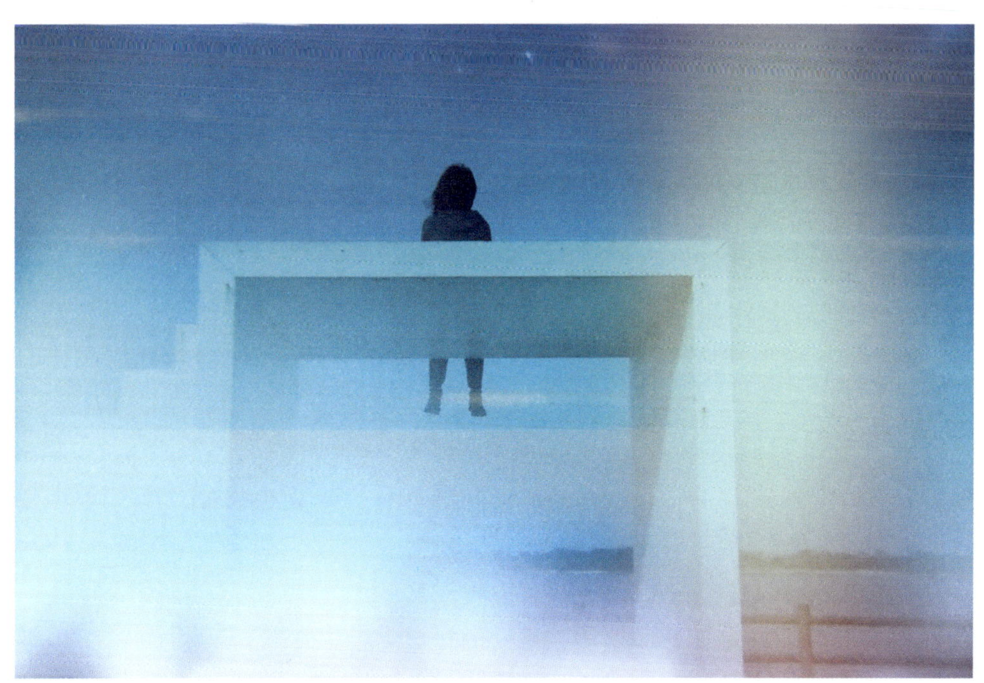

—— interview 25 ——

NAGA

How long have you been customizing cameras for?

I have been doing it for about 5 years, I started by fixing them, and then started to work with twin lens cameras. I was previously in design school, and saw that there were a lot of cool looking cameras in the past, and that was the impetus.

When did you discover toy cameras?

I found toy cameras about 5 years ago too, there was a bit of a film boom, although that has finished and it is now digital cameras and iPhones, just like overseas.

What kind of customizations have you done?

I have customized a camera that I know was made in UK but it isn't clear what the maker is. I worked with a few cameras that use discontinued film that you can't buy anymore. I will customize them so that they can take other formats of film, and when you shoot with them, they will expose the image to the sprockets. When you crop the sprockets off the image, the photo is really sharp as the lens is really good. I also customize digital cameras so they that have easy to see viewfinders.

On toys, I have added motor packs with battery packs on the bottom, for film winding, attached a grip and I would open a small window in the back, so you can see what film you are using. I also put a flash on Konstruktor.
It takes slightly softer images with a nice bokeh than the regular Konstruktor.
It is easy to focus. With the transparent type, I made it black in parts and it didn't work the first 3 or 4 times, and it would leak light.

You work in the toy industry, are there similarities between what you do in your day job and these camera hacks?

No, actually, but in the past, I really loved plastic models and even won competitions for it. I was also working in design as well.

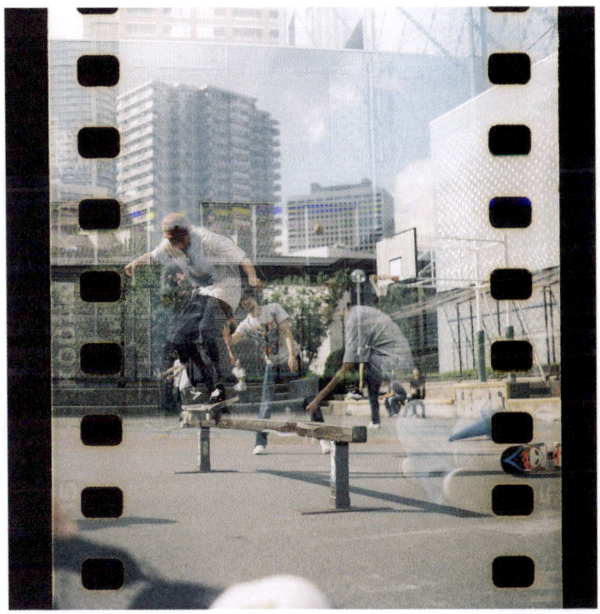

TAKEN WITH A CUSTOMIZED SAWYER'S MARK IV

You travel a lot; are you always taking photos while you are on your voyages?

My trips are mostly for tourism, and I always shoot with film. I find film more fascinating, and I like that analog atmosphere. It

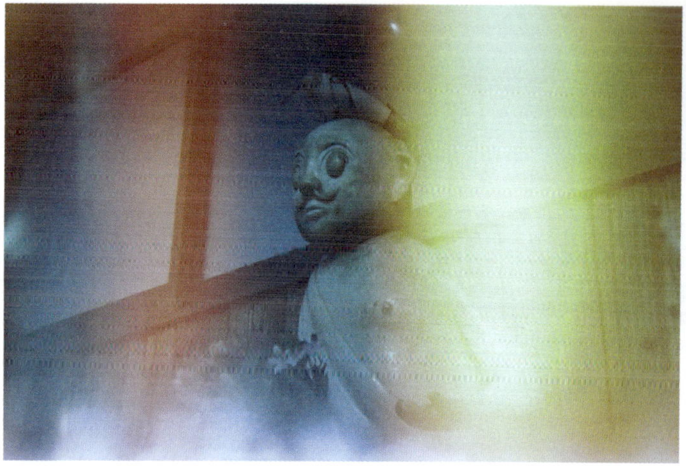

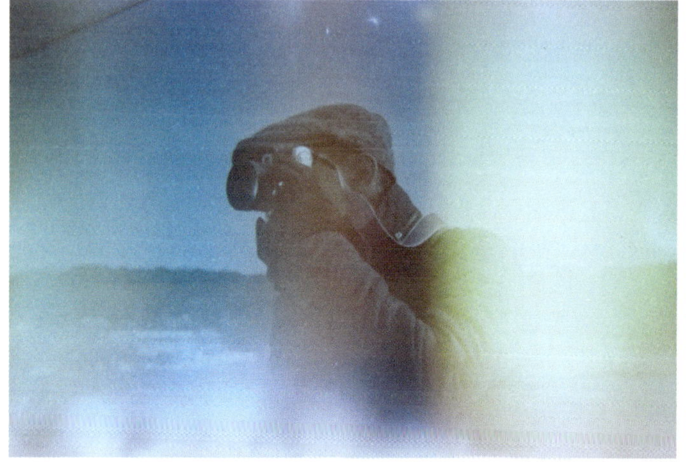

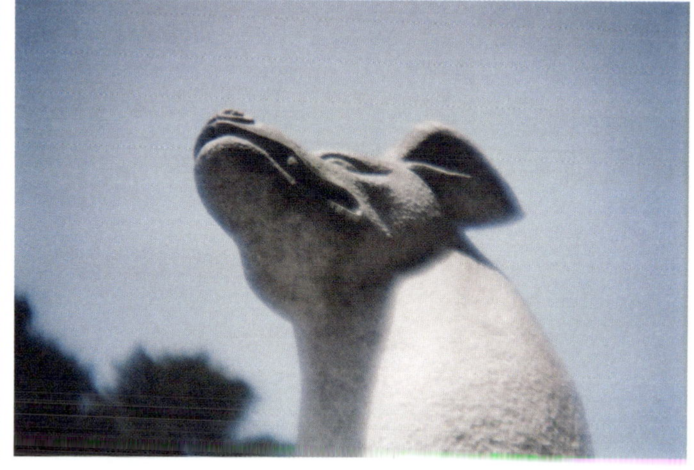

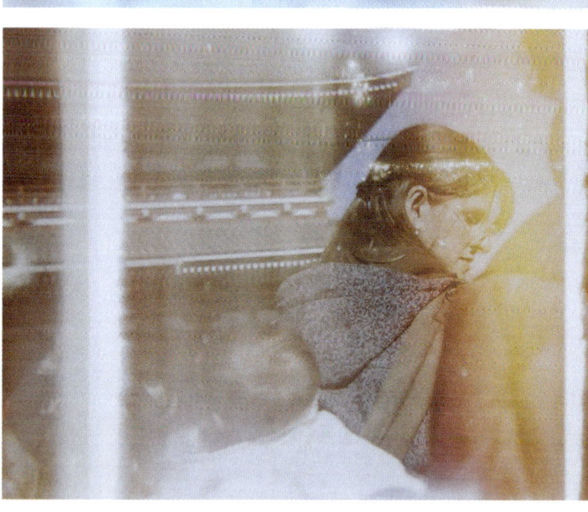

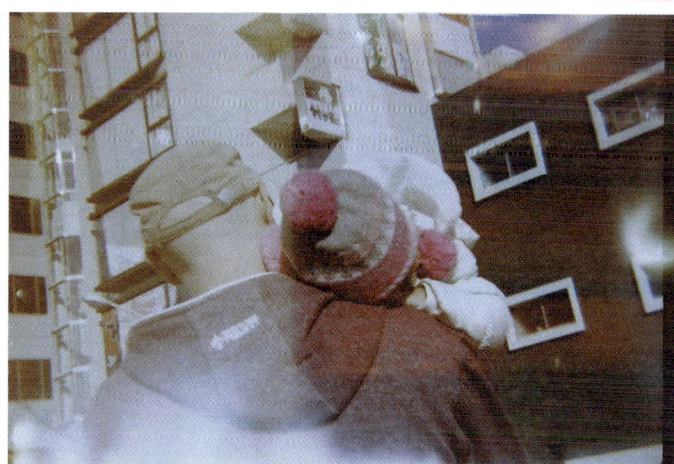

is a hassle to use film, but I feel like I am actually doing photography, rather than if I were to use a digital camera. We are lucky in Japan - if you compare it to overseas, you can buy film easily, even though the places selling it has decreased if you compare it to before.

Where are you planning to go next?

Japan is an island country, so I want to go to various islands like Naoshima and the Seto sea. There are a lot of interesting islands in Japan, for example, there is an island overrun with rabbits. During the war, it was a place for experiments, and now there are ruins and rabbits everywhere. It is very filmic but it has an unusual atmosphere. I also want to go to Gunganjima, people were paying fishermen and going in secretly, it is rife with ruins.

Where can you recommend within Japan?

I have been all over Japan, I want people to know the joy of travelling and I always try and get my friends to go. The people in Tohoku are really kind, it has a particular atmosphere unique to the region. If someone goes over, they will prepare so much food that you can't eat it all. There is also place called Gujohachiman in Gifu prefecture, which is has a river going through the town like some European towns. It is pristine and people jump into the river during summer. I also liked the churches of Nagasaki; they have an unusual atmosphere. In Tottori, there is also a Shigeru Mizuki road, with his (manga) characters and yokai (ghosts) everywhere.

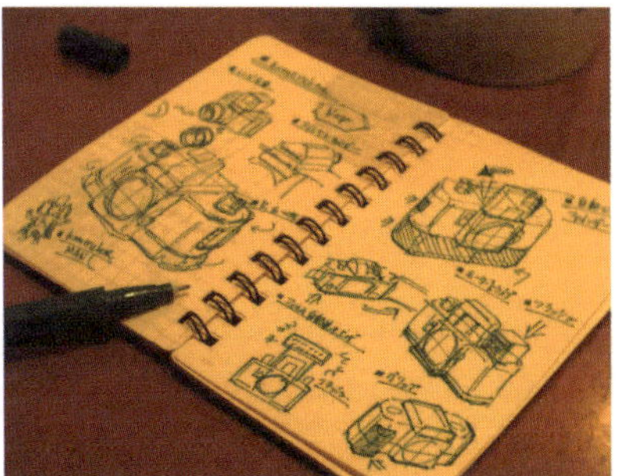

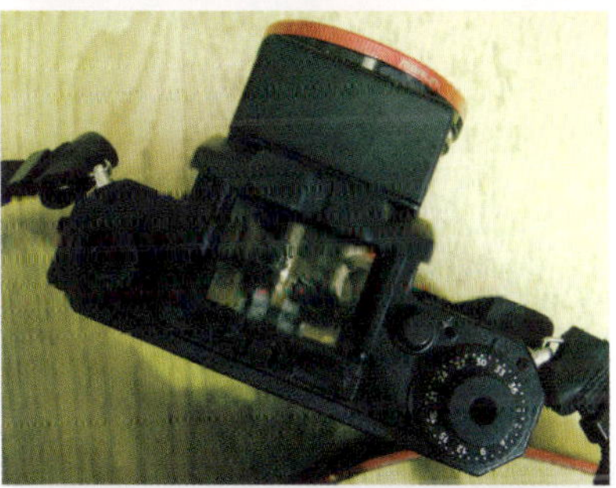

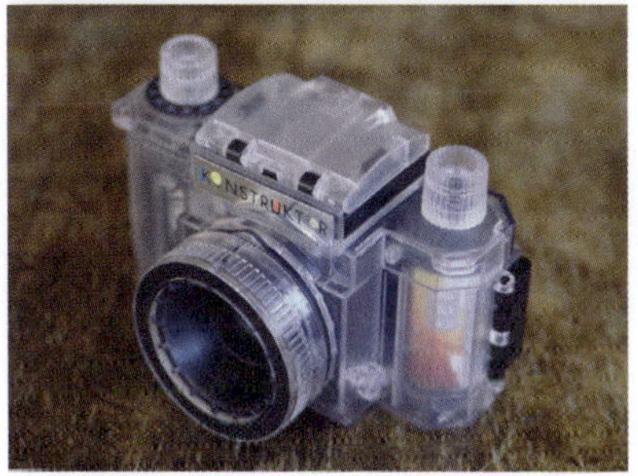

◀ *TAKEN WITH THE CUSTOMIZED KONSTRUKTOR C*

KONSTRUKTOR —— This is a 35mm SLR camera with a detachable 50mm f/10 lens that comes in a kit that is assembled at home, and is fantastic for people wanting to learn the mechanism of a toy camera. It has a manual exposure control and focusing and a hooded waist level viewfinder. It is quite functional as a completed camera, but the real joy is in making it.

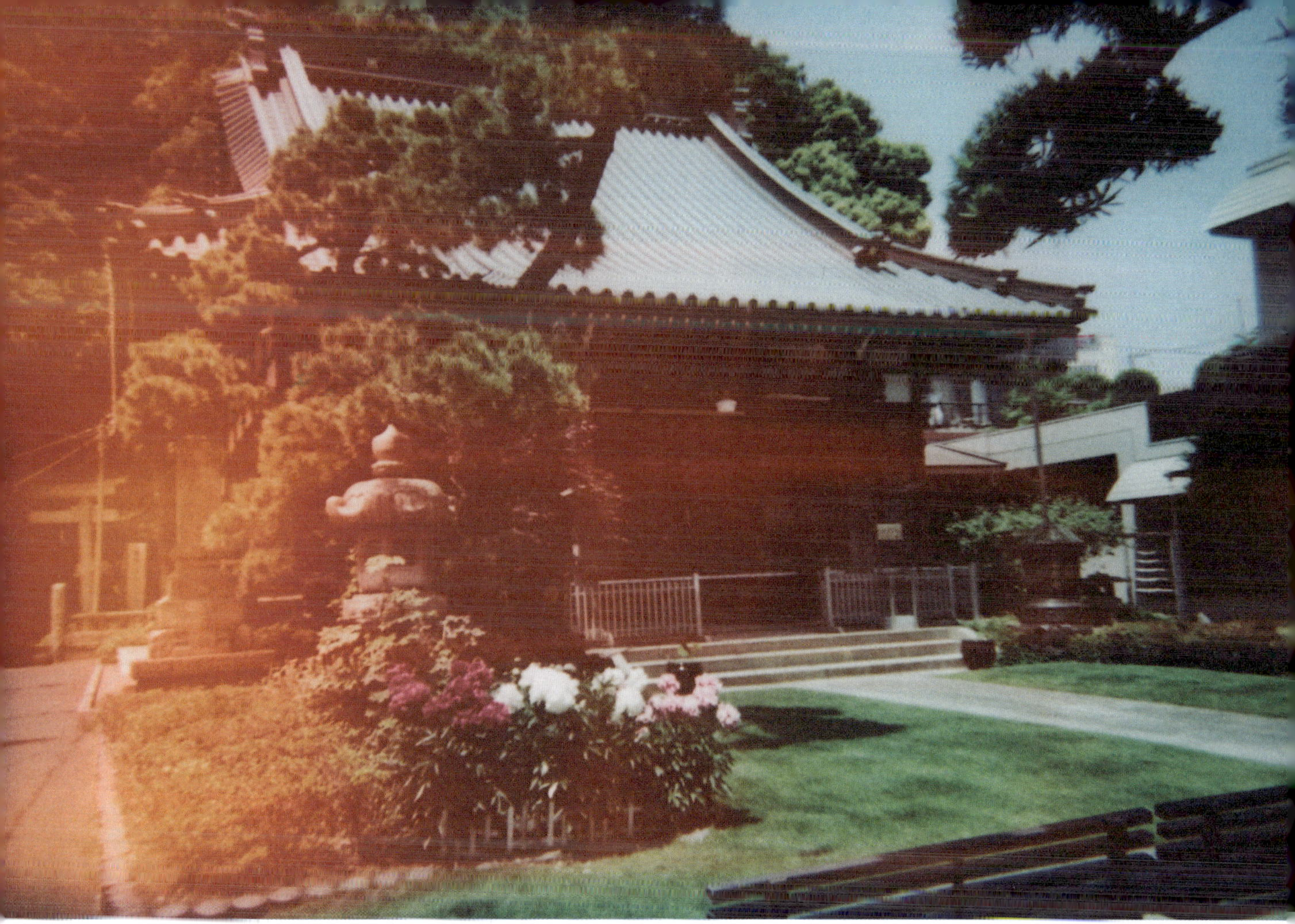

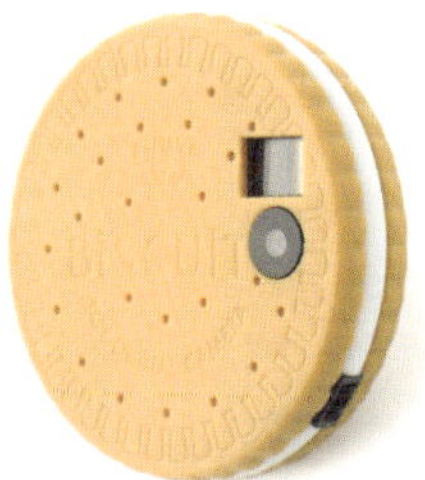

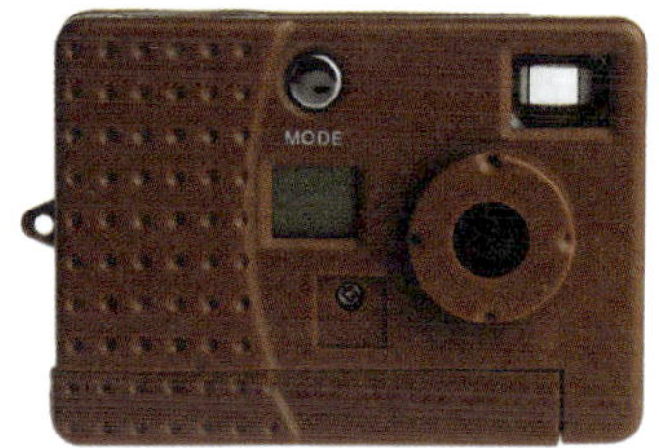

MODE

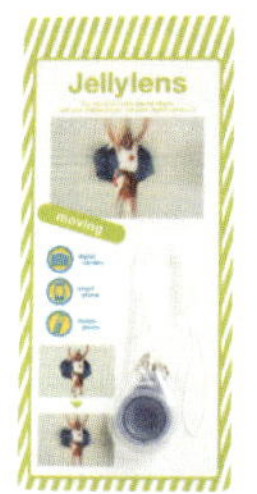

Jellylens

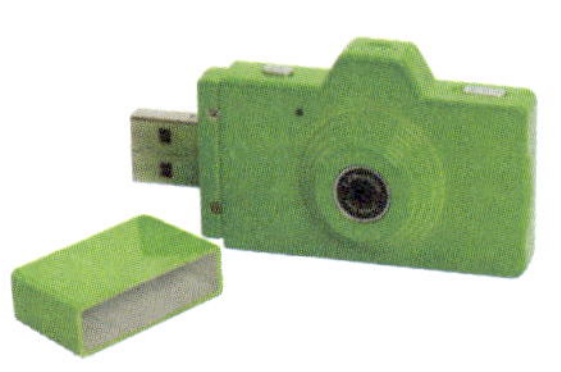

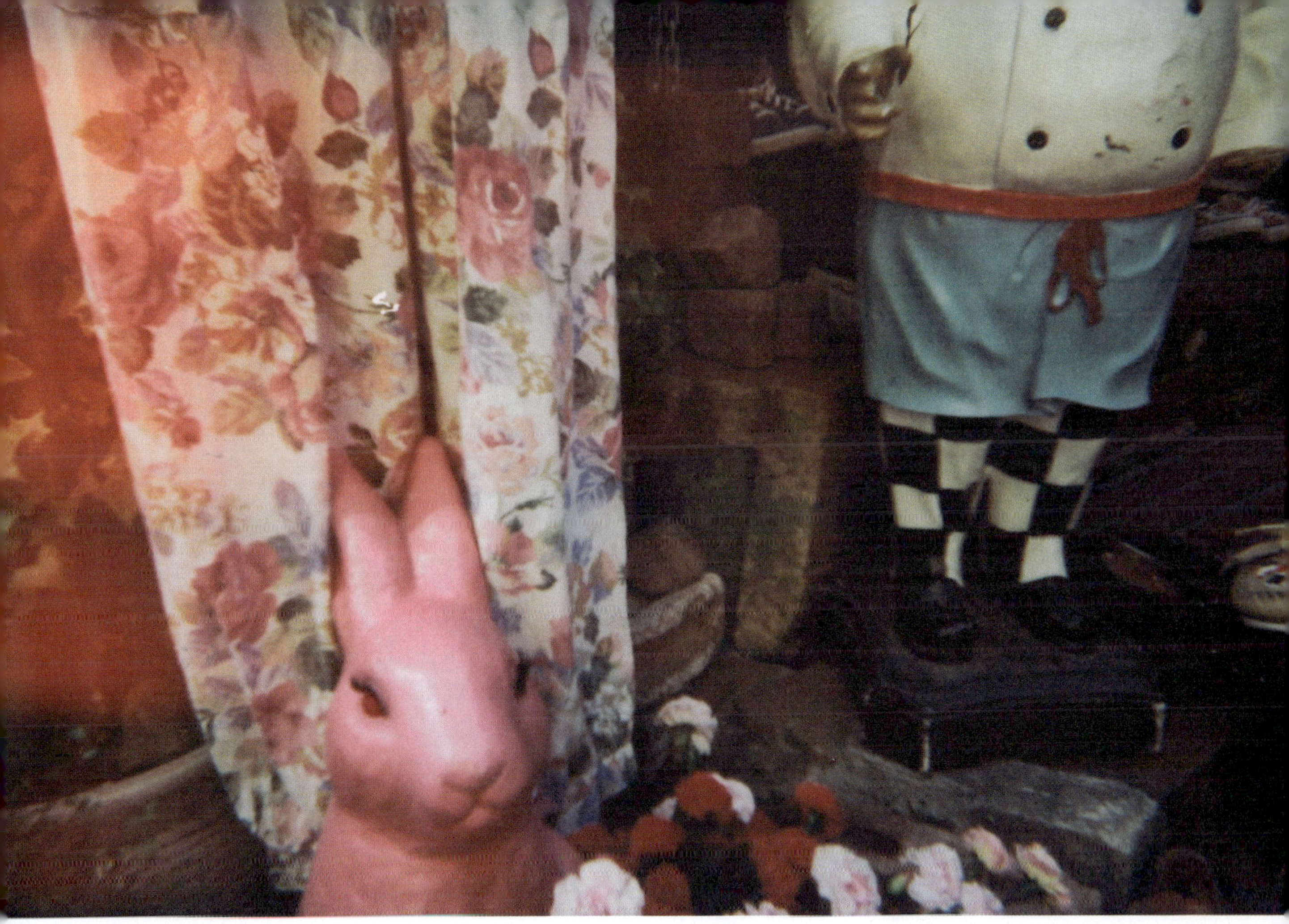

GHST WRLD PHOTO

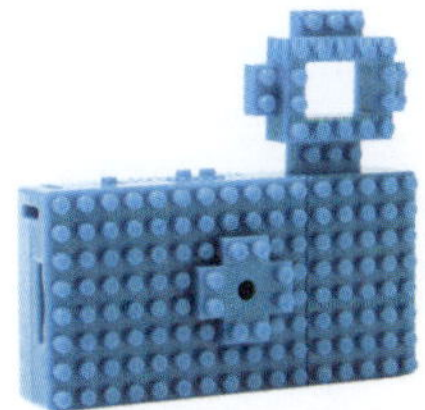

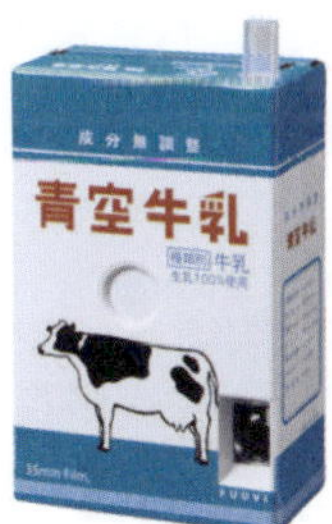

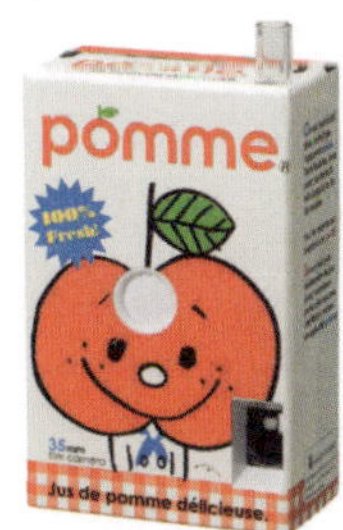

FUUVI —— Japanese company Fuuvi has a range of gorgeously designed digital cameras in the shape of chocolates, biscuits, fruit juice and milk cartons.

Pick is tiny, at 3cm long, with a F2.8 lens and shoots at ISO 100. It shoots 2 megapixels photos and video at 720x480 px at 30 fps.

Bee is modeled after a 8mm video camera, with a 2.8 lens, and shoots silent video at 640x480 px, ISO 100.

The Megane is a pair of lensless fashion glasses that shoots what you see. It takes both movies and 2048 x 1536 px stills.

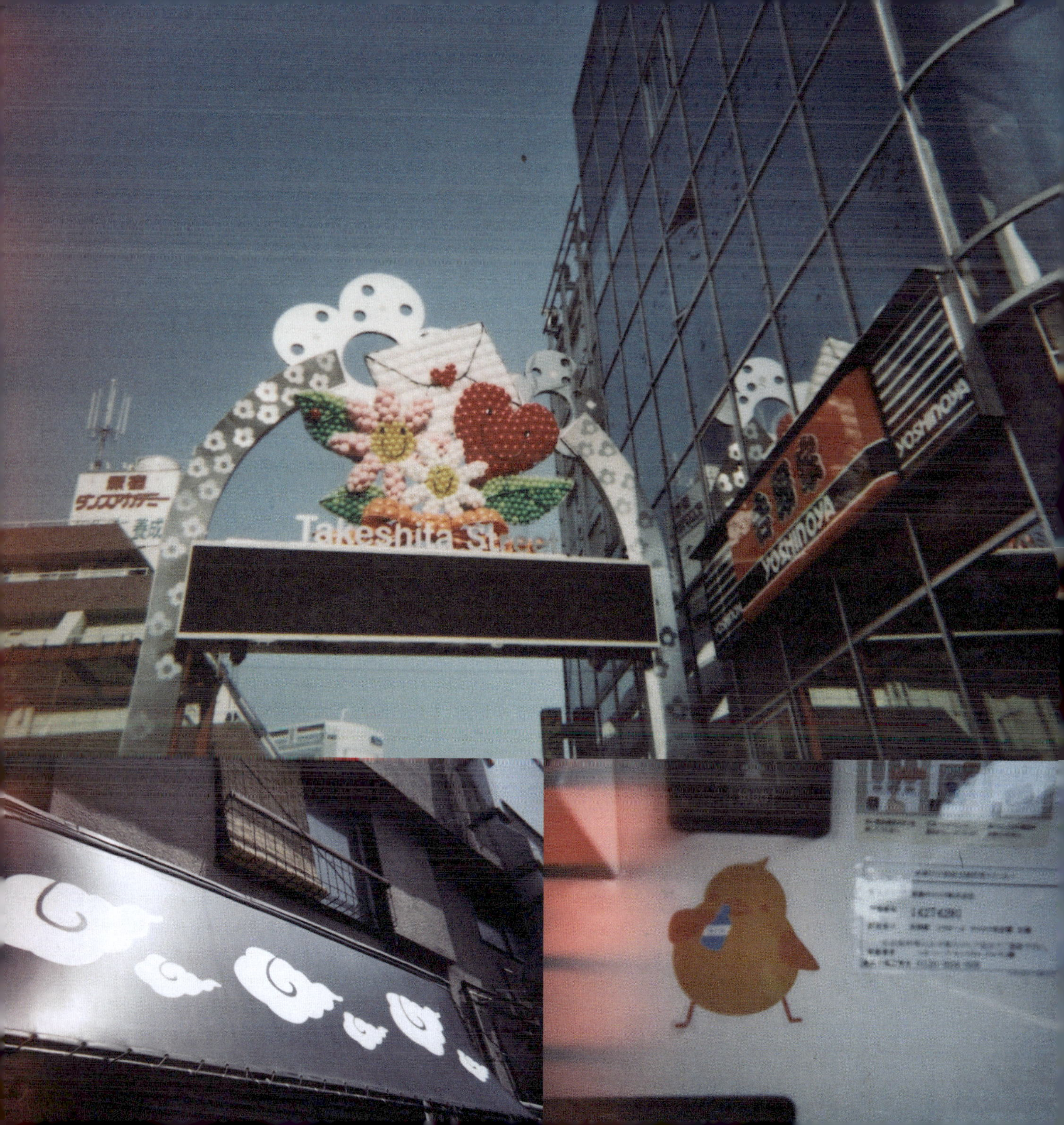
Takeshita St
YOSHINOYA
YOSHINOYA

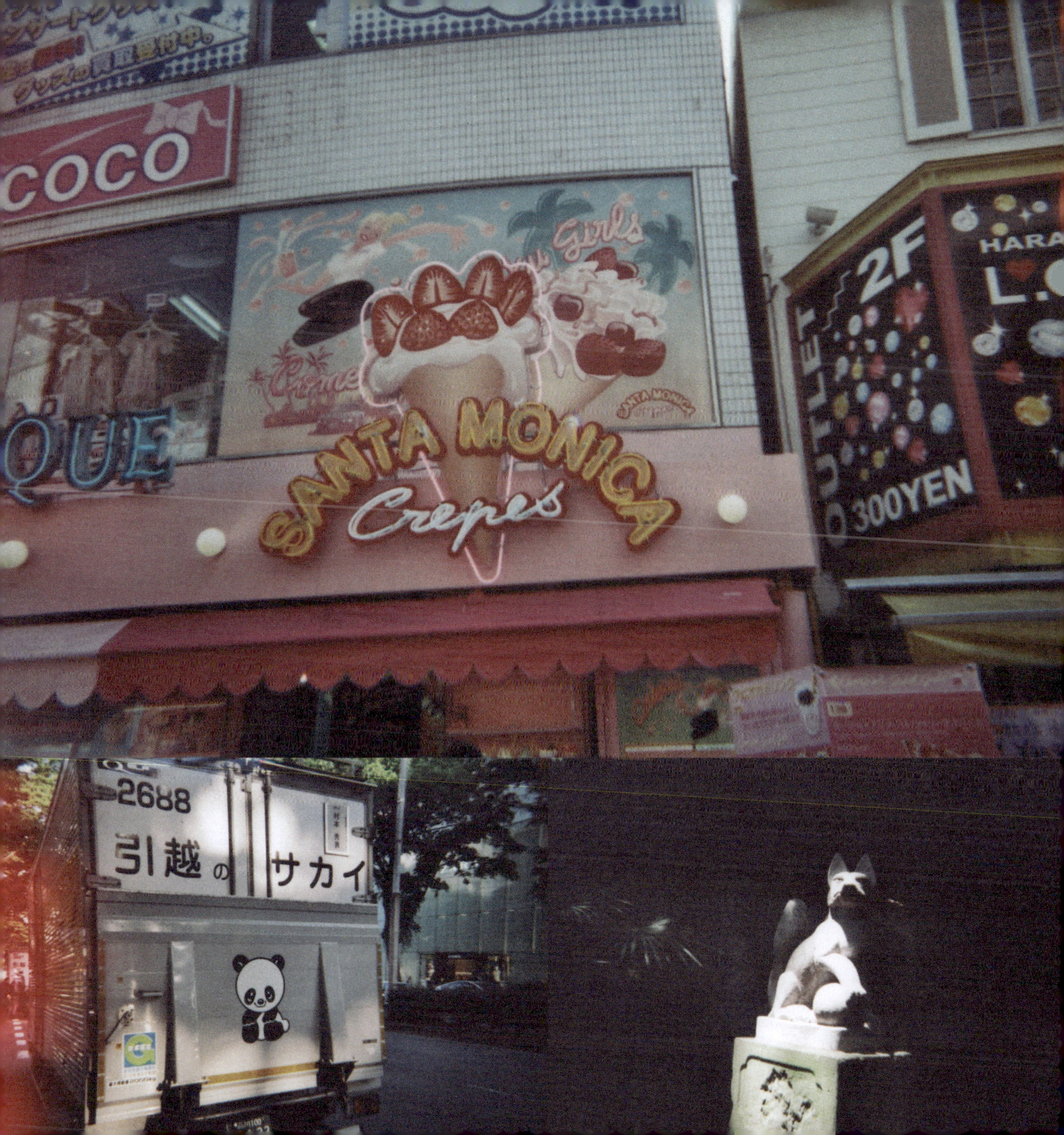
COCO
SANTA MONICA
Crepes
QUE
OUTLET
2F
300YEN
HARA
2688
引越のサカイ

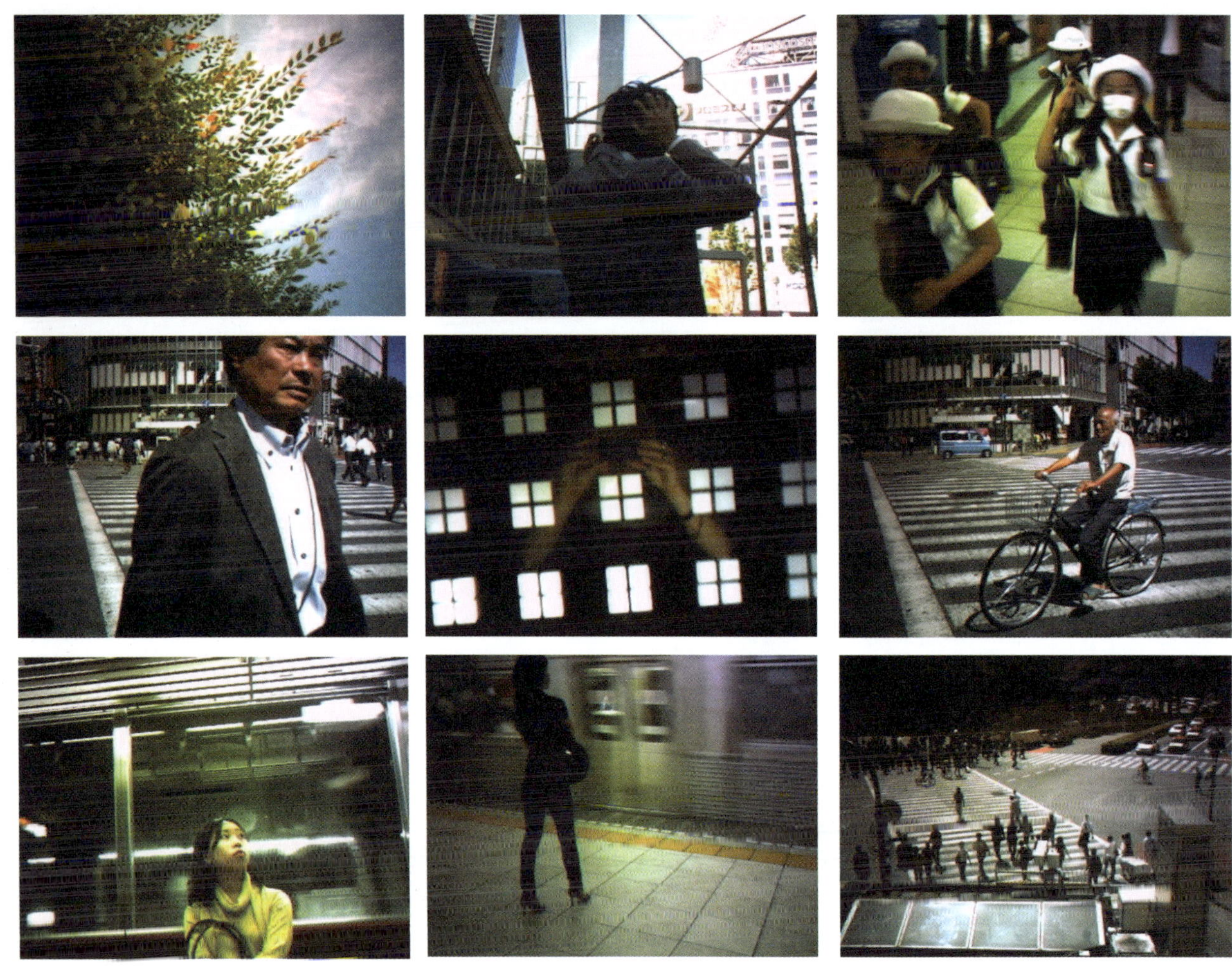

— interview 26 —

KATHERINE OKTOBER MATTHEWS

Can you tell us about your background as a photographer?

I started taking pictures pretty casually, as a way of documenting my travels. I never studied photography in a formal way, I just wanted to have photos of exceptional experiences. Eventually, that 'hobby' grew into a bigger and bigger part of my life. It probably had to do with living abroad for the last 12 years. Over time, I gradually experimented with different formats and cameras as well as pushed myself to work with concepts or artistic goals in mind.

Where did you first come across a Harinezumi and what made you want to use it?

I was already into some of the older Russian toy cameras (in particular I love the Lubitel, but I've also shot with a Smena, Holga, Mini Holga), so I was following blogs, forums and Flickr groups, watching the developments coming out from this niche area of photography. For example, people were excited about LOMO revitalizing, The Impossible Project launching, and apps were coming out for mobile phone photography like the Toy Camera app, etc – there was a lot of buzz in the nostalgic cult of lo-fi photography. I read about the Harinezumi when it was announced and there was no question: I had to get one. It was a great marriage between the lo-fi spirit and the digital capabilities, and on top of everything, it could also take video. I happened to take a trip to Tokyo shortly after it was released in 2009, and scoured the city to find one, which turned out to be harder than I thought for such a gadget-oriented city. But I guess that shows just how much of an obscure interest it was! In the end, I stumbled upon one at the gift shop at the Museum of Photography and started shooting with it immediately.

Do you shoot a lot of movies as well?

I don't shoot a lot of moving images, and in fact have only really shot video with the Harinezumi, not with any of my other cameras, even my Canon 5D Mk II, which is known for its exceptional video quality. Ridiculous, isn't it? But the Harinezumi is really perfect for street video in a way that other cameras aren't – it's incredibly small and unassuming, so people ignore it or don't see it at all.

How does adding music (and another sense) to the work change how you experience the images?

Adding music can add cohesion to a series of images, offering them a common theme or emotional thread that leaves the viewer feeling like the images belong together. When a soundtrack is done well, it can even offer a narrative arc to a series of shots, building up tension or creating the sensation of transcendence, an escape from the mundane world. The multimedia aspect of filmmaking offers incredible opportunities to express yourself in multiple ways at one time, but of course, that also means that you need to be in complete control over your intentions to be effective. With bad combinations, or even bad editing of good combinations, the effect can be ruined entirely. It's easy to screw up, and because modern viewers have grown so sophisticated in terms of what they've seen and now come to expect, even 'good' work can seem mediocre. Good isn't good enough anymore.

It's a tricky thing, to determine the medium to best present a project. Some images really deserve to be seen on their own, without the distracting elements of sound or movement; they're quietly beautiful on their own. For example, sometimes artists or even editors present photo series in a slideshow with some silly song in the background, but the two are disjointed, they were clearly not meant to be shown together and it does a disservice to the photos. I think sometimes it just comes from people's fear of silence. They equate silence with boredom or angst, and want to fill it as quickly as possible. As a viewer, I think it's the same thing as having a conversation with a talkative person: you know it's all nonsense.

What are 5 adjectives you would use to describe the atmosphere of the images produced by a Harinezumi?
Sunburned, candied, nostalgic, mysterious, soulful

I've seen your work focusing on places such as Amsterdam and Texas, where you document a subjective experience, places that represent "home" to you. How did being in Tokyo as a tourist change the way you worked?
The topic of 'home' has been a common theme to my work over the last several years because I feel so at odds with it. I explore it because I don't understand it. When I travel, it feels natural to take photos and make notes of things that are surprising or charming or beautiful or ugly. I brought my 35mm camera to Tokyo and was shooting with that, too. Tokyo is an incredible city for a tourist. There's so much going on, so many people and city lights, so many different neighborhoods, so much modernity and also so much history and culture that is impossible to understand as an outsider.

Maybe for the same reason, it's very difficult to get a deep reading of the city, so that's probably the biggest difference between the work I do when I'm travelling versus in a place where I've spent a lot of time. When I travel, I know I'm approaching the city and the people as an outsider, whereas when I photograph the places I live or know very well, I can play with the topic as an insider, even if I'm trying to see it with distance.

How do you feel Londoners and Tokyo-ites relate to their cities? What is the dynamic between the people and the environment?
Megalopolises are funny places, and that's why I tried to create a series from my work in Tokyo, London and New York. They're so far away from each other, both geographically and culturally, and yet, the very nature of being unfathomably huge cities gives them strong similarities. These cities just heave with life, they're bursting with people. And they all end up being 'dog eat dog' to some extent, very ambitious and cutthroat. When you work your way around the city as an outsider, you see the patterns, for example, the rush hour traffic on the subways, the sad little trees built into the sidewalks for decoration, the new city trying to eat the old city alive. Tokyo tries harder than other megalopolises to hold onto its traditions, London acts like it's just a small, polite village that got a bit big, and New York is a screaming beast, constantly trying to rip its own skin off to make room for the next thing.

Were there preconceived expectations before you went? What kind of things were you looking for?
When I go to a city for the first time, for example my first time in Tokyo, I might have preconceived ideas of how different it will be, but they usually disappear pretty quickly once I'm there. Reality is so much stranger than my imagination! When I start photographing, I'm usually looking for exactly those odd things that catch my eye, as well as the things that are so global that I can recognize them anywhere. There's nothing local about loneliness, for example. Each city has its own personality though, so I try to be open to what a place has to offer. Sometimes it's landscapes, sometimes it's dilapidated buildings, sometimes it's portraits. With Tokyo, I was drawn to the intense mixture of old and new architecture, as well as the people on the street or in public, because there are so many of them and for the most part, they're so busy or tired that they don't really notice if you're photographing them.

Were you attracted to, or feel an affinity with the energy of Tokyo or did you find it alienating? The London clip has eye contact and facial expressions whereas the Tokyo clip seems distant, asides from your friend.
The videos are somewhat circumstantial: in Tokyo, I travelled there alone, whereas in London, I went with two friends. I knew someone in Tokyo, but I was by myself for the most part. I often travel alone, which is great for moving around a place to take pictures, though depending on the friendliness of the city it can also be alienating. I found being in Tokyo incredibly invigorating because everything I saw was new or different, but it's also true that I had very little interaction with locals (outside of being in a restaurant or shop). People are polite, but don't really open up to conversation. I don't know if that has to do with reacting to me as a tourist, for example, a result of the language barrier, or whether it's part of the culture and Japanese people would experience it the same way. Possibly both. Artistically, Tokyo was a great place to be for street photography because everyone would ignore me, but I think if I were to spend a prolonged period of time there, it could become very lonely.

In Tokyo-ga, Wim Wender says, "if I had been there without the camera, I would now be able to better remember." Do you agree?
Memory is an impossible puzzle to solve. If I've forgotten something, how do I know that I don't remember it? It's just gone. Sometimes my friends tell me stories of things that I know never happened – but how can you prove whose memory is correct? Photographs don't prove anything because they're not facts, they're narratives.

I am a deliberate photographer – absolutely not one of those people who walk around with a camera in front of my eyes all the time. If something magical is happening, I would rather experience it than photograph it, and will put my camera down when it detracts from the enjoyment of a moment. Do I remember those moments better without the photograph? I really don't know. Somehow I doubt it.

Does it matter if I remember the photograph, rather than the moment? When I take a photograph, I'm documenting the moment exactly as I see it at that time, so how is that different than my memory? Sometimes I remember photographs I didn't take. Is that a fake memory? I don't treat memories as such precious objects, because I don't trust them anyway. More than anything, I value the present moment, and sometimes that means photographing it and sometimes that means being completely present without a camera in my hand.

Why do you look at this lo-fi technology when the market is going towards high precision and improvements in image quality? Is something lost in this quest for perfection?
The problem with this quest for precision is that it's inaccurate. Memories aren't sharp, they're blurry. So when we take sharp photos to remember things, it might make for a nice photo to put on your wall, but it's sterile and in a way, I think always a little disappointing. I've tried many digital cameras over the years, but so far I always return to film cameras or to equipment that's flawed or just lo-fi. When you use a camera for a long period of time, you learn to 'see' how the camera sees, or maybe it's the other way around. But if a camera sees things perfectly clearly, how can you possibly relate to it? That's what I've never understood. A camera has to have a personality that you find sympathetic.

Some people like precision, and I certainly don't think there's something wrong with people shooting in high quality digital. It's perfect for product shots, for example, or fashion photography where they combine perfection with fantasy.

I think the love of lo-fi photography is something of a backlash against the way that modern precision equipment has enabled even amateur photographers to create technically good photographs. Artists want to distinguish themselves, so they use lo-fi equipment to prove their skill with the craft of photography, or maybe some of them prefer the retro aesthetics in a hipster way. The downside of this is that I see a lot of people using toy cameras to take pictures of their feet and they think that just because it's a bit blurry with some light leaks, that makes it profound art. In the end, the medium doesn't determine whether something is good or bad.

And why do you shoot with film, like you did for the Texas project)? Is there something in the process that appeals to you?
It's as simple as this: I have yet to find a digital camera that consistently sees things the way I see them. If I'm shooting with color film, there's a vibrancy there that's just irreplaceable, inimitable. If I'm shooting with black and white, I can fall in love with the grain of the film, and digital noise will just break my heart. Plus, I can't stand all the details that these high quality digital cameras catch. They see even more than I do, so when I look at the pictures I feel so disturbed. I can only think: that's not what I saw at all.

I also prefer the delay of developing film. The instant feedback of digital cameras changes the way people shoot pictures. It's great for learning about photography, but it drives me crazy to see people checking the back of their screen after every photo – photographers should learn how to trust themselves, trust their cameras. Working without being able to see the picture immediately forces you to visualize it in your head, and after a while you learn that trust. You know how to wait for the right moment, and have enough faith to click the shutter and move on.

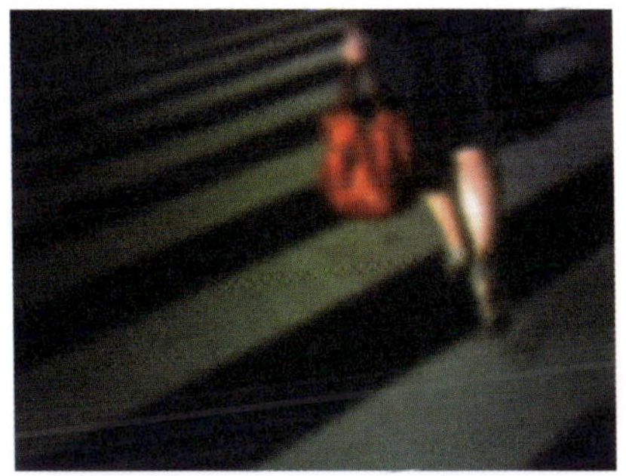

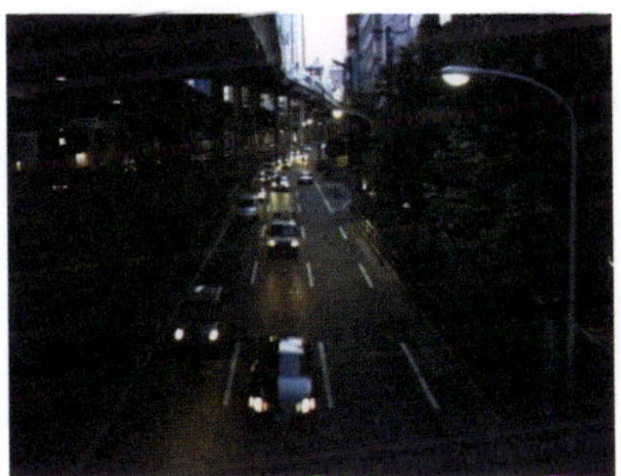

HARINEZUMI —— The Harinezumi is a tiny camera that resembles a 110, and shoots movies with a similar grainy aesthetic quality as Super 8mm videos. It has a cult following with artists and directors, such as Harmony Korine in the film Spring Breakers. It has evolved several times (in version 4 at the moment). The latest model has a zoom, various modes, filters and a multiple exposure function.

TOY TOKYO

Thanks to Christine So at Holga, Grachev Sergey, Anya Likalter, Ayami from Kokeshka Kamakura, Martin Cheung (assistance with art direction), Cakefortiger, Eric Rechsteiner, Anastasiya at LOMO, Lara Day, Henry Hoening, Joyu Wang from the Wall Street Journal, Laurel Chor, Brad Plumb at Kaikai Kiki New York and all the photographers.

Special thanks to my mum, always and my love, Crane.

BEEN TO HONG KONG WITH A TOY?
Accepting submissions for the next issue.
kingyobooks@gmail.com

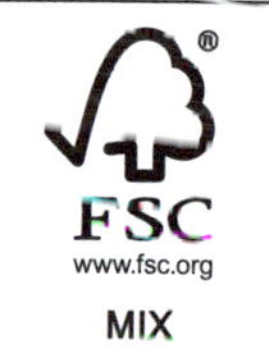

Kingyo Books is committed to using FSC® paper made from responsibly harvested sources.

ISBN 9789881250780
Kingyo Books, Hong Kong.
20th Floor, Central Tower, 28 Queens Rd. Central, Hong Kong
Printed in China.